THE
CRASH
OF **2016**

Also by Thom Hartmann:

ADD: A Different Perception
ADHD Secrets of Success: Coaching Yourself to
Fulfillment in the Business World
Focus Your Energy: Hunting for Success in Business
ADD Success Stories
Think Fast! with Jane Bowman and Susan Burgess
Beyond ADD
The Greatest Spiritual Secret of the Century
Thom Hartmann's Complete Guide to ADHD:
Help for Your Family at Home, School and Work
The Edison Gene
The Last Hours of Ancient Sunlight
The Prophet's Way
We the People: A Call to Take Back America
What Would Jefferson Do?
Ultimate Sacrifice: John and Robert Kennedy, the Plan for a Coup in Cuba,
and the Murder of JFK by Lamar Waldron with Thom Hartmann
Walking Your Blues Away: How to Heal the Mind and
Create Emotional Well-Being
Screwed: The Undeclared War Against the Middle
Class—And What We Can Do About It
Cracking the Code: How to Win Hearts, Change Minds, and
Restore America's Original Vision
Legacy of Secrecy: The Long Shadow of the JFK Assassination
by Lamar Waldron with Thom Hartmann
Threshold: The Crisis of Western Culture
Unequal Protection: How Corporations Became
"People"—And How You Can Fight Back
Rebooting the American Dream: 11 Ways to Rebuild Our Country

As contributor:

Air America: The Playbook: What a Bunch of Left-Wing
Media Types Have to Say about a World Gone Right
Imagine What America Could Be in the 21st Century,
edited by Marianne Williamson
From the Ashes: A Spiritual Response to the Attack on America

THE CRASH OF 2016

The Plot to Destroy America—
and What We Can Do to Stop It

THOM HARTMANN

TWELVE

NEW YORK   BOSTON

Copyright ©2013 by Thom Hartmann

Twelve
Hachette Book Group
237 Park Avenue
New York, NY 10017

HachetteBookGroup.com

Printed in the United States of America

RRD-C

First Edition: November 2013
10 9 8 7 6 5 4 3 2 1

Twelve is an imprint of Grand Central Publishing.
The Twelve name and logo are trademarks of Hachette Book Group, Inc.

The Hachette Speakers Bureau provides a wide range of authors for speaking events. To find out more, go to www.hachettespeakersbureau.com or call (866) 376-6591.

The publisher is not responsible for websites (or their content) that are not owned by the publisher.

Library of Congress Cataloging-in-Publication Data
Hartmann, Thom.
    The crash of 2016 : the plot to destroy America—and what we can do to stop it / Thom Hartmann. — First edition.
        pages cm
    Includes bibliographical references and index.
    ISBN 978-0-446-58483-8 (hardback) — ISBN 978-1-4789-8073-5 (audio cd) — ISBN 978-1-61969-647-1 (audio download)   1. Economic forecasting—United States. 2. United States—Economic conditions—21st century.   3. Financial crises— United States.   4. Rich people—United States.   5. Middle class—United States. 6. American Dream.   I. Title.
    HC106.83.H379 2013
    330.973—dc23
                        2013019837

To Tim Carpenter, cofounder of Progressive Democrats of America, and a true champion of democracy and the people

ACKNOWLEDGMENTS

This book would not have been possible without the help of my friend, colleague, and collaborator in so many things, Sam Sacks. From ideas and suggestions to research to extraordinary editorialist assistance, Sam has helped make this book what it is. Indeed, I'm the author of this book, but you'll find Sam's hand and deft touch throughout it. Partly because of my schedule, but mostly because of Sam's brilliance, I've never so relied on a private editorial assistant for any other book I've written. It's been a pleasure and an honor working with you, Sam. Thank you!

Bill Gladstone, my agent and the CEO of Waterside Productions, also helped bring this book into being, from concept to final publication, and has shepherded it along these many months. Bill has been working with me for decades on my books and is always a source of encouragement, inspiration, and good, solid, sane advice.

The great folks at Hachette and Twelve have been with us on this book from beginning to end, and I'm so grateful for their help, encouragement, and bringing this book to publication. They include: Sean Desmond, Libby Burton, Mari C. Okuda, and Cary Goldstein.

I'm not the first or only author to follow the trail of the themes of this book. There have been many over the years, and many have

Acknowledgments

influenced my thinking. In particular Dr. Ravi Batra, author of *The New Golden Age* and *Greenspan's Fraud* and a frequent guest on my radio show, has taught me a lot. As have Richard Wolff, Robert Reich, Paul Krugman, David Korten, David Cay Johnston, Lori Wallach, Ralph Nader, and so many other brilliant writers, thinkers, and economists I've had the privilege of knowing and interviewing over the years that I'm reluctant to start a longer list of names for fear I will miss some.

Finally, without my wife, Louise Hartmann, none of my many books would have been finished over these decades. Thank you, Louise, for being both my life partner and my business partner!

CONTENTS

INTRODUCTION: Canvas Moon America   xv

Who Stole the Back of the Moon?   xvii

The Crash   xviii

Just One of Us Ducks   xx

Death by Bankster   xxii

Death by Globalism   xxv

The Task   xxvii

PART 1: THE ECONOMIC ROYALISTS AND THE CORPORATIST CONSPIRACY

CHAPTER 1: A Rendezvous with Destiny   3

The Great Forgetting   5

The Economic Royalists   9

A Crash Starts a Nation   11

The Next Cycle: The Civil War   14

FDR Wages War on the Royalists   17

The Road to War: Yesterday and Today   22

War   24

Contents

CHAPTER 2: A Corporate Call to Arms   28

   The Sixties   30

   The Powell Memo   34

   On Campus   38

   The GOP TV Memo and Roger Ailes   40

   The Courts and the Capitol   42

CHAPTER 3: The Crisis Capitalists   45

   Killing Keynes   46

   The Mont Pelerin Society   48

   Shock Troopers   50

   A Global Shift   53

   The "Crisis" Comes to America   54

PART 2: WHY WE CRASHED

CHAPTER 4: A Middle-Class Primer   59

   The Elusive Middle Class   62

   Step One: Progressive Taxation   64

   Step Two: A Social Safety Net   66

   Step Three: Protections for Working People   69

   Step Four: Rules in the Marketplace   70

   Monopoly Endgame   72

CHAPTER 5: Reagan Kidnapped the Jetsons   77

   Tax Cuts of Mass Destruction   78

   More Unequal than Rome   81

   The "Debt" Crisis   82

   Shooting Santa   83

   Republican President Clinton   86

   A Giant Sucking Sound   87

Contents

CHAPTER 6: "Madness"   92

   The Evolution of Madness   94

   Monopolies Return   96

   Global Psychopaths   98

   Bankster Psychopaths   104

   Financialization   106

   The 1920s All Over Again   109

   Even Worse than Before   112

PART 3: "OPPRESSION, REBELLION, REFORMATION"

CHAPTER 7: A Revolution Denied   117

   Jefferson's Cycle of Revolutions   118

   A History of Revolution   121

   The Suicide Pact   123

CHAPTER 8: The Royalists Strike Back   126

   A Tea Party Reimagined   127

   Meet the Kochs   130

   The Rise of the Kochtopus   131

   Fox News Gets in the Game   135

   Thwarted   140

CHAPTER 9: Betrayal on the High Court   143

   Roberts Takes the Case   145

   The Road to Personhood   148

   Delphin Delmas v. Corporate Personhood   151

   The Roberts Court Rules   154

CHAPTER 10: Masters of the Universe   159

   First, Greece   160

   It Spreads   164

Contents

Little Dictators   166

The ALEC Shadow Government   168

Democracy Defamed   173

Cancer Stage   175

PART 4: THE GREAT CRASH

CHAPTER 11: This Is the End   179

Germany Finally Wins World War II   181

Germany Goes Too Far   185

The Divergence and War   189

The China Syndrome   191

The Oil Shock   194

Military Misadventure   196

$1,200,000,000,000,000   199

PART 5: OUT OF THE ASHES

CHAPTER 12: Organized People *v.* Organized Money   205

Move to Amend   207

Take On the Court   212

The Court Takes the Power   215

Depose the Kings!   217

CHAPTER 13: Repair the Fundamentals   220

Medicare Part E   220

Reclaim the Commons   222

Cure Wall Street's Madness   226

Reinvest   228

Card Check   230

Printing Money   232

Contents

Jubilee   234

No Billionaires!   235

CHAPTER 14: Green Revolution   238

Decentralization   240

The Tipping Point   241

Stripping Oil of Its Strategic Value   246

Tipping Point Reached   250

CHAPTER 15: Democratize the Economy   254

The Silent Revolution   255

The Dragon's Mountain   258

The Mercedes and the Labor Union   260

The Seeds   262

CHAPTER 16: Epilogue—A Letter to My Great-Grandchildren   267

About the Author   273

Notes   274

Index   284

INTRODUCTION

Canvas Moon America

Your home is regarded as a model home, your life as a model life. But all this splendor, and you along with it... it's just as though it were built upon a shifting quagmire. A moment may come, a word can be spoken, and both you and all this splendor will collapse.
—Henrik Ibsen, *A Doll's House*, 1879

I was around ten years old, and a total science fiction junkie. *Amazing Stories*—a pulp magazine of science fiction short stories, commentary, and science news—arrived every month, and that meant that on that day all homework and play were forgotten. These were some of the most brilliant stories, written for a penny or so a word by people such as Robert Silverberg, Jack Vance, Poul Anderson, and Frank Herbert, who would go on to become the biggest names in the field of Fantasy and Sci-Fi.

And one particular story haunted me for years. Eight years later, when the first men landed on the Moon, that story was brought back to me as if I'd read it the day before.

In the story, a group of astronauts are finally, for the first time, going to blast off from Earth and circle the Moon. It had never been

Introduction

done before, and because our moon doesn't itself rotate on its axis like we do relative to the Sun, but instead circles us with a single side always facing us, nobody had ever before seen the "dark back side of the Moon." These men would be the first in human history to do so.

The rocket roared to life from the launchpad, the astronauts chatting with Mission Control as they hurtled toward the Moon. When they got close enough, they let the Moon's light gravity grab their space capsule and, with a few deft rocket thrusts, they put themselves into orbit around it. They were unbelievably excited, as were the NASA folks on the ground, chattering back and forth about what they hoped and expected to see.

Was the dark side of the Moon identical to the front, or was it more mountainous? (We now know it is the latter.) Might there be frozen water there, since it has a different exposure to the Sun? Might there even be wreckage there from ancient astronauts, or something else exotic like that? Anything was possible!

As the astronauts began their turn around to the back side of the Moon, Mission Control told them they'd lose communication because the giant mass of the Moon would block their signals, so they prepared for radio silence. But as they made the turn, they could still hear Mission Control.

What they saw as they glimpsed behind the face of the Moon we see on full-moon nights brought an audible gasp from all of them.

One picked up the microphone to radio the ground and tell the horrible story. Another knocked the microphone from his hand with a warning gesture. They continued to circle around the back side of the Moon, and the view became even clearer, ever more undeniable.

"Should we report it?" A debate—virtually a fistfight—broke out in the capsule. What would it mean for earthlings? What if nobody believed them? What if they were quarantined upon returning and imprisoned or sent to a mental hospital?

I remember what they saw that so horrified the astronauts.

The back side of the Moon was missing. They were looking into the concave half ball of the front side of the Moon, which was made of canvas stretched over an elaborate superstructure of two-by-fours, nailed together like the scaffolds that held up roller coasters from that era.

Who Stole the Back of the Moon?

This sci-fi story from my childhood also tells the story of America today on the verge of the Crash of 2016.

On the surface, everything seems OK. Our politicians still talk about promise, hope, and change, and we applaud and feel inspired. The world still uses our money. We still have the strongest military in the world. And our standard of living is still far better than the Third World's (though worse than most of the developed world's). We're still by far the wealthiest nation in the world, with too many billionaires to count: Bill Gates, Warren Buffett, Charles and David Koch, Mark Zuckerberg, and so on. We still have civility in the streets. We have reality TV and fancy (gas-guzzling) cars. We still vote (those with a driver's license and birth certificate can, at least).

As long as you don't look *too* closely at our nation, things seem under control—the United States looks whole. The economically, militarily, and scientifically superior United States, as we've come to know it in the past eighty years, *seems* intact—not only for the whole world to see from afar but also for those of us who live here.

But when you go around to the "dark back side" of the nation, you see the shocking truth. There you see a nation whose core fundamentals have been hollowed out, replaced by balsa-wood stilts and wrapped in a frayed canvas of nationalism and bravado—a cloak similar to that worn by nearly every great superpower that has ever existed on the planet just before its own eventual collapse.

Unlike the canvas Moon, the United States was once full and complete. Many of us still have memories of that golden age of the middle class throughout the 1940s, '50s, '60s, and '70s.

But today that middle class, like the canvas Moon, has been hollowed out. The middle-class neighborhoods still exist across America, but they're teetering on stilts of mortgage and credit card debt.

As then Labor Secretary Robert Reich testified before Congress in 1994, "[T]he net national savings rate, which was at a relatively robust 8.2 percent of GDP during the 1970s, has dropped to a barely visible 1.8 percent as of the early 1990s."[1]

That was just a decade and a half into the Reagan Revolution. Today it's far worse. The AP headline from February 11, 2009, says it all: "Americans Have Negative Savings Rate."[2]

Hollowed out, too, is our nation's democracy. The spectacle of national elections confronts us every other year, but behind the pomp and circumstance our democracy has corroded into an oligarchy, as billionaires finance their own political candidates and corporate-funded think tanks do the work once reserved for elected representatives of writing and passing legislation.

Stripped clean and hollowed out, the United States is more vulnerable today than it's ever been—including during the Great Depression and Civil War. Those fortified pillars that supported a booming middle class are stolen, and without them America teeters on the verge of the next Great Crash.

The Crash

Ultimately, this is a story of how America was dragged into the Crash of 2016.

We are standing today at the edge of the Fourth Great Crash and war in American history. The previous three—each about eighty years apart—were gut-wrenching in their horror and bloodshed, but they ultimately transformed America in ways that made this a greater and more egalitarian nation.

Thomas Jefferson predicted them, as he had lived through one here and observed another sputter and fail in France. Periodic revolutions were necessary for America—or any democratic society—to flourish and grow, he said. And if they were stalled or blocked, then the ensuing crisis would be all the more intense.

Jefferson said it best: "If this avenue [of periodic revolution] be shut to the call of sufferance, it will make itself heard through that of force, and we shall go on, as other nations are doing, in the endless cycle of oppression, rebellion, reformation; and oppression, rebellion, reformation, again; and so on forever."[3]

That cycle, spanning a few generations each time, has indeed been repeated over and over again in America. And right now we're in the midst of it being repeated again.

Numerous anthropologists, historians, and analysts have written about the generational cycles of revolution and crisis, most notably William Strauss and Neil Howe in their brilliant book *The Fourth Turning*, which extensively documents the previous crises, from the American Revolution, to the Civil War, to the Great Depression.

But this book is different. While we provide an overview of history, this book focuses specifically on the crisis that is enveloping us today and will soon overwhelm us—and then, ultimately (over the next decade), fundamentally transform our nation.

We stand today at the edge of the Fourth Great Crash (and Reformation) since Jefferson sparked the First American Crisis by putting quill to paper and drafting the Declaration of Independence in 1776.

In the coming pages, you will meet the actors who set in motion today's cataclysmic chain of events: the architects, the conspirators, and the propagandists who have both shaped the twenty-first-century crisis and are trying so hard to exploit it for their own gain. And you will see how our past may well carry answers to rebuilding our future out of the current crisis.

This crash will unfold in its own unique fashion, different from the three America has previously experienced but also eerily similar.

From the shock of another economic meltdown, to the horror of war, to the dangers of an environmental crisis combined with radical social transformation, and the gridlock of dysfunctional government, the Fourth Crash—the Crash of 2016—is today's moment of truth for America.

For some Americans, the crash is already well under way.

Just One of Us Ducks

In February 2010, we got a glimpse of the sort of inequality-induced violence that may accompany the Crash of 2016 when Joe Stack woke up in his cozy middle-class neighborhood, set his home on fire, and then drove to the local airport just outside Austin, Texas.

He hopped into his single-engine Piper Dakota airplane, took off from Georgetown Municipal Airport, and minutes later, like a missile, dove his plane right into a glassed-facade office building that housed a local IRS tax collection office, instantly killing himself and an IRS agent and former Vietnam veteran, Vernon Hunter, who was working at his desk in the building.

When the American economy first went into meltdown a few years earlier, it was people like Joe Stack who were hit the hardest. He was a software engineer who watched his clients and income dry up, yet he didn't get a bailout the way Wall Street did. His bills piled up, he sank into debt, and the taxman was knocking down the door. Uncle Sam needed to bail out hundred-billion-dollar transnational corporations—many of which, coincidentally, paid no American corporate income taxes.

Joe appeared calm on the surface, a regular guy who lived in a run-of-the-mill middle-class home at Dapplegrey Lane in North Austin. He played guitar in a local band.

But there were clues: He named his band Last Straw and his only album was titled *Over the Edge*.[4] And what seemed like inconspicuous songs were anything but. There was a quiet desperation consuming Joe Stack, and he was nearing a breaking point.

Eventually he hit it. That's when he resorted to becoming our nation's first modern suicide bomber.

It would be easy, and convenient, to write Joe Stack off as a deranged man who, faced with financial troubles, resorted to a desperate act of violence. But he was far from that.

"[Joe] seemed like one of us ducks floating down the river," Stack's brother said. "We just didn't realize he was paddling so furiously under the water."[5]

Eventually Joe Stack got tired of paddling.

In his suicide letter, Stack highlighted the very real problems in Royalist America.

"I remember reading about the stock market crash before the 'great' depression and how there were wealthy bankers and businessmen jumping out of windows when they realized they screwed up and lost everything," Stack wrote.[6]

"Isn't it ironic how far we've come in 60 years in this country that they now know how to fix that little economic problem," he added, "they just steal from the middle class...to cover their asses and it's 'business-as-usual.'"

Taking on the Royalist corruption of government, Stack wrote, "Why is it that a handful of thugs and plunderers can commit unthinkable atrocities...and when it's time for their gravy train to crash under the weight of their gluttony and overwhelming stupidity, the force of the full federal government has no difficulty coming to their aid within days if not hours?"

He went on, "Yet at the same time, the joke we call the American medical system, including the drug and insurance companies, are murdering tens of thousands of people a year...and this country's leaders don't see this as important as bailing out a few of their vile, rich cronies?"

Recognizing the cancer in our nation, he even went after the idea of capitalism itself, writing, "The communist creed: From each according to his ability, to each according to his need. The capitalist creed: From each according to his gullibility, to each according to his greed."

Thanks to this diseased Economic Royalist rule, there are millions of Americans just like Joe Stack who are confronting difficulties—people who are one foreclosure, or one layoff, or one denial of a medical procedure away from reaching their breaking point.

There are still sprawling middle-class neighborhoods across America like the one Joe Stack lived in. But what we can't see is the debt financing, the credit card bills piling up, and the kitchen-table conversations over how the utility bill will be paid that month.

There are still students across America attending colleges, preparing for their jobs in the future. But what we can't see is the massive $1 trillion student-loan bubble handcuffing them to lenders for the rest of their life. Things all look the same on the surface, but just below, the substrate is deteriorating.

We're all ducks like Joe Stack desperately paddling to stay afloat. And day by day more and more of us are sinking.

Joe Stack thought he was doing what needed to be done. As he wrote in his suicide letter, "I can only hope that the numbers quickly get too big to be white washed and ignored and that the American zombies wake up and revolt. It will take nothing less."

Death by Bankster

Norman Rousseau and his wife did everything they were supposed to do. They were responsible homeowners who did business with Wachovia and Wells Fargo (which acquired Wachovia) and put a 30 percent down payment on a home in California back in 2000, and they made every payment from then on, never missing even one single month.[7]

But in 2007, the bank began to exhibit its psychopathic nature. According to a complaint filed by the Rousseaus, the bank approached them about changing their mortgage to an adjustable-rate mortgage. The Rousseaus stressed they were interested only in a fixed-rate loan and that they wanted to pay the same payments throughout the life of the loan.

But they trusted the bank—which was a big mistake. So when Wells Fargo told them that the "new industry standard" is adjustable-rate mortgages, that they could save more than $600 a month in mortgage payments, and that the "worst-case scenario" would be an increase of only a few dollars on their monthly payments, the Rousseaus gave in to the salespeople and took the new mortgage.

But a few years later, in 2009, the Rousseaus knew they were stuck with a bad deal. Their new interest rate *was* higher than it was before 2007, and even higher than what they were told it could increase to. But as responsible homeowners who had done everything they were supposed to do, the Rousseaus still made each and every monthly payment on time.

That's when, judging from the Rousseaus' complaint, Wells Fargo's psychopathy took flight. In May of that year, the bank claimed that the Rousseaus had missed a monthly payment. The Rousseaus said that was impossible, that they had made the payment, and even gave proof that they had made the payment at the bank with a cashier's check that had been cashed by the bank.

But the bank still claimed it never received the payment, and over the next few months the bank repeatedly claimed that the Rousseaus had missed payments, hitting them with a barrage of demands for monies owed including additional fee after fee and penalty after penalty. Every time the Rousseaus thought they had finally convinced the bank that it was wrong, the cycle of abuse would begin again.

During the next few years, this sort of back-and-forth, double-talk, Kafkaesque nightmare continued between Wells Fargo and Norman Rousseau. The fees kept piling up, as did the lies from the bank—and then the eviction notices came rolling in.

By 2012, the financial burden of the whole ordeal had become unbearable, and the Rousseaus—like so many other Americans in the middle of the housing meltdown—were getting wiped out by the increased mortgage payments. That's when Wells Fargo finished them off, setting the eviction date of May 15 for when Norman Rousseau and his wife had to be out of their house.

But two days before the scheduled eviction, Norman Rousseau, apparently unable to bear losing his home after the bank had already taken all his money, pulled out a gun and killed himself. He was one of the first victims of the Great Crash.

So, too, was James Richard Verone.

Verone knew something was wrong when he noticed a strange protrusion in his chest.

He was already dealing with arthritis and carpal tunnel syndrome, only now the pain was too unbearable to handle. Unfortunately, James couldn't see a doctor because he didn't have health insurance after he was laid off as a delivery driver for Coca-Cola—a job he'd held for seventeen years.

With the economy in recession, James could only find work as a convenience clerk, but that job didn't offer any medical benefits. And eventually, as the pain grew and grew, James found himself unable to work. That's when the social safety net that has been under attack for thirty years by the Economic Royalists failed him: He was denied any sort of disability benefits by the federal government.

James was dying and had no options in the United States of America—the wealthiest nation on the planet.

No way to get health care . . . except for one.

In June 2011, James woke up, took a shower, ironed his shirt, and jumped in a taxicab headed for his local RBC bank. He walked inside, slipped the teller a note, and then walked over to a bench in the bank, where he waited, anxiously pawing at his long lock of gray hair and mangy beard.

The note read that he was robbing the bank of one dollar. James knew that the only way he could receive the sort of medical attention he needed was in prison, so he committed the smallest crime he could think of and waited for the cops to arrest him.

He was charged with bank robbery, and exactly according to plan, James was thrown in jail, where he was given the chance of seeing a doctor and received the basic health care that he was unable to receive as a free man.

As James said about his decision to choose jail over freedom, "If you don't have your health, you don't have anything."[8] It's another story that will be common during the Crash of 2016.

Death by Globalism

In the past, diseases such as tuberculosis and malaria have been number one health concerns around the world.

But not anymore.

In today's world, globalization is the number one health risk facing humanity.

A study recently released by the Blacksmith Institute reveals, for the first time ever, the impact of industrial pollutants on communities across the planet. It found that industrial-waste dump sites containing toxic horrors such as lead, mercury, and chromium poison more than 125 million people in forty-nine different low- and middle-income nations around the planet.

The authors of the study say this is a very conservative estimate and that likely even more people are sickened by this rampant industrial pollution. In fact, the report says, industrial pollution is now a bigger global health problem for the world than malaria and tuberculosis.

Richard Fuller, the president of the Blacksmith Institute, warned that it's only going to get worse. "Life-threatening pollution will likely increase as the global economy exerts an ever-increasing pressure on industry to meet growing demands," he said. "The damage will be greatest in many low- and middle-income countries, where industrial-pollution-prevention regulations and measures have not kept pace."[9]

But it's not just the developing world that's being poisoned—it's the United States, too.

In 2012, Chris Hedges warned Bill Moyers, "It's absolutely imperative that we begin to understand what unfettered, unregulated capitalism does, the violence of that system."

In his book *Days of Destruction, Days of Revolt*, Hedges documents what he calls "sacrifice zones." He defines them as "areas that have been destroyed for quarterly profit. And we're talking about environmentally destroyed, communities destroyed, human beings destroyed, families destroyed."[10]

They are places like Camden, New Jersey, which is the poorest city per capita in America. Hedges calls it "a dead city." He adds, "There's nothing left. There is no employment. Whole blocks are abandoned. The only thing functioning are open-air drug markets, of which there are about a hundred."

There are also the "sacrifice zones" of West Virginia, where mountaintop mining is poisoning local populations with sky-high cancer rates, and crippling the environment. Hedges says the Royalists are "rendering the area a moonscape. It becomes uninhabitable. [They are] destroying the lungs of the Eastern seaboard. It's all destroyed and it's not coming back."[11]

There are places all across America that have already crashed.

Hedges warns that "because there are no impediments left" in this cancer stage of capitalism, then "these sacrifice zones are just going to spread outward."[12]

Like Gary, Indiana, which used to be home to buzzing manufacturing plants, but is now a ghost town after those plants were all outsourced to low-wage nations. Half of the population has left the city, and it's one of the ten most violent in America.

This is what crash looks like.

Or it looks like Chicago, Illinois, where the effects of wealth inequality have unleashed unthinkable violence on the streets. There are an estimated 100,000 gang members in the city, according to the Chicago Police Gang Enforcement Unit.[13]

The Task

This crash is coming. It's inevitable. I may be off a few years plus or minus in my timing, but the realities of the economic fundamentals left to us by thirty-three years of Reaganomics and deregulation have made it a certainty. We are quite simply repeating the mistakes of the 1920s, the 1850s, and the 1760s, and we are so far into them it's extremely unlikely that anything other than reinflating the recent bubbles to buy a little time here and there will happen.

While the task ahead is daunting, and the prospects for recovery may seem bleak, you will find out what each of us can do to ensure that this Fourth Crash—like the previous Great Crises—ends with the United States of America being, to quote the Constitution, "a more perfect union."

Part 1 of the book begins our quest to figure out who stole the back side of America and how this theft will result in a gut-wrenching Great Crash around the year 2016. We meet the destructive forces who've looted the United States of America over the last several decades. I describe them the same way FDR did, as "Economic Royalists."

Also in part 1, we learn about a cycle fueling American history that allows the Economic Royalists to rise to power every four generations.

In part 2, we learn of the plot hatched in the 1970s by the modern-day Economic Royalists, who sensed that the cycles of "the Great Forgetting" were just coming around again and that they could successfully sneak back into power and loot the nation once again.

In part 3, we see the aftermath of thirty-plus years of Economic Royalist policies, culminating in the financial panic of 2007–08. But rather than the Royalists being expelled from power for crashing the economy, part 3 shows how they were able to hold on to the reins of government and fling the nation toward another, far more catastrophic crash.

In part 4, we explore the various scenarios confronting us with the Crash of 2016—ranging from social disorder to war. And finally, in part 5, we find redemption in post-crash America with specific direction for how America can emerge from this time of instability and chaos.

So let us begin by looking at what's right in front of us but what so many Americans are working so hard to ignore.

PART 1

The Economic Royalists and the Corporatist Conspiracy

Chapter 1

A Rendezvous with Destiny

In this world of ours in other lands, there are some people, who, in times past, have lived and fought for freedom, and seem to have grown too weary to carry on the fight. They have sold their heritage of freedom for the illusion of a living. They have yielded their democracy.
—President Franklin Delano Roosevelt, 1936

There are very few Americans still alive who heard President Franklin D. Roosevelt, in March 1933, address the nation as he was being sworn into office. Which is why many Americans today believe that when FDR famously said, "The only thing we have to fear is fear itself," he was talking about World War II. But Roosevelt said that long before Hitler had even fully consolidated his own power in Germany.

Instead, the fear—and the war—was here in America. He was speaking of the Great Depression and his "war" against those who caused it.

The week of his inauguration, every state in the country closed their banks. The federal government couldn't make its own payroll. A quarter of working-age Americans were unemployed—some measurements put it at a third—and unemployment in minority communities was off the scale.

While Herbert Hoover, when campaigning against Roosevelt in 1932, had denied there was hunger in America, and said, "Even our hoboes are well fed," the truth was that the single largest "occupation" at the time among Americans was "scavenger": people following food trucks and trains, catching the bits that fell off, or doing what we today call "Dumpster diving."

It was so widespread that farmers guarded their farms with shotguns. Every night when restaurants dumped their uneaten food in trash cans in back or side alleys, crowds gathered to pick through, and often fight over, the leftovers.

Roosevelt spoke bluntly about that situation in Great Depression America.

"Values have shrunken to fantastic levels; taxes have risen; our ability to pay has fallen; government of all kinds is faced by serious curtailment of income; the means of exchange are frozen in the currents of trade; the withered leaves of industrial enterprise lie on every side; farmers find no markets for their produce; the savings of many years in thousands of families are gone."[14]

Dissatisfaction with our economic and political systems had reached such a height that machine guns guarded the Capitol and White House. "Hoovervilles"—tent cities of homeless people—had sprung up in every city of America. Bankers and the wealthy elite traveled with elaborate and heavily armed security details, and it was no longer safe for John D. Rockefeller to repeat his earlier publicity stunt of going out onto a New York City street to hand out shiny new dimes to beggars.

This was America during the last Great Crash, a crash that within a decade led to a world war killing more than 60 million people.

Eighty years later, we are well into the next Great Crash, which future generations will call the Crash of 2016. And this one could be even worse than the last one.

There are remarkable similarities between the Crash of 2016 and the last Great Crash, which began on Black Tuesday in 1929.

In fact, there are similarities between both these crashes, and the other two crashes in American history that both led to horrific wars. The first was the economic disaster of the late 1660s to the early 1770s that led Britain to pass (among other things) the Tea Act in 1773, sparking the Boston Tea Party and the Revolutionary War. The second was the Great Panic of 1857, which preceded the Civil War.

It was roughly eighty years from the Revolutionary War to the Civil War, and eighty years from the Civil War to the Great Depression and World War II. And here we are, eighty years after that great disaster. It takes about eighty years for those who remember to thoroughly die out.

We have to see these similarities, to hear their stories, and to get a handle on how to move around them if we hope to mitigate the damages of the Crash of 2016.

The Great Forgetting

For one, each Great Crash is separated by four generations (there's those eighty years).

Arnold Toynbee and others, over the millennia, have pointed out that when the generation that remembers the last Great War has died out, a nation is set on course—some would say *doomed*—to have another war. While the horrors of war are forgotten, the monuments and "heroes" of war are everywhere.

The same is true of the death of the last person remembering a Great Crash.

Daniel Quinn popularized the phrase "the Great Forgetting," and it's true not only of civilizations but of generations as well. Our memories—as a culture—are largely defined by the practical memories of those who participate in media and government, mostly people from their thirties to their sixties. So, at the most, we as a popular culture remember fifty or so years of history at a slice.

My grandfather was a socialist, my dad a Republican. I'm a

progressive. My grandfather, in the first few decades of the twentieth century, had no recollection of a crisis during a previous "socialist" time, and so at one time thought the Soviet experiment might even work out well. My dad, born in 1929, had no memory of a crisis during the administration of a Republican; in fact, his experience of Eisenhower's presidency had been that of a Great Prosperity. And, born in the 1950s, I don't remember the battles or challenges that my dad saw FDR face.

There are great cycles to all of history, including American history. And this cycle rolls forward as each new generation comes to power without personal memory of the mistakes previous generations made, and without memory of the solutions previous generations employed.

Authors William Strauss and Neil Howe suggested, in their seminal 1997 book *The Fourth Turning*,[15] that the United States would, in the first decades of the twenty-first century, once again enter the catastrophic phase of a historic cycle that happens every fourth generation (roughly every eighty years): an economic collapse followed by a great war.

It was a bold prediction, given the Clinton Prosperity in the late 1990s. But it was prophetic.

Less than a decade later, in the fall of 2006, the Federal Reserve Bank of Saint Louis—the part of the larger Fed that compiles housing statistics—noted that housing starts dropped 14.6 percent that month, bringing the total for the twelve-month federal budget year of October-to-October to a 27 percent crash.[16] To make matters worse, building permits were also in free fall, having dropped 28 percent year-to-year at that point.

This was the housing bubble bursting, which triggered the financial crisis of 2007–08.

The Great Forgetting had again descended on the nation, and eighty years after Black Tuesday 1929, the United States was in two full-scale wars and constructing a massive worldwide war machine built on Predator drones.

A Rendezvous with Destiny

In his First Inaugural Address in January 2009, a young President Barack Obama spoke, just as FDR had four generations earlier, to a nation again gripped by an economic crisis.

It was a balmy 42 degrees in Washington, DC, the day Franklin Delano Roosevelt was sworn in nearly eighty years earlier in the midst of a Great Depression.

But as if the political and economic world had grown colder and harder, it was only 28 degrees on Barack Obama's Inauguration Day, with those on the National Mall exhaling white wisps into the freezing air.

I stood about a hundred feet from President Obama as he was sworn in. Just behind him, George W. Bush rolled his eyes and made silly, exaggerated "flipper" applause motions through much of the speech. Dick Cheney, in a wheelchair and covered with a blanket, barely twitched. Their wives sat behind them.

To my left were the assembled members of Congress and the Supreme Court, in front of me the new president, and to my right was the international press corps. In front of the president were nearly two million people, an ocean of humanity that stretched from the Capitol, where we stood on a second-floor balcony, down the National Mall to and beyond where the Washington Memorial pierced the sky.

He began by talking about how the words dictated by the Constitution to swear a new president into office had "been spoken during rising tides of prosperity and the still waters of peace. Yet, every so often the oath is taken amidst gathering clouds and raging storms."[17]

It was the perfect oratorical device, because that very month over 800,000 Americans had lost their jobs, and over a half million had come to the brink of losing their homes. The stock market had crashed, banks were in a crisis worldwide, and two foreign wars were sucking us dry and devastating our image around the world.

"That we are in the midst of crisis is now well understood," President Obama said. "Our nation is at war against a far-reaching network of violence and hatred. Our economy is badly weakened, a consequence of greed and irresponsibility on the part of some but also our collective failure to make hard choices and prepare the nation for a new age.

"Homes have been lost, jobs shed, businesses shuttered. Our health care is too costly, our schools fail too many, and each day brings further evidence that the ways we use energy strengthen our adversaries and threaten our planet.

"These are the indicators of crisis, subject to data and statistics," Obama continued. "Less measurable, but no less profound, is a sapping of confidence across our land; a nagging fear that America's decline is inevitable, that the next generation must lower its sights."

The cycle had come around again. While the last Great Crash is preserved in our history books, newspaper archives, and old film reels, very few people alive actually *remember* it, thus setting it up to happen again.

But just as Roosevelt had done in his first inaugural by saying, "The people of the United States have not failed," President Obama inspired hope on that day of crisis.

"Today I say to you that the challenges we face are real, they are serious and they are many. They will not be met easily or in a short span of time," he said. "But know this, America: They will be met."

Those final four words brought an eruption of applause from many of the members of Congress, and a roar from the two million people stretching down the National Mall all the way to the Washington Monument. Reporters near me leaned forward in rapt attention.

Sounding like a modern-day Franklin Roosevelt, President Obama pressed on.

"The state of our economy calls for action: bold and swift. And we will act not only to create new jobs but to lay a new foundation for growth.

"We will build the roads and bridges, the electric grids and digital lines that feed our commerce and bind us together.

"We will restore science to its rightful place and wield technology's wonders to raise health care's quality and lower its costs.

"We will harness the sun and the winds and the soil to fuel our cars and run our factories. And we will transform our schools and colleges and universities to meet the demands of a new age.

"All this we can do. All this we will do."

The reality, however, remained the same. There were few still alive, when Obama was sworn in, who remembered Franklin D. Roosevelt's response to the Great Depression.

And, thus, as soon as his speech was over, the president's hopeful and idealistic rhetoric ran headfirst into the Great Forgetting, guaranteeing the Crash of 2016.

But what, exactly, is it that we collectively forget every fourth generation that repeatedly threatens the survival of the United States?

The Economic Royalists

After the last Great Crash, FDR understood he was up against more than an economic crisis. He was also up against a counterrevolution, which had caused the Great Crash and was unabashedly seeking to hang on to the power of our government and economy that they'd held for over two decades. They were America's plutocracy—the wealthy bankers and industrialists who put their own personal enrichment ahead of the well-being of the nation with disastrous results.

In his First Inaugural in 1933, FDR alluded to the "rulers of the exchange of mankind's goods" who had "failed."

He told the nation, "Practices of the unscrupulous money changers stand indicted in the court of public opinion, rejected by the hearts and minds of men."

He added, "True they have tried, but their efforts have been cast in the pattern of an outworn tradition. Faced by failure of credit, they have proposed only the lending of more money.

"Stripped of the lure of profit by which to induce our people to follow their false leadership, they have resorted to exhortations, pleading tearfully for restored confidence.

"They know only the rules of a generation of self-seekers. They have no vision, and when there is no vision the people perish."

Roosevelt understood that while genuine kings and theocrats had been pushed to the fringes of the world in the century and a half since the American Revolution, the forces of plutocracy—economic rule by the *very* wealthy—hadn't really gone anywhere. And they'd been running amok during the previous decade.

By 1936, Roosevelt had a name for them: the "Economic Royalists." Eight years later, against the backdrop of World War II, FDR's vice president, Henry Wallace, referred to these plutocratic forces as "Fascists."

During our Revolution, they were called "Loyalists" and "Tories." In the early days of our new nation, they eventually called themselves "Federalists" and were led by America's second president, John Adams, and our first treasury secretary, Alexander Hamilton.

Early on, they were rather benign; the real cancer came as the nation became richer.

By the last half of the nineteenth century, during the Gilded Age in America, the newspapers called them the "Robber Barons."

Today, these forces of the very wealthy are often simply referred to as "the 1 percent" (even though they actually represent a much smaller number than that—a tiny fraction of the top 1 percent of Americans, economically).

Regardless of their name, their rise to power has always been a harbinger of impending collapse.

Their greed made the War of Independence inevitable. They pulled the strings of both the North and South during the Civil War. And they provoked the stock market crash of 1929 triggering the

Great Depression. In fact, our history is one of constant struggle against this cultural infection.

And while iconic figures and people's movements have arisen throughout history to confront these Royalists, there always comes a crack in the struggle when the Great Forgetting takes hold and the Economic Royalists jump into this opening to take the reins of power and pillage the nation into collapse.

American history proves this point.

A Crash Starts a Nation

In 1776, Adam Smith's *Wealth of Nations* was published and the US Declaration of Independence was signed. This was no coincidence: Both were reactions to a widespread economic depression that had begun in the previous decade. England reacted to its economic distress with a series of efforts to raise revenue—the Stamp Act, the Townshend Acts, and the Tea Act (among others).

Many people today think that the Tea Act—which led to the Boston Tea Party—was simply an increase in the taxes on tea paid by American colonists. That's where the whole "taxation without representation" meme came from.

Instead, the purpose of the Tea Act was to give the East India Company full and unlimited access to the American tea trade and to exempt the company from having to pay taxes to Britain on tea exported to the American colonies. It even gave the company a tax refund on millions of pounds of tea that it was unable to sell and holding in inventory.

In other words, the Tea Act was the largest corporate tax break in the history of the world. And since, at the time, most of the British government and royalty were stockholders in the East India Tea Company, it was also a classic example of crony capitalism.

In response, the colonists dressed like Indians in the middle of the night, boarded ships, and commenced the dumping of hundreds of chests of tea overboard—an act that would eventually light the fuse to war.

The American Revolution began with an act of corporate vandalism.

But independence from Britain didn't defeat the Royalists at home.

Our nation's second President John Adams was sympathetic to their cause (although a man of modest means himself).

John Adams and his Federalists were wary of the common person (whom Adams referred to as "the rabble"), and many subscribed to the Calvinist notion that wealth was a sign of certification or blessing from above and proved a certain minimum level of morality.

As second president of the United States, Adams notoriously passed the Alien and Sedition Acts to lock up political dissenters, and moved the country in a more authoritarian and monarchical direction. As Daniel Sisson documents in his incredible book *The American Revolution of 1800*, there were genuine fears among Americans that these early Royalists would blow up the American experiment of democracy and not cede power to Jefferson and the more egalitarian Democratic Republicans in the election of 1800.

Jefferson himself later said, "The Revolution of 1800 was as real a revolution in the principles of our government as that of 1776 was in form."[18]

Jefferson was Adams's chief political rival, and a champion of a democracy responsive to the people and not the wealthy elite. On October 28, 1813, in a letter to his old rival, Jefferson commented on his distrust of that wealthy elite—in particular in the Senate, which was not democratically elected by the people.

Referring to the "cabal in the Senate of the United States," Jefferson wrote, "You think it best to put the pseudo-aristoi into a separate chamber of legislation [the Senate], where they may be hindered from doing mischief by their coordinate branches, and where, also, they may be a protection to wealth against the agrarian and plundering enterprises of the majority of the people."[19]

Then Jefferson countered in the letter, writing, "I [don't] believe them necessary to protect the wealthy; because enough of these will find their way into every branch of the legislation, to protect themselves."

Instead, Jefferson said, "I think the best remedy is exactly that provided by all our constitutions, to leave to the citizens the free election...In general they will elect the really good and wise. In some instances, wealth may corrupt, and birth blind them; but not in sufficient degree to endanger the society."

And in a final warning about the largely Federalist "cabal in the Senate," Jefferson wrote, "The artificial aristocracy is a mischievous ingredient in government, and provision should be made to prevent its ascendancy...I think that to give them power in order to prevent them from doing mischief, is arming them for it, and increasing instead of remedying the evil."

In a 1786 letter, Jefferson gave his most explicit warning about this threat from plutocracy within, and advocated unwavering vigilance against it.

"Tho' the day may be at some distance beyond the reach of our lives perhaps, yet it will certainly come," he wrote, "when a single fibre left of this institution will produce an hereditary aristocracy, which will change the form of our government from the best to the worst in the world."[20]

He added, "I shall think little [of] longevity unless this germ of destruction be taken out."

With the election of Jefferson in 1800, and a civil war averted, the Economic Royalists were held at bay, but they were never defeated. By the 1820s they'd returned, and this time it was Andrew Jackson who stood up to push them back. Jackson campaigned on a platform of overthrowing the banksters.

In 1832, he vetoed a renewal of the charter of the Second Bank of the United States, defending the first fundamental in his veto message by writing, "It is to be regretted that the rich and powerful too often bend the acts of government to their selfish purposes,"[21] but that he would put an end to that by taking on and humbling the bankers. He was the people's hero for doing so.

The Next Cycle: The Civil War

The Founding generation, who in 1776 had pushed back against the Royalists supporting King George III, and the Economic Royalists of the East India Company, who largely controlled all economic life in America, were all long-dead fourscore years later.

That's when Abraham Lincoln was a lawyer in private practice, working for the railroads. On August 12, 1857, he was paid $4,800 in a check, which he deposited and then converted to cash on August 31. That was fortunate for Lincoln, because just over a month later, in the Great Panic of October 1857, both the bank and the railroad were "forced to suspend payment."[22]

Of the sixty-six banks in Illinois, the *Central Illinois Gazette* (Champaign) reported that by the following April, twenty-seven of them had gone into liquidation. It was a depression so vast that the *Chicago Democratic Press* declared at its start, the week of September 30, 1857, "The financial pressure now prevailing in the country has no parallel in our business history."

The crash highlighted the enormous economic struggle under way between the North's and the South's Economic Royalists.

As the Southern plantation/slave economy was turned on its head with the invention of the cotton gin and calls to end slavery, the Royalists were rising up once again. In the North, too, Economic Royalists were amassing power with booming textile factories and little in the way of protections for workers. Ultimately, in a battle for supremacy over the national economy, the Royalists in the North and South tore the union apart in a bloody Civil War.

Even though the scourge of slavery was defeated in the Civil War, the Royalists, who supported both sides, didn't lose the fight. For the next forty years, they ran roughshod over the American economy, prompting Grover Cleveland, the only Democratic elected president during the era, to proclaim in his 1888 State of the Union Address, "The gulf between employers and the employed is constantly widening, and classes are rapidly forming, one comprising the very rich and powerful, while in another are found the toiling poor."

He added, "As we view the achievements of aggregated capital, we discover the existence of trusts, combinations, and monopolies, while the citizen is struggling far in the rear or is trampled to death beneath an iron heel.

"Corporations, which should be the carefully restrained creatures of the law and the servants of the people, are fast becoming the people's masters."[23]

But those who remembered the previous Great Crash and ensuing Civil War were either all dead or had, at least, passed out of power by 1920, when a nation exhausted by World War I elected Warren Harding president on a platform of "more business in government, less government in business," putting an abrupt end to the Progressive Era that had seen two decades of trust-busting, union-organizing, and anticorruption measures such as the Tillman Act of 1907, which banned all corporate contributions to all political candidates.

In his book *Only Yesterday: An Informal History of the 1920's*, published in 1931, American historian Frederick Lewis Allen described the scene in Washington, DC, in 1921 when the Economic Royalists flocked back to the nation's capital now that they had an ally in the White House with Warren G. Harding.

"Blowsy gentlemen with cigars stuck in their cheeks and rolls of very useful hundred-dollar bills in their pockets began to infest the Washington hotels," Allen wrote. "The word ran about that you could do business with the government now—if you only fixed things up with the right man."[24]

And Harding was the rightest of the right men. Harding's secretary of treasury, Andrew Mellon, a wealthy industrialist and banker, promptly shepherded legislation through Congress that slashed taxes for the superwealthy in America from 73 percent down to 25 percent over the next few years, and the Harding administration followed through on its promise of "more business in government"[25] by rolling back labor protections and financial-industry regulations.

After Harding died, two and a half years into his term, the Royalist agenda was advanced by the Coolidge administration, which coined the term "Coolidge Prosperity," referring to the enormous wealth bubble caused by all the "hot" (low-taxed) money produced by Treasury Secretary Mellon's tax cuts and deregulations.

That hot money inflated a real estate bubble that started down in Florida (but had spread nationwide) and popped when a hurricane wiped out Miami in 1926, pushing investors to move their money into the growing stock market bubble. That bubble popped in 1929, and Republican austerity-based responses triggered the Great Depression just as the third Republican president of the era, Herbert Hoover, was settling into the White House.

He later recounted Treasury Secretary Andrew Mellon's advice during the crisis: "Liquidate labor, liquidate stocks, liquidate the farmers, liquidate real estate."[26] In other words, let everything go bankrupt.

Mellon's friends knew what that meant. Once everything hit bottom, then those who understood the nature and causes of the crash—and why and how the Hoover administration had both prolonged it and let it bottom out—could walk into the devastation and buy up everything for cheap. The Royalists were not going to lose, and some of America's greatest fortunes were made during the Great Depression using just this technique.

Within three years of the crash of 1929, almost one-in-four Americans was out of work, tens of thousands of military veterans, calling themselves the "Bonus Army," were "occupying" the National Mall, and loud voices were variously calling for Fascism and Communism as a solution to our nation's problems. It was a time of genuine crisis.

But FDR believed himself equal to the challenge. Being from the Economic Royalist class himself, he well knew that he had to save capitalism from itself, and in the process he could save the nation as well.

"The money changers have fled from their high seats in the temple of our civilization," Roosevelt said in his First Inaugural Address. "We may now restore that temple to the ancient truths. The measure of the restoration lies in the extent to which we apply social values more noble than mere monetary profit."

This crisis was also an opportunity for FDR.

FDR Wages War on the Royalists

In his famous "first hundred days," fifteen major and dozens of minor pieces of legislation, all designed to restore the economic fundamentals necessary to put America back on track, made it through both houses of Congress and to his desk for signature.

They created the Federal Emergency Relief Administration, passing borrowed federal money out to the states to give both benefits and jobs to the unemployed. There was the Public Works Administration, which immediately set about building major projects such as power-generating plants, water and wastewater facilities, schools and hospitals.

People who'd seen their savings wiped out when their banks had gone bankrupt were reassured and brought back to using banks because of the Federal Deposit Insurance Corporation, which guaranteed that the little guy would never again lose his money.

Tens of thousands of young men were put to work immediately through the Civilian Conservation Corps, which threw together tent cities for workers across the nation and set about planting trees and reclaiming agriculture- and grazing-damaged land.

The Works Progress Administration undertook bigger projects—dams and roads—than the PWA had begun. FDR put into place systems that raised workers' wages and improved working conditions; made collective bargaining possible; moved children out of the workplace; provided long-term, government-backed mortgages for underwater homeowners caught with short-term exploding mortgages; limited working hours; and dumped the gold standard, which had been a roadblock to such a rapid expansion of government spending.

It worked. From 1933 to 1937, in just four short years, FDR pulled the national unemployment rate down from over 24 percent to below 15 percent.

In 1921, more than a decade before she won her Pulitzer Prize for reporting, journalist Anne O'Hare McCormick convinced her editor at the *New York Times* to send her to Italy, where she chronicled the rise of the world's first official Fascist, Benito Mussolini. She knew well what it looked like when executive power was used, and when it was abused.

In FDR, Anne McCormick saw the former but not the latter, and she largely echoed the American zeitgeist of the day.

On March 19, 1933, she wrote a full-page article for the *New York Times* titled "The Nation Renews Its Faith: Out of the Swift Succession of Events That Has Marked Two Weeks of the New Deal, This Fact Stands Out: That the Confidence of the People in Government Has Been Re-established."

"Most of all," she wrote in that article about FDR, "he is an instrument of history." She noted that FDR's first two weeks were "more than a transfer of authority from one party to another." It was, she wrote, "a change of government instead of a change in administration."

People who'd lost hope that the federal government could ever be their advocate, that the first three words of the Constitution, "We the People," had been hijacked by banksters and profiteers, that the government could never work for them, had their faith renewed in American institutions.

"One suspects that he expresses the kind of revolution that fires the American mind," McCormick wrote, "a 100 percent American Revolution, whose manifesto is the Constitution."

And by Roosevelt's force of personality, Congress went along.

As McCormick noted, "One reason for the present meekness of both Houses is that every member is practically buried under avalanches of telegrams and letters from constituents. These messages come to Democrats and Republicans alike. Sometimes profane, always imperative, they are mostly variations of a single order: *Support the President: give him anything he wants.*"

Toward the end of the new president's first month, McCormick again published a full-page *New York Times* article about FDR. On March 26, 1933, she wrote, "Mr. Roosevelt thinks and talks a great deal about government...He believes that at every turning point of history some one rises up who can enunciate and in a sense personify the new direction of the public mind and will. In his view America has reached such a crossroads."

By 1936, the Great Depression–induced "fear" that FDR had warned the nation of in his First Inaugural had largely subsided in America because of the revolutionary economic policies he enacted in his first few years in the White House.

However, solving the Great Crash's economic crisis was just the first task. FDR knew the next task was to remain vigilant against the Royalist counterrevolution enabled by the Great Forgetting.

And so, as he was accepting his party's nomination for a second term as president of the United States, Roosevelt said, "Today, my friends, we have won against the most dangerous of our foes. We have conquered fear."

But, he cautioned, "I cannot, with candor, tell you that all is well with the world." He added, "Clouds of suspicion, tides of ill-will and intolerance gather darkly in many places."

In fact, he'd confronted an attempted coup by the Economic Royalists just two years into his first term.

A front man for a group of American banksters and industrialists,

Gerald MacGuire, approached the popular General Smedley Butler about leading an army of 500,000 men, assembling in Elkridge, Maryland, to march into DC and onto the White House lawn to oust FDR.

Butler said that some of the wealthiest bankers and industrialists in the nation were putting up $3 million—over $3 billion in today's dollars. DuPont and Remington were supplying the arms and ammunition for the assault scheduled to begin the following year in 1935.

But General Butler blew the whistle, and the "Business Plot," as it came to be known, was thwarted.

In sworn testimony before the House Un-American Activities Committee, Butler said about MacGuire, "He did not give me the name of it, but he said it would all be made public; a society to maintain the Constitution, and so forth. They had a lot of talk this time about maintaining the Constitution. I said, 'I do not see that the Constitution is in any danger,' and I asked him again, 'Why are you doing this thing?'"

Coconspirators were named in the hearings, including the Rockefellers, the Mellons, the Morgans, the Du Ponts, and the Remingtons. Butler told the Committee that MacGuire had told him, "You know, the president is weak. He will come right along with us. He was born in this class. He was raised in this class, and he will come back. He will run true to form. In the end he will come around."

And it was true that Roosevelt did come from a wealthy family of considerable economic and political influence in New York. He had also practiced corporate law for a Wall Street firm. But despite his outward appearances of wealth and allegiance to the financial elite, Franklin Roosevelt was, at his core, a progressive.

He came of age during the Progressive Era in the early 1900s when his distant cousin (they didn't know each other personally), Teddy Roosevelt, beat back the Robber Baron Economic Royalists. As he summed up while running for governor of New York for the second time in 1930, "Progressive government by its very terms... must be a living and growing thing, that the battle for it is never ending and that if we let up for one single moment or one single year, not merely do we stand still but we fall back in the march of civilization."

So, when the Economic Royalists declared war on FDR, he declared war right back on them. "Here in America we are waging a great and successful war. It is a war for the survival of democracy. We are fighting to save a...precious form of government for ourselves and for the world," he said in that same 1936 speech.[27]

Summarizing America's multigenerational war against the Economic Royalists, Roosevelt went on, "It was to win freedom from the tyranny of political autocracy that the American Revolution was fought. That victory gave the business of governing into the hands of the average man, who won the right with his neighbors to make and order his own destiny through his own government."

However, Roosevelt added, since our War of Independence, "[M]an's inventive genius released new forces in our land which reordered the lives of our people. The age of machinery, of railroads; of steam and electricity; the telegraph and the radio; mass production, mass distribution—all of these combined to bring forward a new civilization and with it a new problem for those who sought to remain free.

"For out of this modern civilization economic royalists carved new dynasties. New kingdoms were built upon concentration of control over material things."

Roosevelt added, "Through new uses of corporations, banks and securities, new machinery of industry and agriculture, of labor and capital—all undreamed of by the Fathers—the whole structure of modern life was impressed into this royal service."

And then the crash happened.

"The collapse of 1929 showed up the despotism for what it was," Roosevelt said. "The election of 1932 was the people's mandate to end it. Under that mandate it is being ended."

Echoing warnings Jefferson made a century and a half earlier, Roosevelt argued that America's survival depended on constant vigilance against the Economic Royalists.

"These economic royalists complain that we seek to overthrow the institutions of America," he said. "What they really complain of is that we seek to take away their power.

"Our allegiance to American institutions requires the overthrow of this kind of power."

He told his fellow Democrats at that 1936 Democratic Convention that he was totally committed to the fight.

Just looking at what was happening in Europe, where the Great Crash was fueling political extremism and unholy alliances between corporate power and autocratic government, FDR knew the stakes couldn't be higher.

"I accept the commission you have tendered me. I join with you. I am enlisted for the duration of the war," Roosevelt exclaimed.

It would prove to be a war unlike any other the planet had ever seen.

The Road to War: Yesterday and Today

The economic crisis afflicting the world in the 1930s was just the first stage of a cycle that was once again descending on humanity. The next stage is always war.

History tells us that in these times of crisis, the Economic Royalists—the bankers, industrialists, billionaires, kleptocrats, fascists—who know exactly what's going on and whose ill-gotten gains had caused the Great Crash to begin with, immediately try to exploit the crisis to further enrich themselves.

They demand compensation for their losses, extracting bailouts and enacting austerity measures on working people, squeezing what little wealth there is left in the common economy, thus deepening the economic crisis.

Under calls for privatization, they assault democratic institutions, cutting off vital lifelines and services for working people.

Aware that just as nature abhors a vacuum, power does also, they use words such as "freedom" and "free market" to push for weaker government, or weaker institutions of organized people, thus clearing room for organized money to take power.

FDR summed up their strategy in 1936, saying, "In vain they seek to hide behind the flag and the Constitution. In their blindness they forget what the flag and the Constitution stand for.

"Now, as always, they stand for democracy, not tyranny; for freedom, not subjection; and against a dictatorship by mob rule and the over-privileged alike."

As the situation for working people deteriorates further, extremist political parties rise up. Desperate populations flock to racist and nationalistic organizations to place blame on someone or something for their economic plight.

America was not spared this extremism, and there were very real moments in the 1930s when it looked like the nation might go too far. But FDR successfully navigated that fine line between far-left and far-right extremist politics that were on the rise across Europe and Asia. Today, it's often said that in those days of Depression, FDR saved capitalism.

But other nations did succumb.

Like the United States, the German economy had collapsed. After defeat in World War I, a brutal austerity regime under the Treaty of Versailles was imposed on Germany to make the country pay for the damage it had caused all around the continent.

The economist John Maynard Keynes warned of the dangers of austerity at the time, writing, "The treaty includes no provisions for the economic rehabilitation of Europe." He added, "The danger confronting us . . . is the rapid depression of the standard of life of the European populations to a point that will mean actual starvation for some.

"Men will not always die quietly. For starvation, which brings to some lethargy and a helpless despair, drives other temperaments to the nervous instability of hysteria and to a mad despair. And these in their distress may overturn the remnants of organisation."

Speaking directly about Germany, Keynes warned, "Those who sign this treaty will sign the death sentence of many millions of German men, women and children."

War

Thus arrived the next stage of the crash: *war.*

A few months before FDR was sworn in during March 1933, Hitler had been appointed chancellor of Germany. In February of that year, his own forces burned down the Reichstag (the German Parliament building, an act that is comparable to burning the US Capitol), and by blaming it on "communists," Hitler got the political capital he needed to consolidate power for the Nazis.

During the next few years, concentration camps were built. Japan invaded China. Italy, which had gone fascist, invaded Ethiopia. Later, a civil war in Spain would give rise to fascism there, too—a comingling of state and corporation laced with hyper-militarism and nationalism. And in March 1936, Hitler invaded the Rhineland, breaking the Treaty of Versailles that had ended World War I.

By 1936, as he was running for a second term, FDR knew of the peril on the horizon. He was also aware of the cycles of history. And he made an impassioned appeal to this new generation of Americans coming to power during another time of crisis.

"There is a mysterious cycle in human events," he said. "To some generations much is given. Of other generations much is expected.

"This generation of Americans has a rendezvous with destiny."

Today, most of FDR's generation has died out, and a new generation has a rendezvous with destiny that is just as perilous as the previous one. The 2008 stock market crash that triggered this next Great Crash is in our rearview mirror. But the Royalists are on the march in the United States and abroad.

Royalist technocrats have seen to it that any Royalist losses from the financial crisis are recovered. They're quietly toppling democratic governments across Europe in Greece, Italy, and Spain, installing Royalist technocrats to oversee harsh austerity measures that cripple working people in order to pay off bankers who made bad investments.

The cycles of history that led to Europe and the rest of the planet breaking into world war eighty years ago are rolling back around today.

In Greece, a modern-day version of the Nazi Party, Golden Dawn, is gaining more popularity among the austerity-ravaged people. In 2009, that party, which embraces Nazi symbolism, racism, and xenophobia, had zero seats in the national parliament. But after three years of austerity, in the 2012 election, Golden Dawn picked up eighteen seats in parliament.

And Golden Dawn is looking to expand its influence, not just in Greece but all around the continent. As the *Guardian* reported in early 2013, "Greek rightwing extremists have been forging close contacts in Germany in an attempt to strengthen their power base in Europe, according to German officials."

In 2012, the European Union was awarded the Nobel Peace Prize for its efforts over the last half century in preventing another Continental war. But four generations later, with fascism once again on the march in Europe, it's becoming increasingly evident that the Nobel Prize committee spoke too soon.

It's looking more and more like 1936 all over again.

Only this time, in America, we don't have an FDR with a solid majority in Congress. And just like after the crash of 1857 and subsequent Civil War, the Economic Royalists find themselves in power once again.

The Economic Royalists have gained majorities in Congress and state legislatures all around the nation, crippling millions of people with brutal austerity cuts to social services, with union busting, and with privatization of the commons.

As the cycle predicts, extremism is on the rise in America. In

2008, there were just 149 militia groups nationwide. By the end of 2012, there were more than 1,200.

And thanks to the Supreme Court's *Citizens United* decision, there's more money in our political system than ever before, and crony capitalism rivals that of the 1920s.

And unique to this cycle are the even more daunting challenges we confront in a rapidly warming planet.

The legendary Bill Moyers bluntly told me back in 2011, "Our democracy is dysfunctional."

He was right then, and it's only gotten worse.

"We no longer have a government of, by, and for the people—representative democracy. We have government by plutocracy—the rule of the rich for the rich by the rich," Moyers said on my television program. "Plutocracy has one purpose, which is to protect wealth."

The hallmark of plutocracy is monopoly. Fewer and fewer companies owning more and more wealth. Competition is destroyed by unrestrained growth of corporate interests. Big companies buy small companies over and over again, until there are no small businesses left. Private-equity firms take care of the rest, even harvesting small- and medium-sized businesses for a profit.

You could parachute from some great altitude over any part of America, into any American city, and you'd have no idea where you are. The great homogenization has happened; all the cities look the same. There are virtually no unique, regional, family-owned small businesses left; just transnational behemoths whose brands populate every mall, downtown, and suburb of this country.

New Royalists such as the Kochs, the Waltons, and the Adelsons have replaced the Rockefellers, Carnegies, Du Ponts, and Morgans of the past.

Bill Moyers, sounding like President Grover Cleveland, noted, "Democracy is in trouble. Democracy in America has been a series of narrow escapes. We may be running out of luck—representative government is threatened at this moment by wealth, power, and corporate conglomerate interests."

A year later, Nobel Prize–winning economist Paul Krugman explained to me, "We are living through a time where we face an enormous economic challenge."

He warned, "There are a lot of ugly forces being unleashed in our societies on both sides of the Atlantic...We may look back at this, thirty years from now, and say, 'That is when it all fell apart.' And by 'all,' I don't just mean the economy."

Morris Berman, in his *Twilight of American Culture*,[28] suggests we must create a new monastic class to preserve classical wisdom and teachings as we enter a repeat of the feudal Dark Ages. This coming period of chaos and darkness, Berman suggests, could easily last a century or more before the next Renaissance lifts again the wisdom of Plato and Shakespeare into the light.

It's remotely possible that things won't get that bad. But that will depend on "We the People" overcoming the new Economic Royalists, who've taken advantage of this next Great Forgetting and are dragging the nation toward the Crash of 2016.

But the greatest probability is that the Obama administration will do the same thing the Bush administration did when confronted with the forces of the oncoming Great Crash in 2007–08. It will tinker around the edges, inflate as many bubbles as possible, and try desperately to hold things off until the November 2016 elections are safely in the bag. If it doesn't all come apart before then, that will be the time of maximum vulnerability.

Chapter 2

A Corporate Call to Arms

A fascist is one whose lust for money or power is combined with such an intensity of intolerance toward those of other races, parties, classes, religions, cultures, regions or nations as to make him ruthless in his use of deceit or violence to attain his ends. The supreme god of a fascist, to which his ends are directed, may be money or power; may be a race or a class; may be a military, clique or an economic group; or may be a culture, religion, or a political party.
> —Vice President Henry Wallace, *New York Times*,
> April 9, 1944

The 1960s came roughly thirty years after Franklin D. Roosevelt first declared war on the Economic Royalists. A war he won by changing the basic American compact from one of "let the rich do what they want, and the working people are on their own" to one where if you worked hard and kept your nose clean, then you could have that "American Dream," even if it meant the rich had to cough up a little more to "spread the wealth."

In those first five decades after the crash, America became a place where you were protected from old age and disability with Social

Security, protected from joblessness with unemployment insurance, and honored with a living wage thanks to strong new protections for labor unions.

Productivity rose at a steady rate—and in lockstep along with it, working people's wages rose. Average working Americans were getting richer and richer, comparatively speaking. A third of the nation's workforce was unionized, and because union jobs set the wage floor in much of America, well over two-thirds of the workforce had all the benefits of a union job. Working-class people bought homes and cars, had affordable health care, and took vacations. By the 1960s, a solid middle class had emerged.

The Royalists were horrified. The conservative intellectual base, such as Russell Kirk and W. F. Buckley, genuinely feared that if a middle class grew large enough—and politically and economically powerful enough—it would inevitably lead to social chaos.

Average and largely unsophisticated factory-working people—and particularly their teenage children—now had more time and money on their hands. And, the Royalists knew, idle hands—with free college, growing civil and social rights, and economic safety—could jeopardize their excessive profits.

The Royalists of the 1950s and early 1960s predicted there would be even louder calls for even more rights. They saw themselves losing control of our nation's politics and, thus, our nation's economic future.

But the Economic Royalists also knew that the vigilant spirit FDR had instilled in the nation against the forces of plutocracy was waning by the end of the 1960s. Those who were just coming into power with FDR during the last Great Crash in 1929 were, by the late 1960s and early 1970s, retiring and dying off, being replaced with a new generation with little direct memory of why the crash had happened, how it had worsened for three long years, and, most important, who'd caused it. And that generation would be teaching the next generation, which had no memory whatsoever of what caused the Great Crash and the war that followed it.

Taking advantage of this Great Forgetting, a new group of Economic Royalists rose up and plotted their way back into power.

The Sixties

According to the first few paragraphs of the *Wikipedia* entry on the 1960s—*Wikipedia* being a heavy target of right-wing think tanks that pay people to essentially rewrite history all across the Internet— the 1960s was a horrible dystopia.

"The 1960s have become synonymous with the new, radical, and subversive events and trends of the period, which continued to develop in the 1970s, 1980s, 1990s and beyond....

"Some commentators have seen in this era a classical Jungian nightmare cycle, where a rigid culture, unable to contain the demands for greater individual freedom, broke free of the social constraints of the previous age through extreme deviation from the norm."[29]

As a young activist in the 1960s, someone who'd tried drugs, meditation, and "free love"; who'd fought and demonstrated against the Vietnam War; and who'd attended college, built a business, and traveled from one end of the country to the other, I don't remember it as a dystopia. For me and many of my generation (I was born in 1951), the sixties were a time of great spiritual growth, insight, and positive social change.

But from the point of view of establishment, wealthy, white male conservatives, the era was a nightmare. They were under siege from every quarter—from their wives, to their children, to their employees.

African Americans—explicitly kept from the American Dream for over four centuries on this continent—were let into previously white-only schools by the Supreme Court in *Brown v. Board of Education* in 1954. In 1964 and 1965, President Lyndon Johnson and a Democratic Congress built on *Brown* with a series of laws enforcing the civil rights of racial minorities and guaranteeing their political rights.

More than four hundred years of pent-up desire for participation and equality collided with the political conservatives who believed social and political change should happen slowly over time, and the spillover was seen from the Afro hairstyle, to a series of sometimes violent Black Liberation movements, to Martin Luther King Jr.'s nonviolent calls for revolution.

The birth control pill was approved for sale to the public in 1961, leading to an explosion of "sexual liberation"—known at the time as "free love." Perhaps more important, it allowed women nearly absolute control over their reproductive decisions (assisted by the Supreme Court's *Roe v. Wade* decision in 1973), allowing women who wanted to compete with men in the workplace to choose to do so without the burden of pregnancy or fear of social ostracism. Then referred to as the "women's liberation movement," everything about it horrified conservatives, from young women going braless (and even burning bras), to the emergence of *Ms.* magazine in 1971.

LBJ not only gave free health care to seniors with a program called Medicare, but he raised taxes on the very, very rich through a sleight of hand that involved dropping the top rate from 90 to 74 percent but closing up so many loopholes that the highest earners actually ended up paying more in income taxes. If there was to be social justice, after all, *somebody* had to pay for it.

There were over 70 million teenagers during that era, a demographic bulge that in both absolute and relative numbers had never before been seen in America. It was the age of youth, and every marketer in America was pandering to the kids, adding to their feeling of empowerment—and to their willingness to openly confront social and political institutions they saw as corrupt or unfair.

Students for a Democratic Society (SDS) was jump-started in large part by Tom Hayden's "Port Huron Statement" in 1962—long before the Vietnam War was an issue—and concerned itself mostly with the inequality of wealth and power in America, and with American militarism. It explicitly called out American institutional racism and the military-industrial complex (a phrase coined by outgoing Republican President Dwight D. Eisenhower in his 1961 farewell address).

In 1962, Rachel Carson published the fifth-best-selling nonfiction book of the entire twentieth century—*Silent Spring*—and ignited an environmental movement that challenged the right of chemical-industry CEOs to poison the environment for profit. In 1965, Ralph Nader published his blockbuster book *Unsafe at Any Speed*, which ignited a consumer movement and challenged the right of auto industry CEOs to risk consumers' lives simply for increased profits. In just a few short years, corporate bigwigs had gone from being hailed and respected to being reviled and suspected.

In the midst of all this, the Supreme Court in 1961 and 1967 made decisions that prevented illegally obtained evidence from being used against criminals (including kids smoking pot) and required that people (including antiwar protestors) be told the rights they had—among which were the right to a free lawyer—when they were arrested.

While the world of America's wealthy was being shaken, their homes and families seemed to be under assault as well. Newspaper heiress Patty Hearst was kidnapped in 1974 by the Symbionese Liberation Army (SLA) and then participated *with* them in robbing a bank.

Self-styled gurus and messiahs—from Reverend Moon to the Maharishi to the Hare Krishnas—popped up all over the nation, popularized by the Beatles' 1967 embrace of Transcendental Meditation. In every city of consequence in America you would see street corners occupied by young people who had given up everything, left family and friends, and joined one of the many cults that sprang up from coast to coast. They sang, they danced, they sold flowers and incense, they begged. In the spirit of Henry David Thoreau, they were on a spiritual pilgrimage, having rejected the religious institutions of the country.

Conservatives tried to push back against the flood that threatened them. Governor Reagan and others began dismantling opportunities for free college education, as this "gift" seemed to simply breed antiwar dissidents and free-loving potheads. Police cracked down—particularly at the 1968 Chicago Democratic Party Convention—and began extensive intelligence-gathering operations against students involved in politics. From coast to coast, political activists were arrested, and when it wasn't easy to jail them for their political activities, they were set up for drug busts.

W. F. Buckley wrote a series of articles with titles like "Let the Rich Alone" (1967), and Russell Kirk joined in with his 1964 "Religious Instruction: A Natural Right." Dr. Hyrum S. Lewis brilliantly documented the entire process in his book *Sacralizing the Right*.[30]

Senator Everett Dirksen attempted to pass a constitutional amendment providing for prayer in public schools, hoping it would calm down future generations; it failed to get even fifty votes.

None of this made sense to the Economic Royalists. History, they believed—from the Roman Empire to feudal Europe to Victorian England—showed that societies were most stable when the middle class was the smallest—not the largest—class in a nation. At the top there should be a small but very, very, very wealthy (and, thus, powerful) ruling class. Below them, a small middle class of professionals and mercantilists—the doctors, lawyers, bankers, and shop owners—and below them a huge class of the working poor.

As Charles Dickens pointed out in nearly all his books (his father had been thrown in debtors prison when he was a child—he knew the system well), the working poor don't turn universities upside down or go nuts with sex, drugs, or religion. His famous *A Christmas Carol* was the story of Ebenezer Scrooge, a *middle-class* mercantilist who ran a two-person small business. Scrooge discovered that while it was still important to keep his working-poor employee (Bob Cratchit) in poverty, it was OK to give the man a turkey and a small bit of health care for Tiny Tim. But, of course, never was there even a mention that Cratchit should get partial ownership of the business or have any real power or wealth.

But the 1960s changed everything. Hunter S. Thompson ("the Doctor of Journalism") summed up the energy of the decade in his book *Fear and Loathing in Las Vegas*: "There was madness in any direction, at any hour...You could strike sparks anywhere. There was a fantastic universal sense that whatever we were doing was *right*, that we were winning...that sense of inevitable victory over the forces of Old and Evil...We had all the momentum; we were riding the crest of a high and beautiful wave."

From the viewpoint of the Economic Royalists, never in the history of modern civilization had the fundamental social (and, thus, economic and political) order been under such attack. It was the opposite of what happened in the late 1800s when the Royalists seized power after a Great Crash and war, ushering in a Gilded Age for the 1 percent. This time, organized people had beaten back organized money. Or, so it seemed.

But when the Great Forgetting finally came around, that wave, as Thompson had described it, finally broke, and then rolled back.

The Powell Memo

Lewis F. Powell Jr. was just sitting down to breakfast in his suite at the Waldorf Astoria Hotel in New York City, when he received a call from the White House.

The year was 1971—more than forty years since the last Great Crash. The sixties had ended and the Vietnam War had destroyed the Democratic Party, leaving Richard Nixon as president of the United States. And Nixon needed a favor.

A Corporate Call to Arms

A thin, ascetic man with wispy hair and fragile features, Powell had ancestral roots in America's first European settlement, Jamestown, and a lifetime of participation in the law. He deeply loved his Richmond, Virginia, home, and the law practice he had there, which mostly consisted of defending corporate interests and wealthy Southern white men.

He walked comfortably, often in crepe-soled shoes, dressed as a Southern gentleman, and spoke so softly that people sometimes leaned forward to listen. But when he spoke, his words were precise, well measured, and carefully considered.

He was one of the most brilliant jurists of his day, and it's no surprise that the Nixon White House was considering him for a seat on the Supreme Court, a job he turned down at first, but then, when Nixon called him again at the Waldorf Astoria, reluctantly accepted.

As a Supreme Court Justice, Lewis Powell was very much the moderate, and his legacy on the high court would reflect his balanced and authentic interpretation of the rule of law in America.

However, just a few months before he was nominated by Nixon, Powell had written a memo to his good friend Eugene Sydnor Jr., the director of the United States Chamber of Commerce at the time. And Powell's most indelible mark on the nation was not to be his fifteen-year tenure as a Supreme Court Justice, but instead that memo, which served as a declaration of war—a war by the Economic Royalists against both democracy and what they saw as an overgrown middle class. It would be a final war, a *bellum omnium contra omnes*, against everything the New Deal and the Great Society had accomplished.

It wasn't until September 1972, ten months after the Senate confirmed Powell, that the public first found out about the Powell Memo (the actual written document had the word "Confidential" stamped on it—a sign that Powell himself hoped it would never see daylight outside of the rarified circles of his rich friends). By then, however, it had already found its way to the desks of CEOs all across the nation and was, with millions in corporate and billionaire money, already being turned into real actions, policies, and institutions.

During its investigation into Powell as part of the nomination process, the FBI never found the memo, but investigative journalist Jack Anderson did, and he exposed it in a September 28, 1972, column titled, "Powell's Lesson to Business Aired."

Anderson wrote, "Shortly before his appointment to the Supreme Court, Justice Lewis F. Powell Jr. urged business leaders in a confidential memo to use the courts as a 'social, economic, and political' instrument."[31]

Pointing out that the memo wasn't discovered until after Powell was confirmed by the Senate, Anderson wrote, "Senators...never got a chance to ask Powell whether he might use his position on the Supreme Court to put his ideas into practice and to influence the court in behalf of business interests."[32]

This was an explosive charge being leveled at the nation's rookie Supreme Court Justice, a man entrusted with interpreting the nation's laws with complete impartiality.

But Jack Anderson was no stranger to taking on American authority, and no stranger to the consequences of his journalism. He'd exposed scandals from the Truman, Eisenhower, Nixon, and later the Reagan administrations. He was a true investigative journalist.

In his report on the memo, Anderson wrote, "[Powell] recommended a militant political action program, ranging from the courts to the campuses."[33]

Powell's memo was both a direct response to Roosevelt's battle cry decades earlier and a response to the tumult of the 1960s. He wrote, "No thoughtful person can question that the American economic system is under broad attack."[34]

When Sydnor and the Chamber received the Powell Memo, corporations were growing tired of their second-class status in America.

Even though the previous forty years had been a time of great growth and strength for the American economy and America's middle-class workers—and a time of sure and steady increases of profits for corporations—CEOs felt something was missing.

If only they could find a way to wiggle back into the people's minds (who were just beginning to forget the Royalists' previous exploits of the 1920s), then they could get their tax cuts back; they could trash the "burdensome" regulations that were keeping the air we breathe, the water we drink, and the food we eat safe; and the banksters among them could inflate another massive economic bubble to make themselves all mind-bogglingly rich. It could, if done right, be a return to the Roaring Twenties.

But how could they do this? How could they convince Americans to take another shot at what was widely considered a dangerous "free market" ideology and economic framework and that Americans once knew preceded each Great Crash and war?

Lewis Powell had an answer, and he reached out to the Chamber of Commerce—the hub of corporate power in America—with a strategy.

As Powell wrote, "Strength lies in organization, in careful long-range planning and implementation, in consistency of action over an indefinite period of years, in the scale of financing available only through joint effort, and in the political power available only through united action and national organizations." Thus, Powell said, "The role of the National Chamber of Commerce is therefore vital."[35]

In the nearly six-thousand-word memo, Powell called on corporate leaders to launch an economic and ideological assault on college and high school campuses, the media, the courts, and Capitol Hill.

The objective was simple: the revival of the Royalist-controlled so-called "free market" system.

Or, as Powell put it, using Royalist rhetoric, "[T]he ultimate issue... [is the] survival of what we call the free enterprise system, and all that this means for the strength and prosperity of America and the freedom of our people."

On Campus

The first area of attack Powell encouraged the Chamber to focus on was the education system. "[A] priority task of business—and organizations such as the Chamber—is to address the *campus* origin of this hostility [to big business]," Powell wrote.[36]

What worried Powell was the new generation of young Americans growing up to resent corporate culture. He believed colleges were filled with "Marxist professors," and that the pro-business agenda of Harding, Coolidge, and Hoover had fallen into disrepute since the Great Depression. He knew that winning this war of economic ideology in America required spoon-feeding the next generation of leaders the doctrines of a free-market theology, from high school all the way through graduate and business school.

At the time, college campuses were rallying points for the progressive activism sweeping the nation as young people demonstrated against poverty, the Vietnam War, and in support of civil rights.

So Powell put forward a laundry list of ways the Chamber could retake the higher-education system. First, create an army of corporate-friendly think tanks that could influence education. "The Chamber should consider establishing a staff of highly qualified scholars in the social sciences who do believe in the system," he wrote.[37]

Then, go after the textbooks. "The staff of scholars," Powell wrote, "should evaluate social science textbooks, especially in economics, political science and sociology...This would include assurance of fair and factual treatment of our system of government and our enterprise system, its accomplishments, its basic relationship to individual rights and freedoms, and comparisons with the systems of socialism, fascism and communism."[38]

Powell argued that the civil rights movement and the labor movement were already in the process of rewriting textbooks. "We have seen the civil rights movement insist on re-writing many of the textbooks in our universities and schools. The labor unions likewise insist that textbooks be fair to the viewpoints of organized labor."[39] Powell was concerned the Chamber of Commerce was not doing enough to stop this growing progressive influence and replace it with a pro-plutocratic perspective.

"Perhaps the most fundamental problem is the imbalance of many faculties," Powell then pointed out. "Correcting this is indeed a long-range and difficult project. Yet, it should be undertaken as a part of an overall program. This would mean the urging of the need for faculty balance upon university administrators and boards of trustees."[40] As in, the Chamber needs to infiltrate university boards in charge of hiring faculty to make sure only corporate-friendly professors are hired.

But Powell's recommendations weren't exclusive to college campuses; he targeted high schools as well. "While the first priority should be at the college level, the trends mentioned above are increasingly evidenced in the high schools. Action programs, tailored to the high schools and similar to those mentioned, should be considered," he urged.[41]

Next, Powell turned the corporate dogs on the media. As Powell instructed, "Reaching the campus and the secondary schools is vital for the long-term. Reaching the public generally may be more important for the shorter term."

Powell added, "It will...be essential to have staff personnel who are thoroughly familiar with the media, and how most effectively to communicate with the public."

He then went on to say that same system used for the monitoring of college textbooks should be applied to television and radio networks. "This applies not merely to so-called educational programs...but to the daily 'news analysis' which so often includes the most insidious type of criticism of the enterprise system."

Powell didn't know it yet, but somebody in the Nixon administration was already on the same page as him when it came to injecting Royalist ideology into the media.

The GOP TV Memo and Roger Ailes

Today, Roger Ailes is the chairman of Fox News (he literally goes by the name of "The Chairman"). He, alongside his boss Rupert Murdoch, is one of the most influential newsmen in America—even though what he pushes can hardly be considered "news." And like any good foot soldier of the Economic Royalists, he runs an extremely lucrative enterprise.

But the profitability of Fox News pales in comparison to its influence on the political landscape in America—and we can thank Roger Ailes for that. In fact, Roger Ailes has been the man behind the curtain at virtually every watershed moment in the Royalist resurgence in America.

Rolling Stone writer Tim Dickinson notes, "As a political consultant, Ailes repackaged Richard Nixon for television in 1968, papered over Ronald Reagan's budding Alzheimer's in 1984, shamelessly stoked racial fears to elect George H. W. Bush in 1988, and waged a secret campaign on behalf of Big Tobacco to derail health care reform in 1993."[42]

While working in the Nixon White House in 1970, Roger Ailes enthusiastically supported an idea known as "GOP TV."

This plan for the Republican/Royalist takeover of television was largely unknown until recently, when investigative reporter John Cook uncovered a cache of documents from the Richard Nixon Presidential Library. One of those documents, a memo titled "A Plan for Putting the GOP on TV News" outlines in great detail how the Nixon administration could subvert television news and get their Republican-friendly message out across America. It's unclear who originally wrote the document, but Roger Ailes's personal handwriting is all over the margins with his input on how to get "GOP TV" up and running.

The memo begins by noting a substantial change in where Americans are getting their news. "Television news is watched more often . . .

than people read newspapers, than people listen to radio, than people read or gather any other form of communication," reads the memo.[43]

On the margins, Ailes hammers home the point, writing, "44% say TV is more believable than any other medium."

What comes next in the memo is a purpose statement, reading, "Purpose—To provide pro-Administration videotape, hard new actualities to the major cities of the United States," followed by an actual business proposal, complete with estimated costs of production equipment, news crews, and a fancy "customized" editing and delivery truck.

Under a section entitled "The Plan—TV News Operation," the memo details exactly how GOP TV would work. It goes something like this: A Republican politician in Washington, DC, would record a message for their constituents—dishing out their talking points on whatever hot-button issue Congress is focusing on that week.

Next, that message would be edited down to fit into the "crammed" television news environment and duplicated. Here's where the GOP TV truck was necessary. In order to save time, all the video would be edited down in the truck after the shoot as the truck was driving to Washington National Airport to immediately freight the TV reels out to local news affiliates around the country to air that night. The memo estimated the entire process could be done in "four to eight hours."

This was before satellite TV distribution existed, so the plan envisioned in the GOP TV memo was essentially the only way to execute rapid-response Republican messaging on a national scale.

All in all, "GOP TV" came with the fairly hefty price tag of $375,000 for all the equipment plus another $167,000 for a year's worth of operating costs. Ailes surmised in his notes on the memo that the White House or the Republican National Committee could foot the costs.

At the end of the memo, Ailes makes a pitch for his production company in New York to run GOP TV. He writes, "We would as a production company like to bid on packaging the entire project. I know what has to be done...If you are interested I'll have my N.Y office put together a) 90 day pilot costs b) cost to continue on annual basis." Ailes signs off on the memo with, "Best Regards, Roger."

This memo—the blueprint for instilling Royalist ideology into our nation's news media—was discovered toward the end of 2010, just as Fox News was enjoying unprecedented success and influence in steering the national political debate toward Republican aims, giving that party an enormous victory in the 2010 midterm elections. The memo garnered little news attention around the nation.

But the meteoric rise of Fox News and the realization of Roger Ailes's vision of GOP TV cannot be attributed to Richard Nixon's White House, because Nixon's people ultimately rejected the idea— citing concerns that it wasn't economically "feasible."

But thanks in part to the Powell Memo, a generation later there'd be a lot of financial backing for Royalist media, just as Ailes envisioned it.

The Courts and the Capitol

Subverting the national education system and media were necessary for the long-term seduction of the American people by the Economic Royalists. But for immediate change, Powell saw an opportunity in the courts and on Capitol Hill.

"The educational programs suggested above would be designed to enlighten public thinking," Powell wrote.

"But," he added, "one should not postpone more direct political action, while awaiting the gradual change in public opinion to be effected through education and information."

Then Powell bluntly laid it out: "Business must learn the lesson, long ago learned by labor and other self-interest groups. This is the lesson that political power is necessary; that such power must be cultivated; and that when necessary, it must be used aggressively and with determination—without embarrassment and without the reluctance which has been so characteristic of American business."

He concluded, "As unwelcome as it may be to the Chamber, it should consider assuming a broader and more vigorous role in the political arena."

Whether it was exclusively a result of Powell's instructions, or a consequence of the Great Forgetting, or both, corporate lobbying in Washington exploded just after the Powell Memo was sent.

In 1971, only 175 companies had registered lobbyists. By 1982, there were nearly 2,500. Royalists were dumping huge amounts of money lobbying for favorable legislation. At the same time, they were seeding brand-new right-wing think tanks devoted to espousing the same free-market, Andrew Mellon, Warren Harding ideologies that led to the last Great Crash: massive tax cuts, deregulation, and privatization.

The American Legislative Exchange Council was founded in 1973. So, too, was the Heritage Foundation. And in 1977, the CATO Institute was founded, first as the Charles Koch Foundation, and then renamed a few years later as CATO. These Royalist think tanks were (and are) backed by millions of dollars from modern corporate Economic Royalists.

But to Powell, a lawyer, nothing was more important than targeting the courts.

He writes, "Under our constitutional system, especially with an activist-minded Supreme Court, the judiciary may be the most important instrument for social, economic and political change."

He notes, "This is a vast area of opportunity for the Chamber, if it is willing to undertake the role of spokesman for American business and if, in turn, business is willing to provide the funds."

Laying out specifics, Powell adds, "The Chamber would need a highly competent staff of lawyers. In special situations it should be authorized to engage, to appear as counsel amicus in the Supreme Court, lawyers of national standing and reputation. The greatest care should be exercised in selecting the cases in which to participate, or the suits to institute. But the opportunity merits the necessary effort."

In the 1970s, with the Royalists' Chamber of Commerce now focused on the courts, employing high-priced, savvy lawyers, and flooding the Supreme Court chamber with amicus briefs, a string of explosive decisions throughout the decade would give the Royalists what they needed to eventually overthrow FDR's New Deal Revolution that was culminating in the 1960s.

In 1976, in *Buckley v. Valeo*, the Supreme Court ruled that political money is speech, implying that those who have more money have more free speech in our political system. That same year, in *United States v. Martin Linen Supply Co.*, corporations are given Fifth Amendment protections against double jeopardy. And in *Virginia State Board of Pharmacy v. Virginia Citizens Consumer Council*, the Supreme Court ruled that advertising is a protected form of free speech.

A year later, in 1977, in *First National Bank of Boston v. Bellotti*, the Supreme Court overturned state restrictions on corporate political spending, saying such restrictions violate the First Amendment.

In their dissents in the case, Justices White, Brennan, and Marshall argue, "The special status of corporations has placed them in a position to control vast amounts of economic power which may, if not regulated, dominate not only our economy but the very heart of our democracy, the electoral process."

Then came the Federalist Society, founded in 1982 with millions of dollars in funding by the Royalist-allied Bradley Foundation, which built a nationwide network of jurists, attorneys, legal scholars, and politicians to indoctrinate a new generation's legal system with Royalist interpretations: Corporate personhood is real, money is speech, democracy is not sacred, and organized money should always have privilege over organized people.

A new wave was rising, and sweeping across the political and economic landscape in America. Unlike in the 1960s, the Economic Royalists were riding this one.

Chapter 3

The Crisis Capitalists

Instead of citizens, it produces consumers. Instead of communities, it produces shopping malls. The net result is an atomized society of disengaged individuals who feel demoralized and socially powerless. In sum, neoliberalism is the immediate and foremost enemy of genuine participatory democracy, not just in the United States but across the planet, and will be for the foreseeable future.
—Professor Robert W. McChesney, 1999

Just as Lewis Powell's memo was being circulated in corporate boardrooms across America, a social democracy under pressure in Latin America fell. And the Economic Royalists saw an opportunity to remake the world into a neofeudal corporatocracy.

After a military coup in September 1973, the democratically elected socialist president of Chile, Salvador Allende, wound up with a bullet in his head. His country was taken over by General Augusto Pinochet, kicking off a more-than-a-decade-long rule of terror that led to the death and detention of tens of thousands of people.

General Pinochet was adept at running a military state and ruthlessly squashing dissension. But he knew nothing about economics.

And to the Economic Royalists, who were just coming out of the shadows in America, Chile was a blank slate—the perfect opportunity to reintroduce the world to Royalist economics.

Killing Keynes

While Adam Smith was the guy who put economics on the map in the eighteenth century, John Maynard Keynes made it useful for governments.

Keynes saw the importance of a market-based economy, where private citizens were free to buy and sell as they please. He saw that as the best way to amass wealth and improve the lives of everyone in a society. But Keynes knew there was a danger in letting that free market exist completely unchecked, as the Royalists had urged, and argued that unrestrained capitalism will lead to perpetual boom-and-bust cycles—people making huge amounts of money...and then jumping off buildings when they lose it all.

To stabilize the system, Keynes argued that the government should step in. With a number of tools at its disposal, such as the ability to manipulate the money supply and put in place regulations, as well as to spend huge amounts of money, the government can mediate the mood swings of the economy. There would still be recessions, but under the new Keynesian mixed economy, those recessions would be short-lived, and over the long haul the society would experience sustained growth.

A core element of Keynes's theory was that an economy churned because of three basic actions: consumer spending, business spending, and government spending. When a recession crept in, and businesses got wiped out and consumers were laid off and unable to spend money, then it was up to that critical third piece of the puzzle—government spending—to kick in and keep the economy afloat.

When Franklin Roosevelt was elected in 1932, he looked to

Keynes to help get the United States out of the Great Depression. He infused into the economy massive amounts of money in an attempt to get consumers spending again and to give businesses a reason to expand and hire more workers. And it worked.

Sure enough, after the Great Depression, our nation for the first time saw sustained financial stability and the rise of a remarkable American middle class. Because more people had more money in their pockets, they spent more as consumers, and industries all around the nation expanded and further employed more people.

Recessions were short-lived, and economic growth was sustained. Things were working the way they were supposed to. This was the birth of American Social Democracy—or New Deal Economics—a capitalist system that still bred winners and losers but ensured that losers wouldn't be condemned to death and that winners wouldn't have the power to bring down the entire system.

In fact, the entire world adopted a sort of Keynesian economic philosophy, from market economies like in America, where a government simply acted like a referee intervening whenever things got a little too hot or too cold, to economies such as those of the Democratic Socialist states of northern Europe, where the government was much more involved in virtually every aspect of the economy.

But not everyone bought into what Keynes was selling—most notably, a colleague of Keynes's at King's College, Cambridge, Friedrich Hayek, who went in the opposite direction.

The two men knew each other very well; they spent many nights perched atop the roof of the King's College chapel amid German bombing raids during the height of World War II. As the Germans dropped firebombs onto England, Keynes and Hayek were given the task of disposing of, armed only with shovels, any bombs that might land on the chapel before they could be detonated. Keynes was over sixty years old at the time, and Hayek was in his forties—neither man was really qualified for the job. But luckily, they never needed to use their bomb shovels.

Hayek promoted what was called neoliberalism, an economy based solely on free markets. Yes, despite the catastrophic economic damage caused repeatedly by unrestrained free markets, wealth inequality, and dismantled social safety nets, those promoting this destructive ideology never gave up.

Neoliberals like Hayek believed that markets free from democratic intervention could somehow make everyone richer and create an economic utopia, and this belief persists despite its failure everywhere it's been tried around the world.

The neoliberals were overwhelmingly rejected around the world after the last Great Crash and war—banished to the fringes of economic thinking. But, from those fringes, they plotted their comeback.

The Mont Pelerin Society

In 1947, two years after the war ended, Friedrich Hayek gathered a large group of economists, historians, journalists, and businessmen to a meeting in Mont Pelerin, Switzerland.

A man named Milton Friedman was one of those economists in attendance.

He'd graduated high school almost twenty years earlier, in 1928, one year before the stock market crash, and received his college education at Rutgers University and the University of Chicago during the height of the Great Depression.

Friedman was the first member of his family to go to college, and the economic upheaval under way in America motivated him to study economics. As he said, "Put yourself in 1932 with a quarter of the population unemployed. What was the important urgent problem? It was obviously economic and so there was never any hesitation on my part to study economics."[44]

Out of school, Friedman went to work for Franklin Roosevelt's New Deal government, first for the National Resources Committee, then the National Bureau of Economic Research, and then the

Treasury Department. At the time, he believed in the New Deal in a broad sense, and in the Keynesian economic theory underpinning it.

But after the war, as the Great Crash twenty years earlier began receding from collective memory, Friedman found himself drawn to Hayek's religion of free markets.

And so he was on hand in 1947 for the first meeting of what would be known as the Mont Pelerin Society. The purpose was clear. Hayek saw the momentum building around the world for socialist revolutions and more control of markets, and he wanted to cut it off.

Friedman described this meeting, and his tone foreshadows the tone used in an infamous twenty-four-years-later memo by Lewis Powell.

"The point of the meeting was very clear," said Friedman. "It was Hayek's belief, and the belief of other people who joined him there, that freedom was in serious danger."[45]

The reason, Freidman said, was because "during the war, every country had relied heavily on government to organize the economy, to shift all production toward armaments and military purposes. And you came out of the war with the widespread belief that the war had demonstrated that central planning would work.

"And so there were strong movements everywhere," said Friedman. "In Britain a socialist [Clement Attlee] had won the election. In France there was indicative planning that was [in] development. And so everywhere, Hayek and others felt that freedom was very much imperiled, that the world was turning toward planning and that somehow we had to develop an intellectual current that would offset that movement.

"Essentially, the Mont Pelerin Society," said Friedman, "was an attempt...to start a movement, a road to freedom as it were."

But what Hayek was unable to do, mainly because he was operating with the catastrophic consequences of his free-market philosophy still fresh in everyone's mind, Friedman would do—and that's lead a global counterrevolution against controlled capitalism, and in particular against the New Deal.

He took Hayek's message to his alma mater, the University of Chicago, where he and other free-marketeers would banter among themselves in an echo chamber while the rest of the world forged ahead with successful "socialized" economies.

But the "Chicago Boys," as they would soon be called, led by Milton Friedman, would be ready at a moment's notice to reintroduce neoliberalism to the world. He just had to be patient and wait for the Great Forgetting—or a crisis.

Shock Troopers

In his 1962 book *Capitalism and Freedom*, Milton Friedman wrote about crises.

"There is enormous inertia—a tyranny of the status quo—in private and especially governmental arrangements."[46] That "status quo" he was referring to was Kennedy's America when the middle class was on the rise and our nation was the envy of the entire noncommunist world.

"Only a crisis—actual or perceived," Friedman wrote, "produces real change."

Friedman was a crisis guy. He knew how transformational crises could be, and exploited them any chance he got. As he wrote, "Our basic function ... [is] to develop alternatives to existing policies, to keep them alive and available until the politically impossible becomes politically inevitable."

Naomi Klein, in her book *The Shock Doctrine*, chronicles Friedman's exploitations of crises to promote free-market capitalism. "Some of the most infamous human rights violations of this era, which have tended to be viewed as sadistic acts carried out by undemocratic regimes," Klein explains, "were in fact either committed with the deliberate intent of terrorizing the public or actively harnessed to prepare the ground for the introduction of radical free-market 'reform.'"[47]

The Crisis Capitalists

These so-called free-market reforms promoted by the members of the Mont Pelerin Society and later the Chicago Boys do not constitute a legitimate economic theory, as they've never worked anywhere they've been tried, anywhere in the world. They constitute a religion.

Yet this religion actually serves as the intellectual underpinning of the Economic Royalist plan for society. And it would seem to be the spear tip for reclaiming power by the Economic Royalists.

Their first opportunity came in Chile in 1973.

General Augusto Pinochet outsourced the work of building a new economy in Chile to Milton Friedman and the Chicago Boys.

Friedman's "Chicago Boys" were eager to help General Pinochet in Chile. It was their first big gig, and Milton Friedman went to Chile with a plan to radically remake the depressed economy.

They would immediately privatize government industries, cut spending, and open up Chilean markets to free trade. No more Keynesian economics, in which the government kept greed and monopoly under control: The Chicago Boys handed the millionaires in Chile the golden key to the country's treasury and said, "Get to work." There would be no gradual repairs. The Chicago Boys would simply sink the ship and build a new one.

As a result, the Chilean economy collapsed (as has happened every time this sort of thing has been tried, anywhere in the world, throughout world history), and this time there was no longer a social safety net to help people. The unrest in the country grew, and so did the violence.

But to the Chicago Boys, this was all part of the plan. They knew reforms would be painful, and for them it was "no pain, no gain." But the Chicago Boys had a different definition of "no pain, no gain" and it went something like this: If the vast majority of the population doesn't experience the pain of immediate economic reform, then the very few people who make up the wealthy elite won't see their gain of massively greater wealth.

Orlando Letelier was a diplomat and economist who escaped Pinochet's bloody coup in Chile and fled to Washington, DC. In 1976, three years into the Chicago Boys' experiment in Chile, Letelier penned an article in *The Nation* entitled "The Chicago Boys in Chile: Economic Freedom's Awful Toll." As the title suggests, Letelier exhaustively outlined Friedman's failures in his home country.

Letelier points out that, two years into Pinochet and the Chicago Boys' rule, inflation had reached 341 percent—higher than anywhere else in the world. The price of goods increased by 375 percent. GDP decreased by 15 percent. Agriculture production sputtered to a grinding halt. Export values dropped 28 percent and Chile acquired a $280 million trade deficit. And to top everything off, Chile's unemployment rate skyrocketed from 3 percent—among the lowest in that hemisphere—before Friedman stepped foot in the country to more than 10 percent and, in some parts of the country, as high as 22 percent after Friedman left.[48]

Letelier concluded by writing, "Three years have passed since this experiment began in Chile and sufficient information is available to conclude that Friedman's Chilean disciples failed."

But judging the success of an economy based on economic indicators isn't how the Chicago Boys rolled. They judged success another way, as Letelier indicated: "But they have succeeded, at least temporarily, in their broader purpose: to secure the economic and political power of a small dominant class by effecting a massive transfer of wealth from the lower and middle classes to a select group of monopolists and financial speculators."

All of these economic pains took place under the backdrop of a dictator willing to kill anyone who showed the slightest opposition to Friedman's economics. And that included Orlando Letelier, who was assassinated in 1976, when a Pinochet hit squad rigged his car with a bomb.

Despite the wave of violence and abysmal economic indicators, the Chicago Boys were happy with what they accomplished. It would be a common theme elsewhere around South America and the former Soviet bloc, as so-called crises were exploited and new economies "of, by, and for the rich" began to develop under the guidance of the Chicago Boys and others who subscribed to Friedman's economic "shock therapy."

According to the criteria of the Economic Royalists, Friedman's Chilean experiment was a resounding success. And with the Great Forgetting taking hold, the corporatist intellectual community around the world was warming up to the same old Royalist policies that had wrought so much pain generations earlier.

A Global Shift

Just as Friedman was busy running the nation of Chile into the ground in 1974, his mentor, Friedrich Hayek, emerged from the shadows to be recognized by the central bank of Sweden with their Nobel Prize for Economics.

The bank intended to solely honor Swedish socialist Gunnar Myrdal. Myrdal is perhaps best known for his book *An American Dilemma: The Negro Problem and Modern Democracy*, a book written about race relations in America in 1944 that would serve as the basis for the US Supreme Court's decision in the *Brown v. Board of Education* case.

But the bank feared that it would be criticized for "home cooking" by selecting a fellow Swede, so they threw Hayek into the ceremony as well. That decision didn't sit too well with many in the global economics community, including Myrdal, who thought of Hayek, with his free-market ideology, as a radical wingnut. As did most people at the time.

But Daniel Yergin, author of the book *Commanding Heights*, recounts this story and sheds some light on its significance saying, "[T]he award documented the beginning of a great shift in the intellectual center of gravity of the economies profession toward a restoration of confidence in markets, indeed a renewed belief in the superiority of markets over other ways of organizing economic activity." Yergin noted, "Within a decade and a half, the shift would be largely complete."

Two years later, the Nobel economics prize was awarded to Milton Friedman alone in 1976. The changing of the guard was complete.

As with Hayek's coronation, no one was happy with the decision to honor Milton Friedman that year. Chile was in chaos, and tens of thousands had been murdered at the behest of Pinochet. As a result, Sweden was flooded with protestors condemning Friedman and the Swedish Central Bank.

Friedman's wife, Rose, recounted the couple's trip to receive the award in a 1998 article entitled "One Week in Stockholm," which ran in the *Hoover Digest*. Rose describes a hostile environment in which she and her husband were under constant threat. She wrote, "From that moment until we left, we were never without our two bodyguards. In addition, our room was under surveillance day and night by other police. Not even a maid, we discovered, was permitted to enter our room without a police escort!"[49]

Former recipient of the prize Gunnar Myrdal, who had shared the honors with Hayek two years earlier, was appalled and called for the abolishment of the Swedish Bank's Nobel Prize for Economics.

But despite all the grievances, the neoliberalism movement was now afoot and had gained legitimacy—and the Royalists were thrilled. As Daniel Yergin noted, "a great shift" was now under way.

Three years later, Margaret Thatcher, a devout follower of Friedman's economic philosophy, would rise to power in the United Kingdom, deregulate her nation, open up the markets, and cut government spending.

The "Crisis" Comes to America

My wife, Louise, and I had moved to Detroit in the summer of 1973 so I could take a job with RCA that offered health insurance, as Louise was pregnant with our first child. We lived in Westland, a western Detroit suburb on the glide path to the Detroit airport, in a tiny rented house.

In early October 1973, Egypt (with the help of Syria) attacked Israel in what is now known as the Yom Kippur War. Israel fought back and routed their opposing forces, taking large chunks of Egyptian land during the Six-Day War. Because the United States was backing Israel, the Arab world was outraged, and a couple of weeks after the October 6 attack, OPEC's ministers met and announced they were cutting off their exports of oil to the United States and a few other countries. That embargo lasted until March 1974, although its effects continued to echo for years.

In no particular order, I remember President Nixon announcing rationing and asking gas stations to close on the weekends. In December 1973, the month our first child was born, I was working really hard at keeping the gas tank of our van filled, because the hospital was miles away in the more upscale Detroit suburb of Livonia, and finding gas was getting harder and harder. There were long lines, and some stations were closed altogether.

A strike by truckers had further disrupted gas supplies, and also led to supermarket shelves being emptied. Fights broke out at gas stations, as we had to wait in line for hours to get gas. I remember sitting in our van one day after work (when the lines were particularly long) for about two hours when two guys ahead of me got out of their cars to engage in a fistfight. The news told stories from around the nation of people firing guns, although I don't think anybody was actually shot.

Even though we had no money in the stock market, it was impossible not to notice the news screaming, in January 1974, about how the Dow was collapsing. During the next eleven months, it lost almost half its value. Businesses were failing all across the country, and retirees who'd put their savings into the stock market were wiped out.

This crisis persisted through the late 1970s, plaguing President Jimmy Carter's first term. Under the pressure of economic hardship, doubts crept into the American psyche. People questioned whether the institutions born out of the New Deal were now failing and new institutions had to be built.

The Powell Memo had organized the business class under Royalist principles, while neoliberalism as promoted by the Mont Pelerin Society and the Chicago Boys had brought the political and economic class in line with the Royalists.

Carter was crushed in the 1980 election. Ronald Reagan rose to power and brought Milton Friedman on as an economic adviser.

The sun had set on an era of Keynesian stability and New Deal economics that benefited the middle class. The 1970s crisis-induced crack in the national psyche was just big enough for Ronald Reagan and the neoliberal shock troopers to step through it and carry forward an Economic Royalist revolution to tear down everything.

The long fuse to the Crash of 2016 was lit.

PART 2

Why We Crashed

Chapter 4

A Middle-Class Primer

Communism is a hateful thing and a menace to peace and organized government, but the communism of combined wealth and capital, the outgrowth of overweening cupidity and selfishness, which insidiously undermines the justice and integrity of free institutions, is not less dangerous than the communism of oppressed poverty and toil, which, exasperated by injustice and discontent, attacks with wild disorder the citadel of rule.
—President Grover Cleveland, 1888
State of the Union Address

Before we get into how exactly Ronald Reagan and the Economic Royalists set out to destroy the middle class and, thus, set up the next Great Crash, we have to understand how a middle class is created in the first place.

A big shift happened in America during my grandfather's life, which enabled my father to have a life that was unavailable to most of my grandfather's peers. My dad had the good fortune of coming of age in the late 1940s and early 1950s, when the New Deal and the GI Bill were in full effect.

It took the leadership of FDR for government to again play a role in creating a middle class. If the average person—not just the skilled tradesman or the college-educated or the businessman—but the *average* person was to have the American Dream of a middle-class life, it would take more very specific interventions by government.

After my dad graduated from high school and came back from two years in Japan right after World War II, if there had not been explicit policies put into place by FDR, Harry Truman, and Dwight D. Eisenhower, he would have faced the very real possibility of being one of the working poor for the rest of his life.

But in 1949, he enrolled in the GI Bill to get a free education, and began going to college in Grand Rapids, Michigan. His goal was to work his way up to a PhD—he certainly had the intellect for it—and to become a college history professor. But the next year, he met my mom, they fell in love and got married, and thirteen months later I was born as Dad was finishing up his second year of college.

The expense of having a new son meant that Dad could no longer go to school full time, so he dropped out and got a job at the Alcoa steel plant in Grand Rapids, along with a part-time job selling cameras in a local department store. Working fourteen hours a day—eight of them in a cloud of asbestos (which is what ultimately killed him)—he was able to just barely get by, although for a while my mom had to move in with his parents when I was an infant. Two years after I was born, my brother Steve was born, and the load on both Dad and Mom increased even more.

They moved to Lansing to stay with my uncle Stan and aunt Doris, and Dad got two jobs, one selling Rexair vacuum cleaners and the other selling World Book Encyclopedias, both door-to-door. But America was still recovering from the war, and the door-to-door-salesman business was tough. One of my earliest memories is going to the "cheese store"—a government-surplus warehouse where my parents could get free (or nearly free) surplus blocks of American cheese and giant bags of macaroni, as well as powdered milk by the bucket.

A Middle-Class Primer

I still have a love-hate relationship with macaroni and cheese, as it was my main meal for months, and to this day I hate the taste of powdered milk. Mom got pregnant again when I was four, and when I was five years old, my brother Stan was born. And Dad had to find a *real* job.

Fortunately, Lansing was an epicenter for the booming auto industry. General Motors and Fisher Body had major factories in town, and Dad got a job first at Lansing Die Sinking and then at Metal Machining Company. While he'd learned to be a competent machinist, he was no journeyman, but he was very, very good with details and bookkeeping. For the next forty years, he and a friend pretty much ran the office of that little fourteen-man business on behalf of the largely absentee owners, keeping the books, buying materials, making sales of finished products, and pitching in with the huge machines when necessary.

The machinists union was good to Dad—the company was a union shop. From the time I was around six, when he got that job, until the day he died in 2006, he, Mom, and their four sons all had full medical and dental insurance (I remember the doctor making house calls!); he had a pension when he retired; and we took two weeks of vacation every year, usually up to Newaygo to visit his sisters and my cousins. Dad made enough to buy a house in 1957 for about $15,000, with a government-guaranteed 3 percent thirty-year mortgage, which was fully paid off by the time he retired. He bought a new car—and paid cash—every three or four years.

He and Mom were obsessive antique and book collectors—they owned more than twenty thousand books, and my bedroom was carved out among the library-like rows of bookshelves in the basement. Dad was proud that he had read nearly every one—every night instead of watching TV, Dad and Mom would read for hours before we all went to bed (when Mom would read to us boys to put us to sleep).

This was all for a guy who had dropped out of college.

Had he been born a half century earlier, or in a nation that didn't have specific government policies, he would have been working twelve-hour days, six or seven days a week, and never been able to afford the house, the car, or the vacations, much less all those antique books that we went searching for every weekend at the Salvation Army.

And my dad's story wasn't unique—the era of the fifties, sixties, and seventies saw the American Dream being realized all across the nation.

My dad lived the American Dream and had a good and happy middle-class life because FDR changed the laws of American commerce. Instead of a "free market," we had a "middle-class market," which is actually pretty rare in human history.

The Elusive Middle Class

In her writings, which have become foundational for libertarian theology, author Ayn Rand suggested that the only purpose of government should be to prevent oppression by force. What she neglected to consider was all the force inherent in nature.

If you are hungry, there is the "force" of biology. If you're homeless, you confront the "force" of wind and storms, ice and snow. If you're sick, you confront the ravages and "force" of disease.

These were the forces that provoked the first governments. The first communities, clans, and tribes. The first nation-states.

It's easy for libertarian elitists, such as multimillionaire TV talking heads or college kids reading *Atlas Shrugged*, to talk about how there should be "no government beyond police, the army, and courts." They all have enough resources that they don't need to deal with the forces of raw nature. And that explains why billionaires would bankroll libertarian-leaning think tanks that will, when the crash comes with its full force, tell us it was "caused" by "big government."

However, in the real world, humans must confront both nature and other humans. Which is why we create governments, and why we create economies.

But it wasn't until 1776, when Thomas Jefferson replaced John Locke's right to "life, liberty, and property" with "life, liberty, and the pursuit of happiness," that the idea of a large class of working people having the ability to "pursue happiness"—the middle class—was even seriously considered as a cornerstone obligation of government.

(That was also the first time in history that the word "happiness" had ever appeared in any nation's formative documents. As Jefferson wrote in 1817 to Dr. John Manners, "The evidence of this natural right, like that of our right to life, liberty, the use of our faculties, the pursuit of happiness is not left to the feeble and sophistical investigations of reason, but is impressed on the sense of every man.")[50]

As Jefferson realized, with no government "interference" by setting the rules of the game of business and fair taxation, there could be no broad middle class—maybe a sliver of small businesses and artisans, but the vast majority of us would be the working poor under the yolk of elites.

The Economic Royalists know this, which gets to the root of why they set out to destroy government's involvement in the economy.

After all, in a middle-class economy, they may have to give up some of their power, and some of the higher end of their wealth may even be "redistributed"—horror of horrors—for schools, parks, libraries, and other things that support a healthy middle-class society but are not needed by the rich, who live in a parallel, but separate, world among us.

As Jefferson laid out in an 1816 letter to Samuel Kercheval, a totally "free" market, where corporations reign supreme just like the oppressive governments of old, could transform America "until the bulk of the society is reduced to be mere automatons of misery, to have no sensibilities left but for sinning and suffering. Then begins, indeed, the *bellum omnium in omnia*, which some philosophers observing to be so general in this world, have mistaken it for the natural, instead of the abusive state of man."[51]

Although this may come as a sudden realization to many, we've really known it all our lives.

In fact, in the six-thousand-year history of the "civilized" world, a middle class emerging in any nation has been such a rarity as to be historically invisible.

The United States has had two great periods of what we today call a middle class. The first was from the 1700s to the mid-1800s, and was fueled by virtually free land for settlers (stolen from the Indians) and free labor (slavery in the South and indentured immigrants in the North).

The result was (as de Tocqueville pointed out) the most well-educated, politically active, middle-class "nonaristocrats" in the world.

The second period didn't take hold until after World War II, during my dad's lifetime. Unlike the first, which was fueled by free land and slaves, the second had to be carefully constructed with specific (and what some might define as "socialist") policies put in place during the New Deal, which asserted more democratic control over the economy and workplace in order to hold the Royalists in check.

Step One: Progressive Taxation

To both stimulate and balance that domestic economy, FDR reinstituted progressive taxation, which gave workers more to spend and gave the rich an incentive to pay their workers better to maintain a stable workplace (since if they took the money themselves, it would just mostly go to taxes), thus stimulating demand for more goods and services.

Progressive taxation has a long history: As Jefferson said in a 1785 letter to James Madison, "Another means of silently lessening the inequality of property is to exempt all from taxation below a certain point, and to tax the higher portions of property in geometrical progression as they rise."[52]

FDR eventually hiked the top income tax rate paid by the super-rich in America to 90 percent. This had a twofold effect.

First, it held income inequality in check and ushered in an era of equal income growth among all classes. Unlike the Gilded Age, when the economy grew at a blistering pace but the gains were afforded only to the Robber Barons, the period between 1947 and 1979 saw unparalleled equitable growth.

During these thirty-plus years, the poorest fifth of Americans saw a 116 percent increase in their incomes. The middle fifth, a 111 percent increase. And the top 5 percent saw an 85 percent increase. All income classes shared in the prosperity of the times when the top marginal income tax rate was above 70 percent.[53]

The second effect of a high top income tax rate is to bring stability to the economy.

Writer and political/economic commentator Larry Beinhart figured out the truth about taxes, which is that they can be very destructive if kept too low.

He looked at the history of tax cuts and the history of economic bubbles and busts and found a relationship between the two. Whenever top marginal tax rates were relatively high—above 60 percent usually—the economy was at its most stable. Economic bubbles were kept in check since the superwealthy didn't have enormous amounts of hot money to go speculate in the market; debt and deficits were lower, giving the government enough resources to sew a strong social safety net; and working people's wages grew steadily. As a result, the economy as a whole saw sustained growth.

But when those top marginal tax rates dropped, the opposite happened. The very wealthy had a lot of extra money with which to go play in the markets and to place enormous bets on everything from start-up tech companies, to oil and food commodities, to real estate, setting up boom-bust cycles that made some people mind-bogglingly rich during the boom, but left most Americans holding an empty bag when the bust happened.

This was the lesson we thought we learned after Treasury Secretary Andrew Mellon cut the top rate from 73 percent to 25 percent in the 1920s, setting up a frenzy of market speculation and the eventual Great Crash of 1929.

And, as studies from the Center for American Progress show, when the top marginal income tax rate is above 50 percent, economies perform better as a whole. During the past fifty years, average annual GDP growth and employment growth was the highest when the top marginal income tax rate was between 75 and 80 percent. The lowest was when the top marginal income tax rate was 35 percent.[54]

But progressive taxation provides another benefit to the middle class.

Step Two: A Social Safety Net

With more revenue coming in to the government thanks to progressive taxation, the middle class can be protected by a strong social safety net.

In announcing his third run for the White House in 1912, President Teddy Roosevelt laid out the basis for what would become the New Deal a generation later. He named it the "Square Deal," and said:

> We stand for a living wage ... [which] must include:
> Enough to secure the elements of a normal standard of living;
> A standard high enough to make morality possible;
> To provide for education and recreation;
> To care for immature members of the family;
> To maintain the family during periods of sickness;
> And to permit of reasonable saving for old age.

With the Social Security Act of 1935, FDR created Social Security and laid the groundwork for states to implement unemployment insurance programs, borrowing some of the policies in his cousin Teddy's Square Deal. For the first time, our nation's elderly population could enjoy a decent quality of life after retirement and be reassured that those who fell on hard times and lost their jobs wouldn't be swept into destitution.

In his 1936 Democratic National Convention speech—the same speech in which he first called out the Economic Royalists—Franklin Roosevelt quoted an old English judge who once said, "Necessitous men are not free men."

What Roosevelt was touching on was that if you have necessities that are not met—if you're in *need*—then you're not free. If you're hungry and don't have food, you're not free. If you're homeless, you're not free. If you don't have health care, you're not free. If you don't have a job, you're not free.

Roosevelt went on to say, "Liberty requires opportunity to make a living—a living decent according to the standards of the time, a living which gives man not only enough to live by, but something to live for."[55]

For a middle class to take hold, basic necessities must be met. And so, in 1944, FDR went a step further and proposed a Second Bill of Rights. He explained the need for it by saying, "It is our duty now to begin to lay the plans and determine the strategy for the winning of a lasting peace and the establishment of an American standard of living higher than ever before known."[56]

He noted, "We cannot be content, no matter how high that general standard of living may be, if some fraction of our people—whether it be one-third or one-fifth or one-tenth—is ill-fed, ill-clothed, ill-housed, and insecure."

And thus he proposed his Second Bill of Rights, which included the following:

The right to a useful and remunerative job in the industries or shops or farms or mines of the nation;

The right to earn enough to provide adequate food and clothing and recreation;

The right of every farmer to raise and sell his products at a return which will give him and his family a decent living;

The right of every businessman, large and small, to trade in an atmosphere of freedom from unfair competition and domination by monopolies at home or abroad;

The right of every family to a decent home;

The right to adequate medical care and the opportunity to achieve and enjoy good health;

The right to adequate protection from the economic fears of old age, sickness, accident, and unemployment;

The right to a good education.

FDR's Second Bill of Rights never came to fruition. But in 1965, President Lyndon Johnson's "Great Society" built upon FDR's "New Deal" Social Security Act and created Medicare—a single-payer health care system for Americans sixty-five and older. And LBJ's Great Society cut poverty in half in a decade.

After World War II, our nation spread freedom to more and more Americans by caring for one another and by everyone—even the rich, who paid an income tax rate over 70 percent after their first million or so and sometimes above 90 percent—pitching in to create a social safety net.

Then there was the GI Bill, which sent millions of young men like my dad to college and technical schools in the late 1940s and early 1950s.

What happened was that more and more Americans were free to chase down their dreams—to be artists and inventors, to find that perfect job, to teach and to build. They were free to spend more time with their families and to take vacations. The explosion of innovation and opportunity, and the rise of the American middle class, was the result of that freedom.

A Middle-Class Primer

Step Three: Protections for Working People

When George Washington took office, remembering how difficult it was for him to find an American-made suit to wear to his inauguration, he tasked his treasury secretary, Alexander Hamilton, to come up with a plan to make America more self-sufficient—to produce its own goods and services and not have to rely on Britain anymore.

The full title of Hamilton's plan was "Alexander Hamilton's Report on the Subject of Manufactures: Made in His Capacity of Secretary of the Treasury." In it, Hamilton proposed an eleven-point plan to foster American manufacturing. Once enacted, that plan transformed our nation from an infantile dependent into a world superpower.

The premise of the plan is so simple that I can sum it up in four words: "Put American manufacturing first." This is done by giving American industries subsidies—or what Hamilton called "bounties"— to be globally competitive, and then protecting those industries by putting high tariffs—or taxes—on any new imports from foreign countries. The key to a good trade policy, just as in any business model, is to sell more stuff than you buy. So protect your sellers, and restrict the buying of things elsewhere if you can instead make them yourself. That was the basis of Hamilton's plan.

This plan wasn't anything new. Hamilton borrowed it from King Henry VII's "Tudor Plan," enacted in the fifteenth century to turn England into an economic powerhouse. And King Henry borrowed it from the Dutch, who borrowed it from the Romans, who borrowed it from the Greeks thousands of years ago. It's a tried-and-true method for economic prosperity that has existed for thousands of years.

By the 1900s, the United States was emerging as an economic powerhouse in the global market, realizing Hamilton's plan for producing and exporting more goods than we buy abroad.

A trade surplus of roughly $500 million in 1900 ballooned to $10 billion through the 1940s and '50s. Thanks to Hamilton's plan, the United States had built up an enormous manufacturing base that was able to sustain tens of millions of high-paying blue-collar jobs to produce the world's goods—from refrigerators to clothes to cars.

In addition, the Wagner Act of 1935 guaranteed Americans the right to form a union and bargain collectively with their corporate employers in these now booming manufacturing plants. Prior to the Wagner Act, unions were practically unheard of. Even attempting to unionize in the workplace would get you fired, at best. At worst, it could get you killed.

But with these new protections in place, union membership grew from single-digit percentages to nearly a third of all American workers. And with the growth in unions, middle-class wages grew, too, and so did the middle class's share of total national income.

The middle class thrived on a sturdy manufacturing base and strong labor unions negotiating fair wages.

Step Four: Rules in the Marketplace

The final step to securing a middle class is to set rules for the marketplace in order to keep the Royalists in business from getting too powerful and to prevent them from misbehaving.

For example, there was the Sherman Antitrust Act of 1890, which was intended to limit the size of corporations.

In response to the Robber Baron monopolies, Presidents Howard Taft and Woodrow Wilson went trust-busting.

Most notably, Taft would take a hacksaw to John D. Rockefeller's Standard Oil Trust, cleaving it up into thirty-three separate companies. And the American people loved Taft for doing it.

But being too big wasn't the only sin. Operating against the best interests of the public as a corporation could get you shut down, too. Our nation has a long history with the "corporate death penalty." Beginning in the early 1800s, laws were passed in several states to make it easier for legislators to revoke corporate charters if businesses were operating against the public's interest. And this routinely happened.

In Ohio, Mississippi, and Pennsylvania, banks were shut down for being "financially unsound." In New York and Massachusetts, the corporations that ran the turnpikes were given a corporate death sentence for not keeping the roads in good repair.

By 1825, twenty states had amended their constitutions to make it easier for the state to "revoke, alter, or annul" corporate charters whenever a corporation "may be injurious to citizens of the community."

And in just one year, 1832, the state of Pennsylvania sentenced ten corporations to death, revoking their charters for "operating contrary to the public interest."

This continued into the late 1800s, when whiskey trusts, sugar corporations, and oil corporations were all put to death in several states across the nation. In New York, workers petitioned the state supreme court to slay the beast that is Standard Oil for labor abuses. In 1894, the court obliged and revoked Standard Oil's corporate charter in that state.

And after the stock market crashed in 1929, FDR turned to the banks. He created the Securities and Exchange Commission (SEC) to regulate, for the first time, the purchasing and selling of shares on the stock market. He also created the Federal Deposit Insurance Corporation (FDIC), which insured people's bank deposits. And with the Glass-Steagall Act, FDR built a wall between commercial and investment banking to make sure the banksters couldn't use your checking account deposits to place risky bets on the stock market.

With these new reforms, Wall Street's delirium was held in check. And for nearly sixty years, America went without a catastrophic economic crash. It was the longest such period of stability in the nation's history.

But rules in the marketplace needed to be coupled with rules in the political arena. That meant taking Teddy Roosevelt's advice:

"We must drive the special interests out of politics. The citizens of the United States must effectively control the mighty commercial forces which they have themselves called into being. There can be no effective control of corporations while their political activity remains."[57]

In 1907 Teddy passed the Tillman Act (still on the books today), which banned corporate contributions in political elections. Violators of the law could face prison time, and corporations violating the law could be shut down.

The effect of all this government involvement in the workplace led to the greatest period of sustained growth in our national history, and gave rise to the golden age of the middle class through the middle of the twentieth century.

But just as the United States has had two great eras of a middle class, it has also had two dark eras of Economic Royalist rule, in which the middle class was mowed down by corporate behemoths. The first was the Gilded Age after the Great Crash of 1857 and Civil War, which put an end to the first era of the American middle class.

Monopoly Endgame

There's an easy way to understand why a strong middle class with a lot of good-paying jobs and purchasing power is also good for economic stability.

Consider the game Monopoly. If your opponent scoops up Boardwalk, Park Place, North Carolina Avenue, Pacific Avenue, both utilities, the four railroads, and an array of other properties on the board—that's it, the game's over.

The other players, who were once middle-class property owners, will go bankrupt as they are forced to pay higher and higher costs for rent and services, utilities, and transportation. Eventually, one player has all the money, and the losers are left standing out in the cold.

But what if the Monopoly game didn't end there?

What if the once-middle-class-but-now-broke players kept rolling the dice and kept going around the board, using their credit cards and lines of credit to stay in the game?

While they're running up massive personal or small-business debt, the monopolist who owns everything is finding it harder and harder to collect income from the increasingly impoverished players. They can't afford to pay rent, they can't pay utilities, and they can't ride on the railroads.

Eventually, when the consumers run out of both cash *and* credit and can no longer spend any money, even the monopolist goes broke. Then not only is the game over, but the game is over in a massive disaster.

This is remarkably similar to how real-world economics works when it's deprived of a stable middle class.

The board game Monopoly was invented when America's Gilded Age was in its final death throes. The game's inventor, Lizzie Magie, named it "The Landlord's Game." But as she said, "It might well have been called the 'Game of Life,' as it contains all the elements of success and failure in the real world, and the object is...the accumulation of wealth."[58]

Lizzie was a Georgist (one who follows the teachings of economist Henry George), and believed that things found in nature, particularly land itself but also things like mineral wealth, are part of the commons and thus should really be owned by "we the people," not private profiteers.

It was an ideology directly born out of the times—the Gilded Age—when Robber Barons used monopolies in steel, oil, rail, and finance to dominate the American economy. They built vast fortunes by owning all the stops on the Monopoly board of America, while working people's conditions collapsed to the point where we went into the Great Depression.

Carnegie, Astor, Rockefeller, Morgan, and a few dozen other recognizable names built massive monopolies while ruthlessly destroying any upstart that dared try to compete. There was big money to be made in post–Civil War America, now crisscrossed by the railroads. The nation's GDP nearly doubled, growing at the fastest rate ever. But that wealth didn't trickle down; they'd mastered monopoly.

The rest of America was going bankrupt.

In the census of 1900, per capita income was less than $5,000 annually in today's dollars.[59] And more and more Americans who were once self-employed had their lives uprooted and were thrown under the juggernaut of the Robber Barons. In 1850, prior to this so-called Gilded Age, most Americans worked for themselves. But by 1900, the majority of Americans worked for someone else—in many cases the monopolists.

In his 1888 State of the Union Address in which President Grover Cleveland said the "citizen is…trampled to death beneath an iron heel," he also called out the corruption of Congress by the Robber Barons.

"We discover that the fortunes realized by our manufacturers are no longer solely the reward of sturdy industry and enlightened foresight," he said, "but that they result from the discriminating favor of the Government and are largely built upon undue exactions from the masses of our people."[60]

President Cleveland's 1888 reality was our most prominent Founding Father's worst fear. On December 20, 1787, Jefferson wrote to James Madison about his concerns regarding the first draft of our new proposed Constitution, namely that it didn't include a Bill of Rights and, in particular, include a "restriction of monopolies."

And this was why Lizzie Magie invented that early version of what we today call the board game Monopoly. It was her hope, and that of many, that the stranglehold of the Economic Royalists of the era could somehow be broken. She said, "Let the children once see clearly the gross injustice of our present…system and when they grow up, if they are allowed to develop naturally, the evil will soon be remedied."[61]

Early on, even before Parker Brothers acquired the patent on Monopoly, turning it into the game we know today, well-to-do college students would play the game in fraternity houses at the behest of far-left economic teachers such as Scott Nearing, whose autobiography was titled *The Making of a Radical*. The game was meant to answer a question about the current economy.

An early instruction manual for the game of Monopoly in 1925 reads, "At the start of the game every player is provided with the same amount of capital and presumably has exactly the same chance of success as every other player. The game ends with one person in possession of all the money. What accounts for the failure of the rest, and what one factor can be singled out to explain the obviously ill-adjusted distributions of the community's wealth which this situation represents?"[62]

It was a similar question asked by Henry George, whom Chrystia Freeland refers to in her book *Plutocrats* as "the most famous American popular economist you've never heard of."[63]

George was the author of the book *Progress and Poverty*, in which he sets out to answer a fundamental question of the Gilded Age: Why are so many people living in poverty while others are getting so rich in an expanding economy?

George writes in *Progress and Poverty*, "The present century has been marked by a prodigious increase in wealth producing power." Yet, working people were not sharing these gains.[64]

"We are coming into collision with facts which there can be no mistaking," George writes. "From all parts of the civilized world come complaints of industrial depression; of labor condemned to involuntary idleness; of capital massed and wasting; of pecuniary distress among businessmen; of want and suffering and anxiety among the working classes."

He goes on, "Some get an infinitely better and easier living, but others find it hard to get a living at all. The 'tramp' comes with the locomotives, and almshouses and prisons are as surely the marks of 'material progress' as are costly dwellings, rich warehouses and magnificent churches."

America was split in two. Not between North and South, but between the Robber Barons and everyone else.

Eventually, the nation learned the lesson that not only is the accumulation of vast amounts of wealth in the hands of an elite aristocracy not good for working people, it's also not good for economies as a whole, which is exactly what the game Monopoly teaches us.

But first, it took a horrific crash.

The period from the 1870s through the late 1890s, when the Economic Royalists came out of the Great Crash of 1857 and Civil War still in power, were the longest, deepest, and most brutal Great Depression in American history, far worse than what we saw in the 1930s. And at the same time, the rich got richer in a way that wasn't again seen until today. America in that era more resembled Victorian England than that idealistic, egalitarian society envisioned by our revolutionary Founding Fathers.

The peak of the crisis was the crash of 1893.

A fifth of American workers lost their jobs. And countless lost their savings, too, as more than 150 national banks failed alongside more than 170 state banks and 177 private banks. It was the worst economic depression the nation had ever suffered.

What the Robber Barons failed to understand is that by crushing the middle class, they signed their own suicide pact as well. They destroyed their consumers—or their playing partners on the board game of Monopoly. And when working people hit rock bottom and can no longer afford to buy anything in the economy, then everything shuts down.

Eventually, future generations heeded Lizzie Magie's advice in the game Monopoly. The Robber Barons were crushed during the Progressive Era of the early 1900s, and FDR rebuilt the middle class with the New Deal.

But as the cycles would again have it, a second dark period of Royalist rule began in the 1980s, when Ronald Reagan moved in to the White House.

Chapter 5

Reagan Kidnapped the Jetsons

MS. MORNIN: That's good, because I work three jobs and I feel like I contribute.

THE PRESIDENT: You work three jobs?

MS. MORNIN: Three jobs, yes.

THE PRESIDENT: Uniquely American, isn't it? I mean, that is fantastic that you're doing that.

    —President George W. Bush, Omaha (Neb.) Town Hall,
February 2005

In a 1966 article, *TIME* magazine looked ahead toward the future and what the rise of automation would mean for average working Americans.

It concluded, "By 2000, the machines will be producing so much that everyone in the U.S. will, in effect, be independently wealthy. With Government benefits, even nonworking families will have, by one estimate, an annual income of $30,000–$40,000. How to use leisure meaningfully will be a major problem." And that was $30,000–$40,000 in 1966 dollars, which would be roughly $199,000 to $260,000 in 2010 dollars.[65]

Ask anybody who was teenage or older in the 1960s, this was the big sales pitch for automation and the coming computer age. There was even a cartoon show about it—*The Jetsons*—and everybody looked forward to the day when increased productivity from robots, computers, and automation would translate into fewer hours worked, or more pay, or both, for every American worker.

And there was good logic behind the idea.

The premise was simple. With better technology, companies would become more efficient. They'd be able to make more things in less time. Revenues would skyrocket, and Americans would bring home higher and higher paychecks, all the while working less and less.

So by the year 2000, we would enter what was then referred to as "The Leisure Society." Futurists speculated that the biggest problem facing America in that Jetsons future would be just how the heck everyone would use all their extra leisure time!

And, of course, there were also those who were worried about what kind of degeneracy would emerge when a nation has lots of money and lots of free time on its hands.

This didn't happen. And it didn't happen because Ronald Reagan stole the Leisure Society from us and he handed it over to the Economic Royalists.

Tax Cuts of Mass Destruction

In 1981, the Royalists went right to work taking down that first pillar on which FDR rebuilt the American middle class: progressive taxation.

Taking advantage of the oil-shock crisis, neoliberal shock troopers immediately ushered through a revolutionary change to the tax code with the Economic Recovery Tax Act of 1981.

The first major piece of legislation signed by Reagan, it slashed the top marginal income tax rate down from 70 to 50 percent, cutting estate taxes for wealthy businesses and slashing capital-gains and corporate-profit taxes.

Reagan succeeded, a few years later, in dropping the top income tax rate even lower, to 28 percent—where it hadn't been since before the Great Depression. It was the second largest tax cut in history. And it was nearly identical to the largest tax cut ever, Treasury Secretary Andrew Mellon's in the 1920s, the one that created the bubble known as the Roaring Twenties, which eventually burst in 1929.

The Great Forgetting had certainly arrived. The economic mistakes of the 1920s were coming back around. And, again, the influx of all this hot money in the market, coupled with a robust deregulation agenda through the 1980s and 1990s, would trigger a series of painful financial panics.

The reason why the Leisure Society could be imagined by *TIME* magazine is because, ever since 1900, working people's wages tracked evenly with working people's productivity.

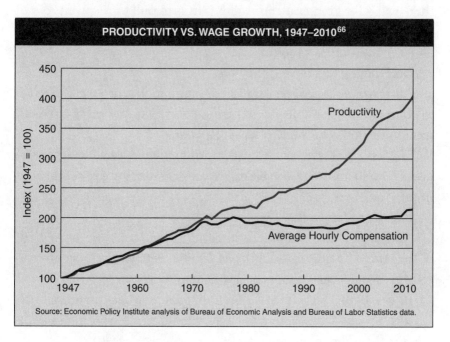

PRODUCTIVITY VS. WAGE GROWTH, 1947–2010[66]

Source: Economic Policy Institute analysis of Bureau of Economic Analysis and Bureau of Labor Statistics data.

So, as productivity continued to rise, which was likely, due to increasing automation and better technology, so, too, would everyone's wages. And the glue holding this logic together was the current top marginal income tax rate.

In 1966, when the *TIME* article was written, the top marginal income tax rate was 70 percent. And what that effectively did was encourage CEOs to keep more money in their businesses, to invest in new technology, to pay their workers more, to hire new workers and expand.

After all, what's the point of sucking millions and millions of dollars out of your business if it's going to be taxed at 70 percent?

According to this line of reasoning, if businesses were to suddenly become way more profitable and efficient thanks to automation, then that money would flow throughout the business—raising everyone's standard of living, increasing everyone's leisure time.

But when Reagan dropped that top tax rate down to 28 percent, everything changed. Now as businesses became far more profitable, there was a far greater incentive for CEOs to pull those profits out of the company and pocket them, because they were suddenly paying an incredibly low tax rate.

And that's exactly what they did.

All those new profits, thanks to automation, that were *supposed* to go to everyone, giving us all higher paychecks and more time off, went to the top—to the Economic Royalists.

Suddenly, the symmetry in the productivity/wages chart broke down. Productivity continued increasing since technology continued improving.

But wages stayed flat.

And, again, since higher and higher profits could be sucked out of the company and taxed at lower levels, there was no incentive to reduce the number of hours everyone had to work.

In the 1950s, before that *TIME* magazine article predicting the Leisure Society was written, the average American working in manufacturing put in about forty-two hours of work a week.

Today, the average American working in manufacturing puts in about forty hours of work a week. This means that despite the fact that productivity has increased 400 percent since 1950, Americans are working, on average, only two fewer hours a week.

If productivity is four times higher today than in 1950, then Americans should be able to work four times less, or just ten hours a week, to afford the same 1950s lifestyle when a family of four could get by on just one paycheck, own a home, own a car, put their kids through school, take a vacation every now and then, and retire comfortably.

That's the definition of the Leisure Society: ten hours of work a week, and the rest of the time spent with family, with travel, with creativity, with whatever you want.

But all of this was washed away by the Reagan tax cuts.

Combine this with Reagan's brutal crackdown on striking PATCO (Professional Air Traffic Controllers Organization) members that kicked off a three-decades-long assault on another substantial pillar of the middle class—organized labor—and life has been anything but "leisurely" for working people in America.

More Unequal than Rome

Instead of leisure, working people got feudalism.

As a result of the Reagan tax cuts, that era from 1947 to 1979, in which all classes of Americans saw their incomes grow together, ended. A new era, in which only the wealthiest among us got rich off a booming economy, commenced.

According to census data, the typical hourly wage for an American worker increased a mere $1.23 over the past thirty-six years, after accounting for inflation. From 1979 to 2008, the middle 20 percent of Americans saw their incomes grow only 11 percent. That's compared with a 111 percent growth in the thirty years prior.

The poorest 20 percent of Americans, meanwhile, saw their

incomes actually decrease by 7 percent between 1979 and 2008. In the thirty years prior, their incomes had grown by 118 percent.

Meanwhile, with the wonders of automation and Reagan's tax cuts, the top 1 percent have seen their incomes increase by 275 percent since Reagan's election (and it's much higher for the top 0.1 percent and massively higher for the top 0.01 percent).

Today, workers' wages as a percentage of GDP are at an all-time low. Yet, corporate profits as a percentage of GDP are at an all-time high.

The top 1 percent of Americans own 40 percent of the nation's wealth. In fact, just 400 Americans own more wealth than 150 million other Americans combined.

Wal-Mart Stores, the world's largest private employer, personifies this inequality best. It's a corporation that in 2011 brought in more revenue than any other corporation in America. It raked in $16.4 billion in profits. It pays its employees minimum wage.

And the Wal-Mart heirs, the Walton family, occupy positions 6 through 9 on the Forbes 400 Richest People in America list, own roughly $100 billion in wealth, which is more than the bottom 40 percent of Americans combined. The average Wal-Mart employee would have to work 76 *million* forty-hour weeks to have as much wealth as one Wal-Mart heir.

Through some interesting historical analysis, historians Walter Schiedel and Steven Friesen calculated that inequality in America today is worse than what was seen during the Roman era.

So the Royalists, just like the Roman emperors, got their Leisure Society.

But there was an extra benefit for the Royalists buried in the politics of the Reagan tax cuts.

The "Debt" Crisis

In his First Inaugural Address in 1981, Ronald Reagan warned of a debt crisis.

"For decades, we have piled deficit upon deficit, mortgaging our future and our children's future for the temporary convenience of the present," he said.[67]

"To continue this long trend is to guarantee tremendous social, cultural, political, and economic upheavals."

At the time, the national debt was a bit under $1 trillion. As a result primarily of his tax cuts, he tripled the national debt to about $3 trillion. He added more to our national debt than every single president before him, from George Washington to Jimmy Carter, combined.

In his Farewell Address to the nation in 1989, Ronald Reagan said the high deficits throughout his administration were one of his regrets. But no Republican since has regretted adding more and more debt.

Reagan's successor, President George H. W. Bush, added more than a trillion dollars more. And his son, George W. Bush, added more than $6 trillion.

Since Reagan, Republican presidents have combined to add nearly $10 trillion to our national debt.

And yet, each devoted their inaugural addresses to promising to lower deficits and reduce the national debt. Republican politicians, in the spirit of Reagan, have even resorted to alarmism, talking about a "debt crisis," while at the same time pushing for budget-busting tax cuts for the rich.

This could be written off as run-of-the-mill political flip-flopping and pandering. But it's not. There's a cunning political strategy behind it.

Shooting Santa

Starting with FDR's big win in 1936, with the lone exception of the two-year "Do-Nothing Congress" elected in 1946, Republicans never held a majority in the House of Representatives until 1995. This period coincided with the banishment of the Economic Royalists as well.

The way the political right was able to finally come out of this political slump was by listening to a Republican strategist/faux economist named Jude Wanniski, who wrote a transformative article for the *National Observer* in 1976 that laid out the new Republican path to power.

Titling his article "Taxes and a Two-Santa Theory," Wanniski warned that Republicans "embrace the role of Scrooge, playing into the hands of the Democrats, who know the first rule of successful politics is Never Shoot Santa Claus."[68]

He said, "As long as Republicans have insisted on balanced budgets, their influence as a party has shriveled."

Republicans first learned this lesson in the 1930s and '40s after the New Deal, when Democratic president Franklin Roosevelt played the role of Santa Claus and gave the American people Social Security and unemployment insurance. At the time, Republicans played Scrooge, arguing that we couldn't afford it. They played the role of Scrooge in the 1960s, too, as Democratic president Lyndon Johnson played Santa Claus as well, and gave the American people Medicare and other Great Society programs to cut poverty.

And what did Republicans get for playing Scrooge? Electoral defeat after electoral defeat.

Wanniski said Republicans need to play Santa Claus, too. They should be the Santa Claus of tax cuts!

Wanniski wrote, "The only thing wrong... is the failure of the Republican Party to play Santa Claus... The Two–Santa Claus Theory holds that Republicans should concentrate on tax reduction."

When Democrats give "gifts" like Social Security and Medicare, Republicans can counter with gifts like massive tax cuts, which is exactly what they did when Ronald Reagan was elected in 1980 and picked Wanniski as an adviser.

But there was another dimension to Wanniski's strategy that he doesn't explicitly lay out in his article. And that's this: If Republicans, by playing Santa Claus on their own, successfully pass their tax cuts (as Reagan and Bush 2 did) without cutting spending, then the government will be starved of revenue until eventually it can't afford the Democratic Party's social services such as Social Security, unemployment insurance, and Medicare—all things that Republicans have labeled "gifts," yet are fundamental to the survival of a middle class.

If Republicans scream and yell enough about the deficit they've created with their tax cuts, then maybe it will force the Democrats to reverse roles, play Scrooge, and eventually shoot Santa Claus.

I asked Ronald Reagan's former budget director, David Stockman, about Wanniski's theory and whether it had motivated the Reagan tax cuts.

Stockman referred to Wanniski as a "raving wildman," and said the Two-Santa Theory wasn't the basis of Reagan's economic program.

But, Stockman admitted, when it became clear that the tax cuts weren't actually working, and that the deficit was exploding, then the White House noticed.

"The White House became divided between the rational people, who realized that things were out of balance, the numbers weren't working, the tax cut was too big, and that we needed to take some of it back. On the other side there were the true ideologues, who insisted, 'Let's just ride it out and continue to defend this massive tax cut that we couldn't afford.' "[69] In other words, the White House was divided between rational Republicans and the Economic Royalists.

Stockman admitted that the Royalists won the debate within the White House. "Unfortunately there are very few people left in the Republican Party who were on the fiscally conservative side of the debate."

He went on, "More and more and more, Republicans took on the catechism of tax cuts anytime, anywhere, for any reason. You never have to pay the bills of government...and just blame it on the Democrats anyway."

Just as Wanniski had laid out. The plan worked.

Republican President Clinton

The irony is that the Economic Royalists in the Reagan administration didn't do the real harm to the social safety net that had once supported the American middle class.

It was a Democratic president who did it.

Bill Clinton was elected in 1992 after campaigning on a promise to bring a sea change to America similar to the one that Franklin Roosevelt had brought, back in 1932. Clinton's agenda was called "A New Covenant," and he summed it up in a 1991 speech at Georgetown University when he said, "To turn America around, we've got to have a new approach...we need a new covenant, a solemn agreement between the people and their government to provide opportunity for everybody...a new covenant to take government back from the powerful interests...and give it back to the ordinary people of our country."[70]

But the New Covenant never got off the ground. As Adam Curtis uncovers in a documentary series he did for the BBC entitled *The Trap*, just a few weeks before Bill Clinton was to take the oath of office, he was paid a little visit by two notorious Royalists, the CEO of Goldman Sachs at the time, Robert Rubin, who would later become Bill Clinton's treasury secretary, and Alan Greenspan, the chairman of the Federal Reserve. Rubin and Greenspan sat the young president down and explained to him that the Royalists were in charge.

Twenty years had passed since the Powell Memo was first circulated around corporate America. A Democrat just elected to the presidency made no difference to the shadow government of lobbyists, corporate-funded think tanks, and political fund-raisers. Clinton chose political expediency. He chose to carry the Royalist agenda forward.

In his First Inaugural in 1993, Clinton pledged, just as the Royalists wanted him to, to "cut our massive debt."

Later in his presidency in 1996, sounding like Ronald Reagan, Clinton would declare that the "era of big government is over."[71] It was as though the Royalists had finally made the New Deal say "uncle."

And then Clinton shot Santa when he "reformed" welfare. Buying into Reagan's completely fraudulent myths of "welfare queens," Clinton signed into law the Personal Responsibility and Work Opportunity Reconciliation Act of 1996. The law undid LBJ's Great Society legislation, which had succeeded in cutting poverty rates in America from 22 percent in 1963 down to 12.6 percent in 1970.

For the first time since the sixties, families in poverty were not guaranteed a lifeline. They eventually had to prove they were working in order to qualify for assistance. This sounded like a good idea in theory, especially during boom times such as the nineties, when there were lots of jobs available. But during recessions, when three or four people are looking for every one job opening, then a work requirement for welfare does a lot of harm to already struggling families.

The stats have borne this out. In the sixteen years after welfare reform, even more people have been kicked off benefits, yet poverty has increased. Before reform, 70 percent of impoverished families had access to a lifeline. But after reform, by 2009, only 30 percent did.[72]

This attack on the Great Society was the first of a long series of attacks on the social safety net.

But Clinton's greatest betrayal of the middle class came when he didn't listen to Ross Perot.

A Giant Sucking Sound

The year Reagan was sworn in, we were the richest nation in the world, and other than a few wobbles during the two world wars, our national debt had been relatively steady in inflation-adjusted dollars since the administration of George Washington.

We were the world's largest creditor—more countries owed us money than any other nation on earth. Today, we are the world's largest debtor nation, and our national debt nearly outweighs our annual GDP.

And here's another startling figure: The year Reagan was sworn into office, 1981, the United States was the largest importer of raw materials in the world and the world's largest exporter of finished, manufactured goods. We brought in ores and shipped out everything from TVs and computers to cars and clothing. Today, things are totally reversed: We are now the world's mining pit, the largest exporter of raw materials, and the world's largest importer of finished, manufactured goods.

This has resulted in an enormous trade imbalance, one that has grown from a modest $15 billion deficit in 1981 to an enormous $539 billion deficit by 2012.

From 1791, when our nation's first treasury secretary, Alexander Hamilton, created an eleven-point plan for American manufacturers, all the way until just the last few decades, the United States protected its manufacturing base with high tariffs on imports and government support for domestic industries.

This "protectionist" approach to trade transformed the United States into the world's largest exporter of manufactured goods, which built and sustained an enormous middle class of Americans working in factories collecting high wages.

Then the forces of globalization crept in, extolling the virtues of a world economy free from national boundaries and protections for domestic manufacturing.

With the Reagan Revolution in the 1980s, Alexander Hamilton's eleven-point plan, yet another pillar on which the middle class was built, was scrapped. In 1986, Reagan lowered tariffs. He also secured a free-trade deal with Canada in 1988. He vetoed protectionist trade bills throughout his presidency. And he doubled America's spending in the global economy.

But Clinton really did a number on working people.

In the 1992 presidential debate, third-party candidate Ross Perot famously warned about a "giant sucking sound" of American jobs going south of the border to low-wage nations once trade protections were dropped.

Perot was right, but no one in our government listened to him.

Tariffs were ditched, and then Bill Clinton moved in to the White House in the 1990s. He continued Reagan's trade policies and committed the United States to so-called free-trade agreements such as GATT, NAFTA, and the WTO, thus removing all the protections that had kept our domestic manufacturing industries safe from foreign corporate predators for two centuries.

In the 1960s, one-in-three Americans worked in manufacturing, producing things of lasting wealth. Today, after jumping headfirst into one free-trade agreement after another, only one in ten Americans works in manufacturing.

Over the last decade, fifty thousand manufacturing plants in the United States have closed down and 5 million manufacturing jobs have been lost. They didn't disappear, they just moved away to low-wage factories, such as Foxconn, in foreign nations.

I saw the damage firsthand when I was returning home from a weekend trip to New York City on the Amtrak regional train that runs about hourly from Boston to Washington, DC. I was sitting in business class, looking out the window and talking on the phone with my old friend Earl Katz, an activist and documentary-film producer.

A few months earlier, while in Germany, I'd taken a long train ride from Frankfurt to Kulmbach, involving three changes of trains during the course of the four-hour trip. The German trains were new, gleaming, the interiors done in twenty-first-century plastic-and-teak paneling, the carpets quiet and elegant, the power seats highly adjustable with state-of-the-art audio. Even the bathrooms were elegant. And the train was traveling at well over one hundred miles an hour, and perfectly smooth.

The Amtrak train, on the other hand—even with the most expensive seat in the train—was old and decrepit. The bathroom was ancient in its technology, the tracks so rough that it was hard to walk from car to car without being pitched into some poor, unsuspecting person's lap, the carpet and seats soiled, the doors between cars loud and clunky. And for much of the trip, the train was going between fifty and seventy miles an hour, and bumping, jerking, and screeching all over ancient and poorly maintained tracks.

But the most shocking difference was what I saw out the windows.

On my trip across Germany, I'd seen vibrant factories, towns where about a third of all the rooftops were covered with solar panels (Germany has gone from no solar power production to the point where home rooftop panels produce more power than ten nuclear reactors in less than a decade), gleaming modern office buildings (built to strict energy-saving standards), and everywhere the bustle of prosperity.

On the other hand, on my trip down the East Coast, I saw mile after mile of ancient, decrepit redbrick or cement factories that were covered in graffiti, cracking with weeds, dotted with boarded-up or broken windows looking at me like toothless old men staring unfocused out at the train through Salvation Army secondhand glasses.

Occasionally I could see the remnants of a name painted on the factory or etched into the concrete or brick rooflines or cornices, names that had been proudly put into place in the late nineteenth or early twentieth century. They spoke of the long-ago manufacture of steel and car parts and lawn mowers and machine tools, of sweaters and socks and jeans.

During one particularly poignant stretch, after passing dozens of empty factories the train passed what must have been at least a mile of empty houses. Most of them looked like they were formerly elegant brick row houses that, if they were in DC or New York today, would fetch a million dollars each. Yet these had once provided middle-class housing to the men and women who'd worked in the now-closed factories. Now they were mostly reduced to smashed-out windows, graffiti-tattooed walls, and rotting ceilings.

I was describing what I was seeing to Earl, who himself knew it all too well. "It looks like the end of America," I said.

"It's certainly the end of the American middle class," Earl said in a soft, sad voice. "You can see it all across the country."

This is the early stage of crash.

We're not just talking about decaying railroads and buildings; we're talking about decaying fundamentals—the pillars on which you can build a healthy economy, an expansive middle class, and a strong democracy.

All of it, sucked out of the country.

There was a moment of hesitation when Clinton signed the free-trade death warrant for the middle class.

According to Bob Woodward, during a meeting in the Oval Office regarding these trade deals, Clinton said sarcastically, "Where are all the Democrats? I hope you're all aware we're all Eisenhower Republicans."[73]

He added, "We're Eisenhower Republicans here. Here we are, and we're standing for lower deficits and free trade and the bond market. Isn't that great?"

It's true, the political left had abandoned FDR's fight against the Economic Royalists. They had assumed the position of New Deal Republicans such as Dwight Eisenhower.

And perhaps that wouldn't be so bad. After all, Eisenhower believed in the New Deal. He told his brother Edgar in a 1954 letter, "Should any political party attempt to abolish social security, unemployment insurance, and eliminate labor laws and farm programs, you would not hear of that party again in our political history." He added, "There is a tiny splinter group, of course, that believes you can do these things. Among them are . . . Texas oil millionaires, and an occasional politician or businessman from other areas. Their number is negligible and they are stupid."[74]

The only problem is, while the Democrats turned into Eisenhower Republicans, the Republicans turned into something completely different.

When George W. Bush took office in 2001, the Economic Royalists would step up their assault. There would be no Leisure Society, only a cataclysmic crash.

Chapter 6

"Madness"

I made a mistake in presuming that the self-interest of organizations, specifically banks and others, were such that they were best capable of protecting their own shareholders and their equity in the firms.
—Former Federal Reserve Chairman Alan Greenspan,
October 2008

One of the great chroniclers of the last era when the Economic Royalists were in control was economist John Kenneth Galbraith, who was born in 1908 and watched it all unfold as a young man. In 1954, while he was a professor of economics at Harvard University, he wrote the international bestseller *The Great Crash 1929*.

In it, he noted that the nine years of hot money (from low taxes on the rich) and minimal regulation had led to a hollowing out of the American economy, along with a massive transfer of wealth from the working class to the very rich.

He noted there was "little question" that in 1929 "the economy was fundamentally unsound." There were, he said, five major weaknesses that "had an especially intimate bearing on the ensuing disaster."[75]

Galbraith listed them as being the following:

(1) The bad distribution of income
(2) The bad corporate structure
(3) The bad banking structure
(4) The dubious state of the foreign balance
(5) The poor state of economic intelligence

Most important, though, Galbraith noted that it was a lack of any sense of conscience or remorse—of responsibility—among the movers and shakers in the business and governmental worlds that caused the Great Crash. Our nation's governance and industry had been taken over by people who had absolutely no commitment to the community of humankind, nor even to the community of our nation, nor to the neighborhoods in which they worked or ran their businesses.

Without using the word, which was then relatively obscure and ambiguous, Galbraith suggested we'd been taken over by psychopaths—people who were unable to understand the damage their actions were causing to the economy as a whole. Bluntly, he referred to it as "madness."

Galbraith went on to describe the effects of this madness. "The sense of responsibility in the financial community for the community as a whole ... is nearly nil. Perhaps this is inherent.

"In a community where the primary concern is making money, one of the necessary rules is to live and let live."

Galbraith noted that when the mad—as in "insane"—people take over an economy, just the simple act of pointing it out is dangerous. The result is that the psychopaths—he refers to them as "the foolish"—are even further empowered and not only make off with more of our nation's wealth but also hollow out our institutions of both governmental and corporate regulation in order to make their heist easier:

> To speak out against madness may be to ruin those who have succumbed to it. So the wise in Wall Street are nearly always silent. The foolish thus have the field to themselves. None rebukes them.

Only in the wake of that Great Crash, Galbraith and most other economists note, did we figure out that our economy had been dangerously hollowed out by the twin combination of well-meaning ideologues and the psychopaths they empowered.

The Evolution of Madness

Could it be that there's a subset of that eighty-year crash/war cycle that produces a corresponding rise and fall in the number of psychopaths who are running American business and government?

Darwin's finches say yes.

Charles Darwin, in the 1830s, famously sailed aboard the exploration ship HMS *Beagle* to the Galápagos Islands, where he observed a broad variety of species of finches (among other things). Some finches, for example, were adapted to eating large, hard seeds and had correspondingly larger beaks. Some ate small seeds, and so had smaller beaks. Some ate seeds inside cacti and had longer and thinner beaks.

This variety of finches had all presumably evolved from one or two initial species that had been blown all the way to the Galápagos by a storm or carried in some other way. From this he developed his theory of how evolution produces speciation, and published it in his book *The Origin of Species*.

But Darwin didn't have the time to visit and revisit the island where he'd found the finches, so he didn't have an opportunity to see how his finches would change over time in response to changes in their environment. That job fell to Peter and Rosemary Grant, who spent decades annually visiting Darwin's finches and watched extraordinary changes, chronicled in Peter Grant's book *Ecology and Evolution of Darwin's Finches* and later more widely popularized by Jonathan Weiner in his best-selling book *The Beak of the Finch: A Story of Evolution in Our Time*.

The Grants, in annual visits to Daphne Major, one of the Galápagos Islands, watched evolution—which Darwin had assumed worked slowly, over aeons—transform the finches of the island several times in response to severe environmental stresses.

The first time was in 1977, when a drought hit the island hard. This island was already a relatively barren and sparse environment, and the drought decimated the smaller and less hardy vegetation, browning the island and killing off the source of smaller seeds. The result was that the finches with smaller beaks, who couldn't crack open the remaining larger seeds, died off.

In 1978, the offspring of the survivors of that drought had universally larger beaks—an environmental adaptation that took less than a year to happen.

It happened again—differently—during a two-year period of unusually rainy weather, 1984–85. All that moisture favored the smaller plants, which exploded across the island, and the finches with smaller beaks were able to eat those seeds without expending as much energy flying around carrying larger, heavier beaks like their relatives. And, sure enough, by 1986 small-beaked finch populations were back up to high levels.

Not only did evolution happen but it also cycled back and forth in response to a changing environment.

To the extent that economics can be described as an ecosystem— and the resemblances are many—it's not hard to see how different economic environments are suited to different types of people.

In the wake of an economic crash, psychopaths would not be favored. Instead, the environment would be best adapted to people who are not perceived as risk takers, who have a high level of social commitment, and who are slow-and-steady builders of businesses. Classically, these were the CEOs and senior executives who followed business models that were prevalent in the half century following the Great Depression—CEOs who took only thirty times what their bottom-paid employee received, who typically had been more than twenty-five years with their own company before reaching the level of CEO, and who were not compensated in a way that was tied to stock prices.

During this period, CEOs were answerable to the workers (via labor unions), the company (via its board of directors), and the community (via local/state/federal government and community pressure). They were paid exclusively by salary and bonus—the tax code did not provide for compensating CEOs with stock or stock options. It was also during this period that some of the largest, strongest, and most resilient of American corporations were built.

Similarly, there were protections built into our business systems to allow for competition—particularly small, local competition—thus giving entrepreneurs an opportunity to step into the marketplace. If big corporations got too big, they were broken up, using the Sherman Antitrust Act of 1890 (among others).

But, eventually, the Great Forgetting took hold. And the Royalists and their madness crept back in.

Monopolies Return

Under the watch of the Royalists, the Reagan administration was philosophically opposed to the government breaking up companies. Over the next few decades, the monopolies of the Gilded Age returned.

On Wall Street, the twenty biggest banks own assets equivalent to 84 percent of the nation's entire GDP. And just twelve of those banks own 70 percent of all the banking assets. That means our entire banking system relies on just a few whales that must be saved at all costs from going belly up, or else the entire system goes belly up.

And consider our food industry. According to Tom Philpott at *Mother Jones* magazine, agriculture oligopolies exist from farm to shelf. Just four companies control 90 percent of the global grain trade. Just three companies control 70 percent of the beef industry. And just four companies control 58 percent of the pork and chicken industry.[76]

"Madness"

On the retail side, Wal-Mart controls a quarter of the entire US grocery market. And just four companies produce 75 percent of our breakfast cereal, 75 percent of our snack foods, 60 percent of our cookies, and half of all the ice cream sold in supermarkets around the nation.[77]

And then there's the health insurance market. Just four health insurance companies—UnitedHealth Group, WellPoint, Aetna, and Humana—control three-quarters of the entire health insurance market. And as a 2007 study by the group Health Care for America Now uncovered, in thirty-eight states, just two insurers controlled 57 percent of the market. In fifteen states, one insurer controlled 60 percent of the market.

Since there's no functional competition in such a market, prices continue to get higher and higher while the profits for these whales skyrocket, too.

In the cellular phone market, just four companies—AT&T Mobile, Verizon Wireless, T-Mobile, and Sprint Nextel—control 89 percent of the market. And in the Internet market, just a handful of corporations—AT&T, Comcast, Time Warner, and Verizon—control more than half of the market.

From newspapers to television, radio to movies, monopolies dominate the markets.

If we were to give the Internet oligopolies the same treatment Richard Nixon gave AT&T in the 1970s, then maybe we Americans would have the same superfast Internet speeds and supercheap rates enjoyed by most of the rest of the developed world. For example, South Koreans get Internet speeds two hundred times faster than what most Americans get, and pay only $27 a month for their service. Professor Susan P. Crawford, author of *Captive Audience: The Telecom Industry and Monopoly Power in the New Gilded Age* and former board member of ICANN, told me that while the average American consumer pays around $90 a month for a cell phone with a data plan, the European average is just $19 (and the coverage is better and the data is both faster and unlimited).[78]

Rising health-care, food, and energy costs can all be traced back to this problem of monopoly in America.

It's a Second Gilded Age, and it's headed for another Monopoly Endgame. And this time it will be worse than before.

We are no longer dealing with the Robber Barons, who savaged working people through the last half of the nineteenth century. And we aren't talking about the Economic Royalists of FDR's day, who plotted a coup. This is a new form of Royalist.

As Pulitzer Prize–winning journalist Chris Hedges told me, "The Robber Barons, however feudal they were, ran their enterprises within the nation-state itself. Now, we have corporate entities which seek the lowest possible wage around the world, in essence the prison labor in China, and are forcing the rest of the planet's workforce to compete with this slave labor."[79]

He went on describing the Royalists at work today. "It's similar to the age of the Robber Barons but in fact worse because there is no loyalty to the nation-state. The corporations are actually hollowing the country out from the inside...We're creating a kind of neofeudalism."

Global Psychopaths

In his book *The Collapse of Globalism*, author John Ralston Saul lays out the primary driving ideology of globalism, which was unleashed on the world on a scale not previously seen before with the creation of GATT, the WTO, and NAFTA.

"The force of Globalism," Saul writes, "through trade agreements, deregulation and privatization, would seriously weaken the ability of nation-states to act with any political independence."[80]

For most of American history, businesses—for-profit and nonprofit— had mission statements that were broader than simply serving the interests of the shareholders and CEOs, and referred instead to the long-term interest of the company, its workers, and its customers.

And perhaps most important, the long-term interest of the nation it belonged to. After all, if your nation goes to hell, so does your market—a collapse isn't good for business.

But globalism changed the game. Globalism is the breaking down of economic borders. What globalism does is peel away those government protections of national industries, and let global Economic Royalists dive in and feast on the goods. Once government is out of the way, Saul explains, the transnational corporations rise to power. "Richer than a majority of nation-states on the planet, free of the geographical and social obligations of these old states, beyond the embarrassing demands of nationalism, freed in fact from the emotional, immeasurable demands of the citizenry, the transnational would be able to organize world affairs in a more rational, efficient manner."

Without the "demands of nationalism," corporations can skate by without hiring American workers, they can dodge taxes, and they can spew toxic chemicals all over our commons. Instead of nationalism, corporations are bound by efficiency, which in turn yields higher profits. And it's far more efficient and profitable to hire low-wage workers in India, to spend millions lobbying to avoid billions in taxes, and to skirt regulations that keep people working on oil rigs alive and prevent ecological disasters.

Clinton opened the door to globalism, but George W. Bush oversaw the looting of America by global psychopaths.

As a result of so-called free trade, every single month since 2001, our nation has shed, on average, fifty thousand manufacturing jobs. And in that same time period, over fifty thousand manufacturing plants—like the ones that used to line the rail tracks up and down the East Coast—have been permanently shut down.

At a blistering pace, American industries are being sold to the highest foreign bidders, be they Chinese business tycoons, Saudi princes, or Russian oligarchs. In the time it takes you to read just one page in this book, $240,000 worth of American industry is sold off to a foreign interest.[81]

In the past thirty years, foreign investors bought roughly $3 trillion worth of American industry.[82] That means $3 trillion worth of assets that were generating profits for America, hiring American workers, and making things with a "Made in America" stamp on them are now in the possession of foreign nations, so if they continue to operate, all their profits go overseas. It's like a giant liquidation sale in a nation that's on the verge of going out of business.

To highlight just how in peril the United States' economic dominance in the twenty-first century is, consider this trend: In the first decade of this new century, some of the biggest transnational corporations in America—corporations that employ one-fifth of all American workers—have been shipping jobs away en masse. Since 2000, these transnationals have laid off 2.9 million Americans, and hired 2.4 million foreign workers.[83]

Some of the most well known American companies, from all sectors, are contributing to this trend. Caterpillar, Cisco, Chevron, GE, Intel, Merck, Oracle, Stanley Works, and United Technologies have all outsourced at least 45 percent of their workforce to another country. GE has more than half of its workforce in other countries and yet GE's CEO, Jeffrey Immelt, was appointed to head President Obama's Economic Recovery Advisory Board to provide guidance on how to fix our economy.

And this outsourcing of our manufacturing base is creating enormous trade deficits.

For example, consider South Korea, where our automobile trade deficit alone is a whopping $10.8 billion. In 2009, South Korea exported $11.72 billion worth of cars into the US economy. We, on the other hand, were only allowed to export about $492 million worth of cars into theirs.[84]

Or India, where in 2010 we ran up a $10.3 billion trade deficit.[85]

Or China, where our 2010 trade deficit is a mind-boggling $273 billion—the largest trade deficit between two nations ever recorded in the history of the world.

"Madness"

Our trade relationship with China is particularly worrisome. While other nations are just banking off our dumb trade policies promoted by American CEOs who've sold their allegiance to Davos-promoted globalism instead of the United States, China is preparing to be the next world superpower.

Loose lips sink ships, but corporations that have developed some of America's most advanced technologies are more than willing to sell off that technology to the Chinese government if they can just have a little taste of Chinese consumerism.

Leading IT manufacturers and defense industries are blatantly helping to grow the technological capacity of China in return for deeper market penetration and higher profits. In 2020, China will roll out its first full-size commercial airliner built thanks to technology largely developed by Boeing and Airbus.[86]

Of course, American transnational corporations have historically cavorted with nations whose interests were similarly opposed to those of the United States—morally at least. American CEOs made deals with Mahmoud Ahmadinejad in Iran—as was the case with foreign subsidiaries of Koch Industries, America's second-largest private corporation. Other corporate interests worked with Nazi Germany and Apartheid South Africa. They signed contracts with dictators like Mu'ammar Gadhafi in Libya (even while our military was bombing Gadhafi).

Trade expert and former Commerce Department official in the Clinton White House Patrick Mulloy wrote in a 2006 report by the United States-China Economic and Security Review Commission, "The interests of the U.S.-based multinational corporations, which have done so much to influence our current policies toward China, are often not aligned with the broader interest of our nation."

Again, with nationalism off the table, it's only about profits at whatever cost. Mulloy concludes, "Focused on 'shareholder value'...[corporations] are not charged to consider the larger impact of their decisions on the American economy and workers, and the impetus they give to China's growing international, political, and military strength."[87]

Eamonn Fingleton, an economist, best-selling author, and former editor at *Forbes*, who predicted both the Japanese stock market crash in 1987 as well as the tech-bubble crash in 2000, described this wild American sell-off by saying, "For just a few years of profits, America is giving away a technological inheritance that took generations to accumulate...the big gainers are...just a few thousand top corporate executives," the guys hanging out at Davos, "who reap huge returns via bonuses and stock options."[88]

Thanks to them, our nation's current account deficit, primarily our trade imbalance, in 2006 was 7 percent of GDP. That's the highest peacetime current account deficit ever recorded—second only to Italy in 1924, a year before Benito Mussolini anointed himself dictator of fascist Italy.[89]

There's a lot of money to be made seeking out cheaper and cheaper labor markets. So wealth was growing exponentially, which made both political parties buy into this new global paradigm.

Columnist Chrystia Freeland nailed this mind-set perfectly in her 2011 article "The Rise of the New Global Elite," which ran in *The Atlantic* magazine. She reported that one influential American hedge fund manager argued that it didn't matter if the US economy was in peril, because "if the transformation of the world economy lifts four people in China and India out of poverty and into the middle class, and meanwhile means one American drops out of the middle class, that's not such a bad trade."[90]

And yet, millions were being uprooted around the world as a result of these new globalized markets. Subsistence farmers in South America and India were shut out of trade, put out of business by massive transnational agribusiness, and forced into the slums.

Meanwhile, entire communities near Detroit and Camden that once buzzed with manufacturing plants and middle-class trappings were also leveled by the forces of globalism.

"Madness"

There were voices speaking out. People warning that the Royalists were not bringing with them genuine prosperity for all, but only prosperity for the few. They argued it was only an illusion that we were all getting rich and everyone's conditions around the planet were improving thanks to deregulation and global free trade. In reality, they warned, just as Spengler and Galbraith had warned before the last Great Crash, our cultural core was decaying.

As Galbraith noted, when the madness takes hold, "the wise remain silent."

Sir James Goldsmith didn't remain silent. He questioned the logic of the time in his book, *The Trap*, when he wrote, "Many believe that the problems we face can be resolved by doing what we always have done, but doing it more effectively. They believe that we are going in the right direction but we should redouble our efforts to achieve our objectives."[91]

Goldsmith then posed three questions to those who thought the Royalists were on the right track:

- How is it that nearly two hundred years after the birth of the Industrial Revolution, which produced humanity's greatest period of economic expansion, the absolute number of those living in misery, both material and social, has grown exponentially?
- How is it that the world's slum population has developed at a rate vastly greater than that of global population growth?
- And how is it that despite incredible technological innovations the world now faces man-made threats of quite different magnitude from the wars, famines, epidemics and other upheavals of previous dark ages?

Goldsmith asked these questions in 1994. Little did he know things were about to get a lot worse when the psychopathy was allowed to run loose on Wall Street a few years later.

Bankster Psychopaths

Reagan's decision to stop enforcing the Sherman Antitrust Act led to a boom of big companies becoming enormous—a mergers-and-acquisitions (M&A) frenzy, led by "M&A Artists," "LBO Artists" (Leveraged Buyouts), and "Corporate Raiders."

The philosophy that drove the Reagan administration (and had infected the last two years of the Carter administration before it, which deregulated trucking, travel, and several other industries) opened the door for executive-suite psychopaths.

"Chainsaw" Al Dunlap, "King" Carl Icahn, Willard "Mitt" Romney—all made hundreds of millions to billions of dollars strip-mining companies, regardless of the impact of their actions on the employees. Famously, Dunlap bragged about how many thousands of employees he'd fired, and Romney bragged, "I like to fire people."

As Jon Ronson, author of *The Psychopath Test: A Journey Through the Madness Industry*, told *Forbes* writer Jeff Bercovici, for Bercovici's article titled "Why (Some) Psychopaths Make Great CEOs," Chainsaw Al "effortlessly turns the psychopath checklist into 'Who Moved My Cheese?' Many items on the checklist he redefines into a manual of how to do well in capitalism."[92]

The reason psychopaths were making hundreds of millions of dollars in the executive boardroom, Ronson said, was because "the way that capitalism is structured really is a physical manifestation of the brain anomaly known as psychopathy."

A CEO or Corporate Raider, post-Reagan, no longer had any obligations to his community, his employees, or even his company and its customers. Following aggressive lobbying by "experts" advocating for the CEO class, federal tax law was changed so CEOs could be compensated with stock options, producing a generation of CEOs loyal only to stockholders (which included themselves).

By the 1990s, Corporate Raiders and LBO Artists had gotten a bad name, Michael Milken had gone to jail, and Drexel Burnham Lambert had gone bankrupt. Very large companies deployed a variety of strategies from poison pills to loading their balance sheets with debt to avoid the predations of the raiders, forcing them to look to smaller companies to buy, load with debt, and then strip. Instead of making billions like the first-generation raiders, these second-generation raiders were only personally making hundreds of millions.

The industry as a whole decided it needed a new image, and stopped referring to itself as "raiders" or "LBO Artists," instead choosing the Middle America–sounding and ambiguous phrase "private equity."

But the point was the same. In 1985, Mitt Romney explained what his private-equity firm does, saying, "Bain Capital is an investment partnership which was formed to invest in start-up companies and ongoing companies, then to take an active hand in managing them and hopefully, five to eight years later, to *harvest them at a significant profit* [italics added]."

Ronald Reagan's deregulation of the savings and loan (S&L) industry through the Garn–St. Germain Depository Institutions Act of 1982[93] made it easier for very wealthy people to pass on money to their heirs, allowed banks to swindle customers with "adjustable"-rate mortgages, and eliminated much of the regulatory oversight under which S&Ls operated. The result was as predicted by naysayers in 1982: By 1986 the industry had collapsed.

Nonetheless, the relentless drive for more deregulation continued. As laid out in the Powell Memo, hundreds of millions of dollars were funneled into "conservative" and "libertarian" think tanks, which issued a nonstop stream of policy papers and proclamations about the wonders of "less government in business," the very thing Warren Harding had campaigned on in 1920.

Then, Kenneth Lay of Enron wanted badly to run a division of his own company as a bank and to gamble on energy derivatives, both without regulatory oversight. Conveniently for him, Wendy

Gramm, who'd worked for Reagan from 1985 to 1988 as head of the Office of Management and Budget's Office of Information and Regulatory Affairs (OIRA), was running the Commodity Futures Trading Commission from 1988 to 1993. Ken Lay appealed hard for the CFTC to exempt Enron from regulation, and Gramm complied. Shortly thereafter, she left her job at the CFTC and went to work on the Enron board of directors, serving on its Audit Committee.

Her husband, Senator Phil Gramm, laid the groundwork both for meeting Ken Lay's goals and for the banking crash of 2007–08 by pushing, in 1999 and 2000, the Commodity Futures Modernization Act and the Gramm-Leach-Bliley Act, which did away with the 1935 Glass-Steagall Act that had banned regular commercial checkbook-banks from gambling in the markets with their depositors' money.

Clinton signed it into law, and the preeminent lesson we learned about Wall Street following the last Great Crash was officially forgotten.

The madness had returned.

Financialization

Since we don't build anything much anymore, as evidenced by the decaying factories across the nation, we have needed to manufacture at least the appearance of wealth in some other way. That means our economy headed into the twenty-first century was (and still is) heavily dependent upon psychopathic banksters.

In the early 1950s, Americans working in factories and building things accounted for more than a fifth of all the wealth created in the United States. At the same time, bankers offering loans and investments created only about one-tenth of the wealth in America.

Today, however, things are different. Manufacturing has plummeted to about one-tenth of our economy. Whereas finance has surged to nearly a third of our entire economy. This is a phenomenon that many economists have called "financialization."

"Madness"

In the mid-1980s, after a decade of financial deregulation flirted with by Jimmy Carter, fully endorsed by Ronald Reagan, and put on steroids by Clinton and the Bushes, banking, which for forty years had been a very, very boring and safe industry, got a makeover and became the Wild West of lawlessness and get-rich-quick schemes.

These stages of deregulation, fueled by a belief that markets should be "free," produced many different ways of manipulating money and investments to return high profits. Remember, new ways to generate high profits were necessary to keep the American economy thriving, since manufacturing profits were no longer being returned to the nation.

And after deregulation, droves of college graduates who might have gone into engineering forty years earlier, or rocket science during the 1960s, flocked to Wall Street to get involved in the new game of exotic financial instruments that would make them billionaires. Welcome to the world of "credit default swaps" and "collateralized debt obligations." Welcome to the "financialized" world.

In his book *Griftopia*, *Rolling Stone* investigative journalist Matt Taibbi examined how these new exotic financial instruments could make the banks a lot of money by preying on the rest of the economy and the middle class.

In 2008, oil prices and food prices were inexplicably on the rise. As far as supply and demand is concerned, there was no reason why prices should have been going up.

Yet, between January 2003 and July 2008, the price of a barrel of oil went from $30 to $149—a 500 percent increase! Again, there was more than enough oil in the world to meet demand. So why was the price going up?

During this 500 percent price hike over five years in oil, Taibbi noticed something odd in the derivatives markets. He writes, "From 2003 to July 2008...the amount of money invested in commodity indices rose from $13 billion to $317 billion—a factor of twenty-five in a space of a little less than five years."[94]

To put that into perspective, Taibbi goes on to say, "the total increase in Chinese oil consumption over the five and a half years... turns out to be just under a billion barrels—992,261,824, to be exact."[95] On the other hand, "during that same time...the increase in index speculator cash pouring into the commodities markets for petroleum products was almost exactly the same—speculators bought 918,966,932." That's right, speculators used their exotic financial weapons to "fake buy" just as much oil as the enormous Chinese dragon economy.[96]

These speculators were really the only game in town. By 2008, actual commodity sellers and buyers were completely marginalized in the market by speculator banksters, who accounted for 80 percent of all futures purchases. And with their price manipulations, these derivative bombs cratered our economy with high gas prices.

Then there were food prices. Started toward the end of the first Bush administration, the Goldman Sachs Commodity Index is the signature derivatives market in the world. And the betting lines for banksters include energy resources such as oil and gas and food such as cattle, wheat, corn, and soybeans, among other things. Food wasn't immune from the speculator frenzy.

Professor and author Frederick Kaufman details the speculator effect on food prices in a 2010 article he wrote for *Harper's Magazine*. "Nothing had changed about the wheat, but something had changed about the wheat market," Kaufman wrote.[97] "Robber barons, gold bugs, and financiers of every stripe had long dreamed of controlling all of something everybody needed or desired, then holding back the supply as demand drove up prices."[98] That's exactly what speculators were doing—buying up huge amounts of wheat contracts and holding on to them until they could be sold at a higher price.

This had catastrophic effects on the global food supply. "The global speculative frenzy sparked riots in more than thirty countries and drove the number of the world's 'food insecure' to more than a billion...The ranks of the hungry had increased by 250 million in a single year, the most abysmal increase in all of human history," Kaufman writes.[99]

When the Supreme Court selected George W. Bush as president, the transition from New Deal regulations to the Coolidge Prosperity deregulation was largely complete. The psychopathic banksters were free to run wild, and went on to create out of thin air over $800 *trillion* worth of unregulated derivatives—more than ten times the annual GDP of the entire planet.

And just like the previous period of madness in 1929, it all crashed.

The 1920s All Over Again

As Noah Mendel, of George Mason University's History News Network, noted, although the term "great depression" had been used periodically from the James Monroe administration to the Hoover administration, "It was only later, once the Depression had subsided and could be remembered as a historical era, thankfully in the past, that the term 'great depression' could fulfill its proper noun potential and take on the capitalized form that we know today."[100]

Many modern economists have discussed the causes of the 2006–07 American housing-market meltdown, but far fewer have told the story of the housing-market meltdown of 1926.

Evoking that same theme of madness as Galbraith, historian Frederick Lewis Allen recalls the first six years of the Roaring Twenties as "the most delirious fever of real-estate speculation which had attacked the United States in ninety years."[101] (Interestingly, he was parenthetically mentioning the housing bubble bursting just before the Civil War.)

With the advent of the automobile and construction of new roads in the second decade of the twentieth century, the state of Florida suddenly became accessible to millions of Americans seeking warmer weather and new fortunes. The stock market was surging through the 1920s, consumer spending soared, and confidence in the economy was at an all-time high. It was the time of "Coolidge Prosperity"—a term birthed by Republicans and echoed in the newspapers of the mid-1920s, when our nation's thirtieth president said that good times were here to stay in America forever, and that every American could become rich thanks to the "free market."

As we would later learn, it wasn't *actual* "prosperity" but instead just another economic bubble created by low taxes and financial deregulation.

But at the time, Americans had no idea, and they flocked to the Sunshine State to get a piece of real estate in a housing market that everyone thought would continue to rise indefinitely—the same assumption that inflated the housing bubble of the George W. Bush years. As Allen writes, "the abounding confidence engendered by Coolidge Prosperity...persuaded the four-thousand-dollar-a-year salesman that in some magical way he too might tomorrow be able to buy a fine house and all the good things of earth."

So, in five years, from 1920 to 1925, the population of Miami grew fivefold. If you were operating under the assumption that real estate prices would continue to soar, then it didn't matter how much of your life savings you staked out on a piece of land in Coral Gables, Florida, because that land would grow in value and you would make tons of money off of it. And people did make boatloads of money— for a short few years.

South Florida lots that sold for $800 at the beginning of the bubble were resold just a few years later, in 1924, for $150,000. Land bought for just $25 in 1896 was selling like hotcakes for $150,000 by 1925.[102] Nobody was actually planning on moving into these new, insanely priced houses and condominiums, though. Ninety percent of the buyers had only one plan for their newly acquired and mortgaged property—to resell at a profit. As Allen writes, "few people worried much about the further payments which were to come."

But then Mother Nature had her say. As could have been predicted (and was by some locals), a hurricane blew through Florida in 1926, killed or injured over two thousand people, and punctured the housing bubble. South Florida imploded.

A 1928 article in *The Nation* magazine written by Henry S. Villard relayed what postboom Florida looked like: "Dead subdivisions line the highway, their pompous names half-obliterated on crumbling stucco gates. Lonely white-way lights stand guard over miles of cement side-walks, where grass and palmetto take the place of homes that were [soon] to be ... Whole sections of outlying subdivisions are composed of unoccupied houses, past which one speeds on broad thoroughfares as if traversing a city in the grip of death."[103]

People who got caught up in the frenzy lost everything. Banks and real estate offices that littered the once-vigorous streets of Miami began, one after the other, to go under. In 1925, at the height of the bubble, bank holdings in Miami totaled over $1 billion—and that was back when a dollar was worth nearly thirteen of today's dollars.[104] By 1929, bank holdings had plummeted almost 90 percent to just under $150 million. It turned out real estate prices couldn't go up forever (a lesson from the 1850s and the 1770s that had been forgotten).

When the Florida housing bubble burst in 1926, the hot money created by Treasury Secretary Andrew Mellon's tax cuts simply shifted to Wall Street. As Allen wrote, "[The] national speculative fever which had turned their eyes and their cash to the Florida Gold Coast in 1925 was not chilled; it was merely checked. Florida house-lots were a bad bet? Very well, then, said a public still enthralled by the radiant possibilities of Coolidge Prosperity: what else was there to bet on?"

The answer was obvious, as Allen wrote, "Before long a new wave of popular speculation was accumulating momentum. Not in real estate this time; in something quite different. The focus of speculative infection shifted from Flagler Street, Miami, to Broad and Wall Streets, New York. The Big Bull Market was getting under way."

Predictably, that "Big Bull Market" imploded a few years later, despite Hoover's assurance that if government just stayed out of the way, everything would magically rebalance itself and prosperity would return. Instead, it was the third act of the three-act play we've seen over and over again, from the onset of capital markets to today: boom, bust, Great Depression.

And, almost exactly eighty years after that Great Crash of 1929, it all happened again.

Even Worse than Before

Economist Steve Keen, author of *Debunking Economics*, defined the "madness" in our banking system as inherent. He told me, "It's the structure of finance itself. There's inherent instability in a capitalist system."[105]

He explained that capitalism demands a banking system and that that banking system is wired to misbehave, since there's always an "inherent temptation" to create and sell as much debt as possible—whether it's in the form of oil derivatives, mortgages, or student loans.

"They will always want to lend more money...the banking sector profits by creating debt," Keen said.

If the banking sector simply lent money to businesses to fund productive investments and homeowners who could actually afford a home, then, Keen estimates, bank profits would be only 5 to 10 percent of total profits in America.

But with manufacturing decimated from so-called free trade, and no rules on Wall Street, Royalist banksters lunged for a bigger piece of the profit pie. They force-fed the nation more and more debt.

The peak level of debt financing was less than 10 percent of GDP in the 1920s, before the last Great Crash. But between 2000 and 2008, it was 20 percent of GDP—it was a far bigger bubble.

During this time, Wall Street profits as a share of total profits in

America were upward of 50 percent. As Keen told me, "That's not a sign of a healthy economy. That's a sick economy."

Another debt bubble, even bigger than the one in the 1920s, was being inflated. Keen told me the bubble had started in 1982.

I asked him why, and he said, "You had such a terrifying experience after the Great Depression and the Second World War. You completely tamed that bad behavior in the financial sector and people's willingness to take on debt."

But then people forgot. As Keen said, "If you look at when people started to really take on debt again, it was when the first baby boomer turned eighteen. We lost that memory, and then that same irresponsible behavior that gave us the Roaring Twenties came back."

While my father's generation remembered the Great Depression, I was born in 1951 and have no personal recollection of it. As my "boomer" generation took the reins of business in the seventies and eighties, there was no "remembered" sense of the dangers of reckless banking practices or even of reckless personal debt.

And so, in October 2006, history repeated itself when the second Great American Housing Bubble started to burst. It was worse than 1929.

Savvy investors saw the fuse burning. They knew that the housing-fueled Bush Bubble inflated by the Royalists' assault on financial regulations and Alan Greenspan's dangerously misdirected stewardship of the market, much like the dot-com-fueled Clinton Bubble, had come to an end and that soon it would move from little-noticed Fed figures into their own backyards—into the guts of Wall Street. The business press subtly informed investors, and giant hedge funds in New York and London began to position themselves for the coming market collapse.

The *Financial Times*, for example, in a September 27, 2006, article titled "Hedge Funds Hone In on Housing,"[106] cited that "growing numbers of hedge funds have placed bets on a slump in the US housing sector in recent weeks." The article noted that the funds were rapidly buying insurance against a housing crash in order to "be on the winning side of a housing downturn."

But those insurance bets only made the problem worse. They just shifted ground zero of the now-larger derivative bomb from mega-bank corporations like Goldman Sachs to mega-insurance corporations like AIG. Both were "Too Big to Fail," both were drenched in systemic risk, and both were capable of ending the United States as we know it.

We know what happened next—a serious financial panic.

Fittingly, three years after that panic, a June 2011 article in the *Financial Times* titled "Alfred Hitchcock's 'The Bankers'" noted, "The characteristics that make for good traders and investment bankers are pretty much the same as those that define psychopaths."[107]

The article goes on to ask about the increasingly vital-to-our-economy psychotic bankers. "Surely only someone with a serious personality disorder could have thought it was a good idea to sell a highly risky financial instrument like a CDO-squared to a naive investor who clearly did not understand the risk?"[108]

As a result of these psychopaths, the markets tanked, banks across the country failed (the big ones got bailed out), and millions lost their homes and jobs.

But with the crash of 2007–08, the Royalists were just warming up. Their harvesting of the United States wouldn't be complete until a few years later.

PART 3

"Oppression, Rebellion, Reformation"

Chapter 7

A Revolution Denied

*You never let a serious crisis go to waste. And what I mean by that is it's
an opportunity to do things you think you could not do before.*
— Rahm Emanuel, chief of staff to
President Barack Obama, 2008

The beginning of the end of the Crash of 2016 begins on a cold
January night in 2009—where this book begins—with the
inauguration of Barack Obama.

In fact, the crash was plotted in a dining room a block off of Pennsylvania Avenue about halfway between the White House and the US
Capitol. The Caucus Room, as it's known, is across the street from the
J. Edgar Hoover Building, headquarters of the FBI, right around the
corner from Ford's Theatre, where a president was killed during a time
of national crisis, and two blocks north of the National Mall, which was
"occupied" by the Bonus Army, during another time of national crisis,
in 1931. It's in the back end of the apartment building where Louise
and I resided during the first year we lived in Washington, DC.

It was there, on the night of Inauguration Day in 2009, beneath
soft track lighting and surrounded by polished cherrywood paneling,

that a plot was hatched to make sure the Economic Royalists took advantage of the economic crisis, which they had caused. The stakes couldn't be higher for them.

America was on the verge of a second New Deal. Or, a second Gilded Age. She was in the middle of a revolution.

In fact, Thomas Jefferson had predicted this revolution, and he also predicted what might happen to this nation if those Royalists in the Caucus Room won the revolution.

Jefferson's Cycle of Revolutions

Running alongside the eighty-year cycle of Great Crashes, there's another cycle, one of revolutions.

Because he had lived through a true revolution here, and had watched another one sputter and fail in France, Thomas Jefferson knew that periodic revolutions were necessary for America—or any democratic society—to flourish and grow.

Jefferson even suggested that "every generation" should have its own smaller form of revolution, reconfiguring the nation and its government to adapt to changing needs and changing times.

The concept of *generations* has played a role in many governing documents. The Iroquois Confederation's "Great Law," which was a major inspiration for the American Constitution, famously called for all governmental decisions to be made in the context of their impact on "the Seventh Generation" down the line into the future.

While the definition of the time period represented by a "generation" has been the subject of much speculation over the years, Thomas Jefferson recognized two clear definitions, and repeatedly said that both the Constitution and future legislators should respect each of them.

The first was the personal, familial definition of "generation"— which Jefferson put at nineteen years and today is generally considered to be around twenty years. In that context, with the first

American Revolution officially beginning in 1776, today's young people are about the twelfth generation since our nation's birth.

The second was the generational epochs—blocks of time during which generations overlap and a major transfer of power is made from one to another, along with a period of time long enough for a major change in our understanding of government and a recalibration of our worldview.

Jefferson and his contemporaries spoke and wrote often about the obligations of each generation to its heirs, and about the political crime of any generation placing shackles (financial or legal) on future generations.

Jefferson wrote to his protégé, James Madison, the year the Constitution was ratified and our modern nation birthed: "The question, whether one generation of men has a right to bind another…is a question of such consequences as not only to merit decision, but place also among the fundamental principles of every government."[109] No single generation, he wrote, has the right to saddle the next with problems or debts, and it should be obvious "that no such obligation can be transmitted" from generation to generation.

Laying out his thinking on the issue, Jefferson continued: "I set out on this ground, which I suppose to be self evident, that the earth belongs in usufruct [common ownership] to the living; that the dead have neither powers nor rights over it. The portion occupied by any individual ceases to be his when himself ceases to be, and reverts to the society."

Jefferson's logic that no person or generation should be able to bind the next one was one of his core beliefs throughout his life, and shared by most of his contemporaries. He added, "For if he could, he might during his own life, eat up the usufruct [commons] of the lands for several generations to come; then the lands would belong to the dead, and not to the living, which is the reverse of our principle."

But what was most revolutionary about Jefferson's thinking on this was the idea of *generational revolutions*—that the nation itself must fundamentally change roughly once every biological or epochal generation, and that even that wouldn't prevent larger periodic political transformations of the nation. These were, he believed, not just ideals but a basic force of nature. He wrote:

> On similar ground it may be proved, that no society can make a perpetual constitution, or even a perpetual law. The earth belongs always to the living generation: they may manage it, then, and what proceeds from it, as they please, during their usufruct [shared ownership]. They are masters, too, of their own persons, and consequently may govern them as they please. But persons and property make the sum of the objects of government. The constitution and the laws of their predecessors are extinguished then, in their natural course, with those whose will gave them being.

Jefferson believed that even the laws enshrined in our Constitution came with a time limit, and that once the generation that wrote those laws passed on out of power, those laws must be rewritten by the new generation, or at least every second generation.

"Every constitution, then, and every law, naturally expires at the end of thirty-four years," Jefferson wrote. "If it be enforced longer, it is an act of force, and not of right. It may be said, that the succeeding generation exercising, in fact, the power of repeal, this leaves them as free as if the constitution or law had been expressly limited to thirty-four years only."

A revolution every twenty to thirty-four years? Could Jefferson have actually been proposing—or predicting—that?

In fact, yes.

Jefferson stressed the need for every generation to essentially produce a revolution that would turn the wheel of America forward into the new epoch. He arrived at this conclusion by understanding the weaknesses inherent in the Constitution when it was first drafted, and the need that each new generation must continue to perfect it, or at least adapt it to respond to changing times.

A Revolution Denied

Jefferson noted the absurdity of a rigid Constitution—or at least an interpretation of that Constitution—that does not change as the nation grows and times change, saying, "We might as well require a man to wear still the coat which fitted him when a boy, as civilized society to remain ever under the regimen of their barbarous ancestors.... Let us follow no such examples, nor weakly believe that one generation is not as capable as another of taking care of itself."

Looking back, Jefferson's theory of revolution holds up.

A History of Revolution

The young men of the Revolution of 1776 had become the old establishment of 1800. But the young people of the nation were dissatisfied with how things were going under the presidency of John Adams (elected in 1796), as Adams had steadily been moving the government in a more and more authoritarian and monarchical direction.

The result was that young people who voted in the election of 1800 fostered what historians refer to as "The Second American Revolution of 1800," the first peaceful transfer of power from one party (Adams's Federalists) to another (Jefferson's Democratic Republicans, today called the Democratic Party) of a major nation in history. Jefferson called it a "revolution as significant" as the one of 1776.

This cycle then repeated over and over again, with each new generation bringing with it a new "revolution."

The young people of 1800 came to power in the 1820s, and the election of Andrew Jackson in 1828 was again revolutionary, in that he campaigned on a platform of overturning the existing order. In 1832, he vetoed a renewal of the charter of the Second Bank of the United States, took on the "selfish" "rich and powerful," and humbled the banksters. He was the people's hero, and it was a revolution against the establishment that had rigidified thirty years after the revolution of 1800.

Roughly thirty years later, the children of Jackson's revolution fought the Civil War under Abraham Lincoln.

The next generation came of age and power in the 1880s, while America was once again facing a grassroots revolution, this one against the Industrial Age's rise of the Robber Barons (railroads, steel, oil, finance) in a period we often refer to as "the Gilded Age."

The children of President Cleveland's generation watched, as they grew up, the assassination of an incredibly corrupt President McKinley, which turned power over to his vice president, Theodore Roosevelt. By 1907, the revolution was on again, and Roosevelt pushed through Congress the Tillman Act, which not only made it an explicitly criminal act for a corporation to give money or any other form of support to candidates for federal office but even provided for corporate officers and directors themselves to individually go to jail for the election-influencing crimes of their companies.

A generation later, in 1932, revolution was brewing. Forty-five thousand veterans of World War I were occupying land from the White House Lawn to the Potomac River, demanding that their bonus coupons for service in the war, redeemable in 1945, be cashed in immediately so they could deal with the Great Depression. The relatively moderate governor of New York, a man born of wealth and firmly part of the establishment, Franklin D. Roosevelt, stepped into the White House. And, recognizing the revolutionary times, Roosevelt had by 1936 become such a revolutionary himself that his opponents among the banking and industrial class were openly using the media to call him a communist and a traitor; they even organized an unsuccessful coup d'état against him.

FDR's revolution was resolved with Roosevelt's death and the end of World War II in 1945. So as the wheel of history turned, inevitably there came the next generation's revolution, the one of the 1960s.

The tenth generational revolution in America, led by Ronald Reagan and a new batch of Economic Royalists, was promoted as a revolution against the "free love" and "tune in, turn on, and drop out" ethos of the hippies. But at its core it was a corporate revolt, following an outline drawn up by Lewis Powell (as mentioned previously in chapter 2) against the rising profiles of Rachel Carson, Ralph Nader, and their unrelenting and successful work regulating big business.

Reagan's Royalist revolution was continued and expanded through the presidencies of George Herbert Walker Bush and Bill Clinton, "ending welfare as we know it" and Clinton's declaration that "the era of big government is over."

So, a generation after Reagan, when a young senator from Illinois came along promising change in the midst of another crisis, a nation pregnant with a new generation's revolution found her new president.

A dozen American generations built this nation and sustained it, with each one producing its own revolution.

But Jefferson also knew that at times these revolutions would not be achieved so easily. That old forces—be they those of monarchy, aristocratic slaveholders, or Economic Royalists—would conspire to keep power and deny a new generation its revolution.

He was blunt about the consequences of such a thing happening, writing, "If this avenue [of periodic revolution] be shut to the call of sufferance, it will make itself heard through that of force, and we shall go on, as other nations are doing, in the endless circle of oppression, rebellion, reformation; and oppression, rebellion, reformation, again; and so on forever."[110]

John F. Kennedy echoed this warning 150 years after Jefferson when he said, "Those who make peaceful revolution impossible will make violent revolution inevitable."[111]

The Suicide Pact

Which brings us back to the Caucus Room on the night of President Obama's Inauguration Day.

Newt Gingrich was there. So, too, were some of the most prominent Republican members of Congress, including Representatives

Eric Cantor, Paul Ryan, and Kevin McCarthy. Senators Jon Kyl, Jim DeMint, and Tom Coburn were there. And Frank Luntz, Republican pollster and Fox News regular, was there, too. They all sat around a square table facing each other like a group-therapy session.

After all, Democrats were now in control of the White House, the Senate, and the House of Representatives for the first time since before the Reagan Revolution and they were talking about things like repealing tax cuts for the top 1 percent, reforming health care, passing a carbon tax, and spending huge amounts of money to rebuild America reminiscent of Franklin Roosevelt's WPA.

Hours earlier, a man who campaigned on "fundamentally transforming the United States of America" gave his Inaugural Address to the largest gathering of people the National Mall in Washington, DC, had ever seen.

A new direction is exactly what the nation pregnant with revolution wanted. And the nearly 70 million people who voted for Barack Obama (the most votes ever received by a president of the United States in the history of the nation) *hoped* that he was the man to bring about this revolution—just as he campaigned he would do.

So, the disciples of Reagan sat together eating their steaks and digesting the new political reality of Democrats in charge and everything they'd worked for over the last thirty years being completely wiped out. They talked about how they'd got to this point, what had gone wrong, and, most important, what to do now.

In his 2012 book *Do Not Ask What Good We Do: Inside the U.S. House of Representatives*, Robert Draper recounts the outcomes of this meeting, writing, "The dinner lasted nearly four hours. They parted company almost giddily. The Republicans had agreed on a way forward...show united and unyielding opposition to the president's economic policies...Begin attacking vulnerable Democrats on the airwaves...Win the spear point of the House in 2010. Jab Obama relentlessly in 2011. Win the White House and the Senate in 2012."[112]

A Revolution Denied

Representative Paul Ryan warned that everyone "had to stick together." Representative Kevin McCarthy chimed in, saying, "We've gotta challenge them on every single bill and challenge them on every single campaign."

The seeds of the Powell Memo, planted nearly forty years earlier, had grown into giant spruces of corporatocracy with branches wrapped around our political, economic, and media institutions.

Just as the lessons learned in the Powell Memo were used to take power in the 1970s, they would be used to keep power during another time of crisis.

The Royalists in the Caucus Room gambled that if only this coming Progressive Revolution could be handcuffed for just two years, then maybe the revolutionary spirit of the American people could be broken, or better yet hijacked, and the Reagan Revolution might weather the storm and even exploit this crisis to push their own revolution further. That was the plan at least, and the Republicans in the room were confident they could pull it off.

As Newt Gingrich said after dinner, "You will remember this day. You'll remember this as the day the seeds of 2012 were sown."

Republican Representative Pete Sessions from Texas, in an interview with the *National Journal*, compared the Republican strategy moving forward to a "Taliban insurgency."[113]

And so a suicide pact was drawn up the night that President Obama was sworn in to office, in January 2009. Which meant that even before Barack Obama went to sleep on his first night as president of the United States, he was dealing with an insurgency.

With the help of prominent media outlets, the Royalists, now a political minority, would engage in a scorched-earth strategy to defeat a coming Progressive Revolution, even if it meant crashing the United States as we know it. If they were going down, then the rest of the nation was going down with them.

Which is exactly what happened.

Chapter 8

The Royalists Strike Back

We needed to have the press be our friend ... We wanted them to ask the questions we want to answer so that they report the news the way we want it to be reported.

—Tea Party Senate candidate Sharron Angle,
August 2, 2010

The very first Great Crash in our nation's history—that of the economic exploitation in colonial America, which was followed by the Revolutionary War—was kicked off by a "Tea Party."

We learn about the Boston Tea Party in elementary school. But rarely do we learn what really triggered this event (another consequence of the Great Forgetting).

As was mentioned in chapter 1, the Boston Tea Party was a revolt against the Economic Royalists, who had seized the British government and passed the world's largest corporate tax break at the time, devastating colonial tea sellers.

The purpose of the Tea Act was to increase the profitability of the East India Company to its stockholders (which included the king) and to help the company drive its colonial small-business competitors out of business. Because the company temporarily no longer had to pay high taxes to England and held a monopoly on the tea it sold in the American colonies, it was able to lower its tea prices to undercut those of the local importers and the mom-and-pop tea merchants and teahouses in every town in America.

In response, in December 1773, a group of Bostonians boarded ships belonging to the East India Company and committed one of the largest acts of corporate vandalism in the history of the world—throwing what would be today millions of dollars' worth of tea into the harbor.

War would soon follow.

Today, as the great cycles come back around, and battle with the Royalists reconvenes, the "Tea Party" has returned. Only this time, the Royalists are the ones dressed silly.

A Tea Party Reimagined

It's hard to figure out when exactly the twenty-first-century Tea Party "started."

The sentiment that government should be supersmall, that taxes are evil, and that social safety nets encourage laziness has existed in America since its founding, albeit usually only on the fringes of society. But what exactly caused tens of thousands of Americans around the country to start dressing up in eighteenth-century garb and dangling tea bags from tricornered hats in the summer of 2009 is a little trickier than those simple slogans.

The prominent Tea Party organization, the Tea Party Patriots, attributes the beginning of the Tea Party to a rant by CNBC talking head Rick Santelli in February 2009—less than a month after President Obama took office.* Santelli was reporting from the floor of

---

* Tea Party national press release, November 4, 2010: "Tea Party Patriots wishes to extend a special thank you to Rick Santelli for his rant on February 19, 2009, which started this entire movement. Without Rick's rant, this movement would never have started. Many others will try to take credit but don't be fooled. He was the spark that began this fire."

the Chicago Stock Exchange when he went off on a program being floated by the Obama administration to help struggling home-owners during the height of the foreclosure crisis that was sweeping across the nation.

Santelli went unhinged while live on the air, yelling, "The government is promoting bad behavior...How about this president and new administration? Why don't you put up a website to have people vote on the Internet as a referendum to see if we really want to subsidize the losers' mortgages."

By "losers," Santelli was referring to struggling homeowners who had been hustled into buying adjustable-rate mortgages by predatory salesmen out to make a quick buck in the banking industry.

Never mind the program being proposed by the Obama administration to deal with that crisis was far weaker than the one passed through Congress by Franklin Roosevelt, which backstopped people's mortgages to stop the train wreck of a foreclosure crisis during the Great Depression.

Santelli turned to traders standing nearby and asked, "This is America. How many of you people want to pay for your neighbor's mortgage that has an extra bathroom and can't pay their bills? Raise your hand. President Obama, are you listening?"[114]

The Economic Royalists were listening. And there was already a movement afoot to exploit Santelli's rant for their own gain. Santelli himself gave up this fact when he shamelessly plugged what was likely the first-of-its-kind Tea Party rally, saying, "We're thinking of having a Chicago tea party in July. All you capitalists that want to show up to Lake Michigan, I'm gonna start organizing."

While on the surface Santelli's rant may have seemed like the kickoff of the Tea Party movement, a closer look at the facts shows that a "Tea Party" was already being organized even before President Obama took office.

A 2013 study[115] published in the scientific journal *Tobacco Control* revealed that today's incarnation of the Tea Party goes back a long way—well before the election of Barack Obama.

Talk of a new Tea Party to advance corporate interests in America began in the 1980s and 1990s, when tobacco companies invested heavily in building new broad alliances with other organizations in hopes of fighting back against the emerging antismoking agenda in Congress.

Taking the advice of the Powell Memo, written a decade earlier, tobacco companies such as R. J. Reynolds, Lorillard, and Philip Morris funneled millions of dollars into an organization called Citizens for a Sound Economy (CSE). One funder of CSE is one of the most prominent Royalists of today, David Koch.

The purpose of CSE was to build a coalition of tobacco companies and corporate polluters to oppose regulations on smoking and air pollutants being considered in Congress. It's estimated that at least $5.3 million was funneled into CSE by Big Tobacco.

Then in 1993, a Philip Morris PR flack wrote a "Powell-esque" memo outlining a strategy of fighting any new taxes by joining up with other antitax groups to create a "New Boston Tea Party."

The memo reads, "Grounded in the theme of 'The New American Tax Revolution' or 'The New Boston Tea Party,' the campaign activity should take the form of citizens representing the widest constituency base mobilized with signage and other attention-drawing accouterments such as lapel buttons, handouts, petitions and even costumes."[116]

Ultimately, the tobacco companies failed and were hit with a massive $200 billion settlement in 1998. But in 2002, David Koch's CSE purchased a website domain name: USTeaParty.com. Eventually, plans for this Tea Party were put on hold. After all, a Republican Royalist, George W. Bush, was in the White House, and Royalists were in control of Congress, so there was no reason to cause any trouble.

Only after the Royalists crashed our economy, and were banished from Congress, would the so-called Tea Party be revived. And sure enough, it was revived by CSE. Only, by now, CSE had split into two Astroturf corporate-funded organizations: Americans for Prosperity and FreedomWorks. Unlike "grassroots," Astroturf organizations are propped up by a wealthy elite and rely on corporate cash rather than genuine activism.

Meet the Kochs

Few did more to put the Powell Memo into motion than the billionaire Koch brothers, David and Charles.

They run the massive transnational conglomerate known as Koch Industries, dealing in everything from petroleum refining and distribution, to chemical processing and ranching.

Koch Industries is the second largest privately held company in the United States, taking home nearly $100 billion in annual revenue. And the Koch brothers occupy spot 4 on the Forbes 400 Richest People in America list, each worth $31 billion. Together, they are wealthier than Warren Buffett, who is in spot 2 on the list.

They inherited Koch Industries from their father, Fred Koch, who in 1927 discovered a more efficient way of processing crude into gasoline, which he pitched to Joseph Stalin in the Soviet Union and made a fortune.

Despite his collaboration with the communists, Fred Koch was an unapologetic Economic Royalist. Long before Lewis Powell's memo, Fred helped found the John Birch Society in 1958. It was a group of far-right, fierce anticommunists, who also worked against the civil rights movement in America. They subscribed to the radical economics of neoliberalism, which was still shut out of the mainstream political and economic debate at the time.

But Fred would instill in his sons, Charles and David, this same radical Royalist ideology that would soon gain favor around the world in the 1980s.

Writing in *The New Yorker*, Jane Mayer talks about the political influence on the Koch brothers, such as the John Birch Society to which they were exposed through their father.

"Members of the John Birch Society," she writes, "developed an interest in a school of Austrian economists who promoted free-market ideals. Charles and David Koch were particularly influenced by the work of Friedrich von Hayek... [and his] belief in unfettered capitalism."

She adds, "Charles and David also became devotees of a more radical thinker, Robert LeFevre, who favored the abolition of the state... LeFevre liked to say that 'government is a disease masquerading as its own cure.'"

David Koch even ran for president in 1980 on the Libertarian ticket, but only received 1 percent of the vote. As Mayer writes, "The brothers realized that their brand of politics didn't sell at the ballot box. Charles Koch became openly scornful of conventional politics. 'It tends to be a nasty, corrupting business,' he told a reporter at the time. 'I'm interested in advancing libertarian ideas.'"

And they had a lot of money to do just that.

The Rise of the Kochtopus

When Lewis Powell told Eugene Syndor that the Chamber of Commerce needed to spend more money influencing politics, education, the media, and school curriculums, he might have been better off just addressing the letter to the Koch brothers.

At the onset of the Jimmy Carter presidency, in 1977, they bankrolled the CATO Institute, a think tank devoted to espousing Libertarian—or Royalist—ideology.

Brian Doherty, a senior editor at *Reason* magazine, interviewed the brothers multiple times. He quoted Charles describing the strategy behind their funding to "bring about social change." It was, Charles said, a "vertically and horizontally integrated" endeavor "from idea creation to policy development to education to grassroots organizations to lobbying to litigation to political action."

After CATO, the Kochs spent millions creating the Mercatus Center at George Mason University, devoted to neoliberal economics and climate change denial.

The Wall Street Journal noted, "When it comes to business regulation in Washington, Mercatus, Latin for market, has become the most important think tank you've never heard of." The article goes on to say, "Mercatus, with its free-market philosophy, has become a kind of shadow regulatory authority."

The Mercatus Center is so effective that when oil men George W. Bush and Dick Cheney moved in to the White House in 2001, they sought suggestions for which environmental regulations they should immediately kill off. Of the twenty-three regulations to bite the dust, fourteen were suggested by the Mercatus Center, which has been given more than $14 million by the Kochs since 1998.[117]

But Koch-funded Royalist spin machines aren't exclusive to George Mason University.

At Florida State University, Charles Koch inked a multimillion-dollar deal with the economics department to advance Royalist economics. As the *St. Petersburg Times* reported, "A foundation bankrolled by Libertarian businessman Charles G. Koch has pledged $1.5 million for positions in Florida State University's economics department. In return, his representatives get to screen and sign off on any hires for a new program promoting 'political economy and free enterprise.'"[118]

The article highlights just how pervasive the Koch influence is in the Florida State University deal. "Under the agreement with the Charles G. Koch Charitable Foundation...faculty only retain the illusion of control. The contract specifies that an advisory committee appointed by Koch decides which candidates should be considered. The foundation can also withdraw its funding if it's not happy with the faculty's choice or if the hires don't meet 'objectives' set by Koch during annual evaluations." In other words, the Kochs get final say on new professors—especially ones who don't subscribe to the Kochs' own free-market economic philosophy. In 2009, Charles Koch nixed nearly 60 percent of the university faculty's suggestions.[119]

The Kochs have similar strings-attached deals with public universities all across the country, including West Virginia University, Troy University, Utah State University, and Clemson University. All in all, over 150 higher-education institutions receive some sort of financial contribution from the Koch brothers—often in the form of quid pro quos. Our higher-education system is being used by Economic Royalists such as the Kochs to fund economic brainwashing and a hearts-and-minds assault against the government.

And the Kochs make no secret that their money comes with strings attached. "If we're going to give a lot of money, we'll make darn sure they spend it in a way that goes along with our intent," he told Doherty. "And if they make a wrong turn and start doing things we don't agree with, we withdraw funding."

The Kochs have been behind mind-boggling amounts of political spending.

Koch Industries itself has spent more than $50 million lobbying since 1998. But Jane Mayer, with *The New Yorker*, cautions, "Only the Kochs know precisely how much they have spent on politics."

According to tax records, between 1998 and 2008, the Kochs funneled hundreds of millions of dollars through charitable organizations, with much of that money winding up in the hands of political organizations, too.

Mayer writes, "The three main Koch family foundations gave money to thirty-four political and policy organizations, three of which they founded, and several of which they direct. The Kochs and their company have given additional millions to political campaigns, advocacy groups, and lobbyists."

The National Committee for Responsive Philanthropy produced

a report in 2004 questioning the charitable nature of the Kochs' donations. Their report concludes that the Kochs aren't actually making charitable contributions; they're making investments in ideas that will eventually lead to higher profits. According to the report, Koch foundations "give money to nonprofit organizations that do research and advocacy on issues that impact the profit margin of Koch Industries."

The International Forum on Globalization has mapped the various organizations and individuals that make up the tentacles of the Kochtopus.

They include media personalities such as Rush Limbaugh and Glenn Beck. Think tanks beyond CATO include the American Enterprise Institute, which has received nearly $2 million in Koch cash, and the Heritage Foundation, which has received more than $4 million. Also benefitting from the Kochs are lobbying organizations such as the US Chamber of Commerce and the American Legislative Exchange Council.

And the Kochs provided nearly $6 million in funding for Americans for Prosperity, one of those organizations that split off from CSE's tobacco Tea Party in the first decade of the twenty-first century to form the new Royalist-tinged Tea Party after Barack Obama was elected in 2009.

It takes a lot of money to get the entire political and economic class to buy into an ideology that has repeatedly caused massive economic crashes—especially since the last crash was still fresh in everyone's mind.

As Charles Koch told Doherty, "We have a radical philosophy."

The Tea Party, even if birthed by the tobacco companies, was nurtured by multimillionaire Royalists and billionaires such as Charles and David Koch. They spent millions to set up and promote Tea Party organizations, fund rallies, and charter buses to carry people from all around the country to boost participation.

And by the summer of 2009, what appeared to be a full-on grassroots movement, but in the background was a well-oiled, corporate-funded anti-Obama PR machine, had developed all around the country, complete with mostly elderly white Americans shouting down their congressmen and congresswomen, accusing them of being socialists and pushing secret agendas to raise everybody's taxes and destroy democracy.

But the Kochs weren't operating alone. Born out of the Ailes memo for GOP TV in the 1970s, Fox News was now the most watched cable news network in America. And they did their part to squash any sort of Progressive Revolution, and ensure that the Royalists' counterrevolution succeeds.

Fox News Gets in the Game

Bill Sammon got the memo.

On the morning of October 27, 2009, staffers at Fox News received an urgent message from their boss, the Washington managing editor, Bill Sammon. It had to do with certain wording to be used by Fox anchors when reporting on the health reform debate—in particular, the wording to be used to describe the "Public Option."

Ten months had passed since Barack Obama and a slew of progressive Democrats in Congress were sworn in, promising to break up the Royalists' stronghold in our democracy and economy.

First up was the Royalist dominance in our health care system—the only one in the entire developed world that does not offer health care as a basic human right.

The Royalists knew their grip on our nation's health care system was in danger, so they grabbed ahold of their megaphone to spew disinformation—namely, Roger Ailes.

Fear of "death panels" was one of several myths spun out of the right-wing messaging campaign funded by big for-profit health insurance corporations opposed to any sort of health reform. It was given credence by Sarah Palin in an August 2009 Facebook post in which she wrote, "The America I know and love is not one in which my parents or my baby with Down Syndrome will have to stand in front of Obama's 'death panel' so his bureaucrats can decide, based on a subjective judgment of their 'level of productivity in society,' whether they are worthy of health care. Such a system is downright evil."

The ironic thing about Palin's message was that so-called death panels are actually a very real thing in America. Every single day, death panels at for-profit health insurance corporations determine whether or not it's worth paying out a certain claim or signing on to a certain lifesaving medical procedure. In those cases, a "subjective judgment" is made on how a cancer patient's chemotherapy will affect the corporation's bottom line.

It was exactly this sort of abuse that President Obama's Affordable Care Act was trying to curb. But in the perversion of the health reform debate, somehow that message got reversed. And even though there was no such thing as a "death panels" provision in the health reform bill, it was an issue that dominated much of the health care debate in the summer of 2009.

Another myth was that the president's health reform would amount to a government takeover of the private health insurance industry. Given the antigovernment fervor sweeping the nation after thirty years of bad government under Royalist Republicans, this myth gained a lot of traction.

The Royalists warned that President Obama was taking over the American health care system with all its advanced MRI machines and laser surgeries and cutting-edge medication, and transforming it into a socialized, rationed health care system like the ones that were killing off millions of people in "Communist Europe." It was a myth that everyone who lives outside the United States, in particular in Canada and Europe, regarded as patently absurd. Europeans have far better health care results than Americans, and nearly every single person I've talked to from a nation that has a single-payer system told me they prefer their health care system to mine any day of the week, thank you very much.

But Royalists were able to find a handful of Canadians who'd had a bad experience with their home health care system and paraded them around as victims of "socialized medicine." Eventually, like the "death panels" myth, the government takeover myth stuck, too.

It grew out of the Public Option component of the health reform law.

In some parts of the country there was only one health insurance choice for consumers. One big for-profit health insurance corporation held a monopoly over the local market and could therefore charge whatever they liked and treat their customers however they liked. To inject some competition (the stuff Royalists claim to love) into the market, a government health insurance program was conceived that would serve as a more efficient and compassionate alternative to private health insurance plans. In the proposed health reform legislation, this alternative was known as the Public Option. The idea is simple, give people a choice and let the free market decide.

The Public Option was a far cry from what progressives wanted, which was a single-payer system. But if private health insurance corporations suddenly had to compete, then maybe prices would get lower and quality would get better.

Royalists hated the idea, as you would expect, since their corporate donors knew that more competition in the markets meant less money diverted to the bonuses of health insurance executives such as "Dollar" Bill McGuire, who made a billion dollars working at United Healthcare.

So Fox News took up the cause. The subject of the Bill Sammon October 27, 2009, e-mail was: "Friendly reminder: let's not slip back into calling it the 'public option.'"[120]

This e-mail was later obtained by the media-watchdog group Media Matters. It read in full:

1) Please use the term "government-run health insurance" or, when brevity is a concern, "government option," whenever possible.
2) When it is necessary to use the term "public option" (which is, after all, firmly ensconced in the nation's lexicon), use the qualifier "so-called," as in "the so-called public option."

The e-mail continued with two more "reminders" from Sammon about how to talk about the Public Option:

3) Here's another way to phrase it: "The public option, which is the government-run plan."
4) When newsmakers and sources use the term "public option" in our stories, there's not a lot we can do about it, since quotes are of course sacrosanct.[121]

Fox anchors did as they were told, and suddenly the phrase "Public Option" vanished from the Fox News airwaves.

Why the name change? Why call it a "government option" rather than its legal name, the "Public Option"?

The answer: polling.

About two months earlier, on the same airwaves, Republican pollster Frank Luntz went on *The Sean Hannity Show* and let slip a critical Republican messaging strategy. In regard to the Public Option, Luntz told Hannity, "If you call it a 'public option,' the American people are split... [but] if you call it the 'government option,' the public is overwhelmingly against it."[122] After all, a "government option" implied a government takeover of health care, which meant socialized medicine.

Hannity himself was blown away and immediately noted that Luntz made "a great point" and that from then on Hannity himself would use the term "government option."

A new message was born.

Here was the Washington managing editor of Fox News, Bill Sammon, instructing his news anchors to use poll-tested terms that would help Republicans sway the public's opinion against President Obama's health reform law. It was plain-and-simple propaganda.

A few months later, Fox News's manufactured fear of a "government takeover of health care" successfully forced Democrats to drop the Public Option from the health reform law.

Emboldened, Bill Sammon set his eyes on climate change.

A few months later, in December, the news was about Copenhagen, where world leaders were meeting to chart out a global solution to fight worldwide climate change. And Bill Sammon had another e-mail he needed to get out to his anchors about wording in the climate change debate.

The December 8, 2009, e-mail[123] was titled "Given the controversy over the veracity of climate change data..."

Sammon instructed his anchors:

[W]e should refrain from asserting that the planet has warmed (or cooled) in any given period without IMMEDIATELY pointing out that such theories are based upon data that critics have called into question. It is not our place as journalists to assert such notions as facts, especially as this debate intensifies [emphasis Sammon's].

Like the for-profit health insurance executives, the oil barons believed pending cap-and-trade legislation in the Senate could crimp their profits. And they knew that as long as climate change was in doubt in the public's mind, there would be no urgency to pass climate change legislation. Once again, Fox News came to a monopolistic industry's aid.

Fox News became ground zero for faux climate change science, and the soapbox on which every corporate-funded pseudoscientist could stand, raise doubts about climate change, and collect their paycheck or get their grants from the big oil industry, wealthy industrialists, or foundations with allied ideology.

And it worked, the first comprehensive climate change bill for our nation to consider in decades died in the Senate—the American Clean Energy and Security Act which contained the "cap and trade" provision—a proven method to reduce pollution that had been supported by both Republicans and Democrats dating all the way back to Ronald Reagan's attempts to reduce acid rain in the 1980s.

On Fox News, "cap and trade" was routinely referred to by talking heads as "cap and tax"—another poll-tested term—and characterized as a Socialist plan to seminationalize the American energy market.

Thanks to Fox News, politicians heavily funded by the oil industry kept the status quo in place.

Thwarted

All of this Royalist money and organization worked.

It bought a "false remembering" just as the nation was going through a Great Forgetting in the 1970s. And then two generations later, after another Great Crash, it preserved the status quo of Royalist rule.

Unlike Roosevelt's "first hundred days," President Obama's "first hundred" were far from revolutionary.

The American Recovery and Reinvestment Act was a fifth the size of Roosevelt's first New Deal including the Public Works Administration, passed in 1933. Roosevelt's Second New Deal in 1935, creating Social Security, was even larger. And the federal spending effort of World War II was larger still.

Despite one of President Obama's top economic advisers, Christina Romer, pushing for a $1.8 trillion stimulus, the president whittled down his stimulus proposal to get a few Senate Republicans on board. In the end, only a third of the $787 billion stimulus plan was actual stimulus. The other two-thirds was assistance to states to close budget holes to prevent the layoff of public-sector workers and tax cuts that historically have the lowest bang for the buck in stimulus.

It became clear early on that the president really had no intention of being a revolutionary (with the exception of major steps forward for the LGBT community). The signature legislative achievement of the so-called Obama Revolution was the Affordable Care Act—known as "Obamacare"—which was far from revolutionary.

The Dodd-Frank Wall Street Reform bill paled in comparison to Roosevelt's regulations on Wall Street following the crash of 1929. The so-called War on Terror was expanded, Guantanamo remained opened, and extrajudicial killings increased. And the superwealthy in America, who've enjoyed unreasonably low taxes since the 1980s, kept their low taxes.

But the nation was still pregnant with revolution, and so they joined the billionaires' Tea Party.

But what the average Tea Partier doesn't understand, and what the millionaires and billionaires who fund the movement *do* understand, is that nature abhors a vacuum. So when Tea Partiers clamor for smaller government—or in some cases, no government at all—something must fill the void. And what's always filled the void in the past, from the Gilded Age, to the Roaring Twenties, to Reagan's America, is corporate power and aggregated wealth.

So fast-forward nearly 240 years later after the Boston Tea Party, and today's Tea Party is rallying on *behalf* of some of the very biggest transnational corporations in the world—our own East India Companies.

The private health industry directly benefitted from the Tea Party's assault on the Public Option, and in general "Obamacare." The polluting oil industry secured another decade of higher and higher profits thanks to the Tea Party's denial of climate change and the defeat of a new carbon tax or cap and trade law. Simply, the Tea

Party rallies on behalf of the monarchists of the eighteenth century, the Robber Barons of the nineteenth century, and the Economic Royalists of the twentieth century.

What the Economic Royalists of the 1930s were unable to do with the Business Plot against FDR—that is, successfully launch a coup d'état—the Koch brothers and the Economic Royalists of today were determined to do against Barack Obama in 2010. This time they would use money instead of an army.

But their coup wouldn't be complete without one final gift handed down by the Supreme Court.

Chapter 9

Betrayal on the High Court

[The] activist element of the Supreme Court struck down key protections of our elections integrity, overturned the will of Congress and the American people, and allowed all corporations to spend without limit in order to elect and defeat candidates and influence policy to meet their political ends. The consequences may well be nightmarish.

—Senator Sheldon Whitehouse (D-RI),
January 29, 2010

The day after President Obama's inauguration, Supreme Court Chief Justice John Roberts was called back to the White House. He needed to take care of some unfinished business.

At just past seven thirty that evening, Roberts and President Obama stood face-to-face in the Map Room of the White House. During World War II, President Franklin Roosevelt used the room to discuss war strategy with his generals as they pored over map after map of the European battlefield, hence the name given to the room. Today, some of those maps still hang on the walls.

Previous presidents, such as Calvin Coolidge, used the room for billiards, and to this day, with only a red paisley couch and two matching high-back chairs, a low-hanging polished wooden table, and a few delicately crafted desks and end tables placed near the walls, the room is still barely furnished, and there's more than enough space to drag a pool table into the center of it. The Map Room is now mostly used for interviews and private meetings, but on this night, it was to be used for a do-over of the presidential oath of office.

John Roberts hardly ever makes mistakes, but during President Obama's inauguration the day before, in front of millions of Americans huddled together on the lawn of the White House and Washington Mall, and hundreds of millions of people watching around the world, Roberts made what was likely the most embarrassing mistake of his life, completely butchering the presidential oath of office. Even though he'd been practicing the oath all morning, and had the words committed to memory, when it came time to swear Barack Obama in as the nation's forty-fourth president, Roberts fumbled, putting the word "faithfully" out of order of the other words in the oath and then stumbling through the rest of the lines before wrapping it up and congratulating the new president.

Immediately, Fox News jumped on the garbled oath. Hours after the inauguration, talking head Chris Wallace questioned the legitimacy of the president, telling viewers, "We're wondering here whether or not Barack Obama in fact is the president of the United States," and then speculating that maybe this is a situation that will ultimately end up "going to the courts."[124] I guess the irony of having Chief Justice John Roberts rule on whether or not he'd legally administered the oath escaped Wallace at the time.

So to quash any Fox News–manufactured controversy from the get-go, the White House legal counsel summoned John Roberts back to the White House the next day to readminister the oath. Roberts obliged, and in front of the fireplace of the Map Room, under the watchful eyes of a portrait of Benjamin Latrobe, the man who oversaw construction of the United States Capitol Building, Barack Obama once again recited the presidential oath of office.

Turns out, the Map Room was the most appropriate place for Roberts and Obama to convene for the constitutionally mandated swearing in, because from that day forward the Economic Royalists, led by John Roberts, would lay siege to the United States and successfully turn our prized democracy into an oligarchy.

That oath would be meaningless because, almost exactly a year later, Barack Obama's democratic republic would be transformed into a Royalist oligarchy by the Supreme Court.

Roberts Takes the Case

The Economic Royalists knew the final stage of their coup required the clearing away of all impediments to unrestrained corporate participation in electoral politics. As in, if a corporation likes a politician, it can ensure that he or she is elected every time; if it becomes upset with a politician, it can carpet-bomb his or her district with a few million dollars' worth of ads and politically destroy the candidate. With that power, the Royalists could essentially hand-pick lawmakers from that point forward. And with the case of *Citizens United*, John Roberts knew just how to give the Royalists what they wanted.

Forty years after the Powell Memo instructed that the "judiciary may be the most important instrument for social, economic and political change," the Royalists held a five-to-four majority on the highest court in the land.

And as the Royalists were expanding their influence in the United States, they had the perfect ally in John Roberts. Whether it was his work as a clerk on federal courts, as a lawyer in the White House under both Reagan and George H. W. Bush, or as a millionaire corporate lawyer, there was a common theme to Roberts's approach to American law—a theme that was put on steroids when he ascended to the pinnacle of the American legal system.

As Jeffrey Toobin notes in a *New Yorker* article documenting the rise of John Roberts, entitled "No More Mr. Nice Guy," "In every major case since he became the nation's seventeenth chief justice, Roberts has sided with the prosecution over the defendant, the state over the condemned, the executive branch over the legislative, and the corporate defendant over the individual plaintiff. Even more than Scalia, who has embodied judicial conservatism during a generation of service on the Supreme Court, Roberts has served the interests, and reflected the values, of the contemporary Republican Party."

As a US senator, Barack Obama explained his opposition to Roberts's nomination to the high court, saying on the floor of the Senate, "It is my personal estimation that [Roberts] has far more often used his formidable skills on behalf of the strong in opposition to the weak."[125]

The data would support then Senator Obama's fears. In 2013, a study out of the University of Southern California concluded that the current Supreme Court under the leadership of Chief Justice John Roberts is the most pro-business court since World War II, with the Chamber of Commerce winning nearly 70 percent of the cases it intervened in.[126]

But no Royalist victory was more significant than that of *Citizens United v. Federal Election Commission.*

During the bruising primary election season of 2008, a right-wing group put together a ninety-minute hit-job on Hillary Clinton and wanted to run it on TV stations in strategic states. The FEC ruled that advertisements for the "documentary" were actually "campaign ads" and thus fell under the restrictions on campaign spending of the McCain-Feingold Act, so they stopped them from airing. (Corporate contributions to campaigns have been banned repeatedly and in various ways since 1907, when Republican president Teddy Roosevelt pushed through the Tillman Act.)

Citizens United, the right-wing group, took the case to the Supreme Court, with right-wing hit man and former Reagan solicitor general Ted Olson—the man who'd argued Bush's side of *Bush v. Gore*—as their lead lawyer. Some newspaper reports have placed John Roberts in Florida during the 2000 election-recount fiasco assisting Olson and the Bush legal team in convincing the Supreme Court to stop the statewide recount. Roberts claims he was just taking a vacation. Either way, a decade after the high court handed George W. Bush, and the Economic Royalists, the presidency in 2000, it would hand the entire institution of American democracy to the Royalists in 2010.

This new case, *Citizens United v. Federal Election Commission*, presented the best opportunity for the Roberts court to use its five-vote majority (a consequence of Republican rule in the White House for twenty of the last thirty years since Roberts clerked for Justice Rehnquist on a left-leaning court) to totally reshape the face of politics in America, rolling us back to the pre-1907 era of the Robber Barons.

Although he is handsome, with a nice smile and photogenic young children, Roberts is no friend to average working Americans. If anything, he is the most radical judicial activist appointed to the court in more than a century. He has worked most of his life in the interest of the rich and powerful and was chomping at the bit for a chance to turn more of America over to his friends.

In the *Citizens United* case, the Roberts court listened to arguments, took briefs, and even discussed it among themselves as if they were going to make a decision. But instead of deciding the case on the relatively narrow grounds on which it had originally been argued—whether a single part of a single piece of legislation (McCain-Feingold) was unconstitutional—John Roberts asked for it to be reargued in September 2009 and asked that the breadth of the arguments be expanded to reexamine the rationales for whether Congress should have any power at all to regulate corporate "free speech."

Striking down any and all restrictions on corporate "free speech" was the logical end result of nearly 125 years of Supreme Court decisions, beginning in 1886 with the *Santa Clara County v. Southern Pacific Railroad* case, that conceded more and more constitutional rights that were supposed to be reserved for actual people over to corporations.

The Road to Personhood

After the Civil War, three amendments to the Constitution passed to provide fully for the rights of the newly freed African Americans who had formerly been held in slavery. The Thirteenth Amendment explicitly bans slavery; the Fifteenth Amendment guarantees their right to vote. And the Fourteenth Amendment says that they will have full access to the courts and cannot be denied a level of legal and constitutional protections equal to that of white people.

Here, for example, is the entire text of Section 1 of the Fourteenth Amendment, ratified in 1868:

> *All persons born or naturalized in the United States, and subject to the jurisdiction thereof, are citizens of the United States and of the State wherein they reside. No State shall make or enforce any law which shall abridge the privileges or immunities of citizens of the United States; nor shall any State deprive any person of life, liberty, or property, without due process of law; nor deny to any person within its jurisdiction the equal protection of the laws.*

Notice the word "person" in the text.

For over a thousand years of British common law and a century of American constitutional law, attorneys and legislators understood that there are two kinds of "persons." The first, "natural persons," are human beings. It was for them, for example, that the Magna Carta was written in 1215.

The second type of "persons" acknowledged by law are, broadly, states and nations, churches and nonprofits, and for-profit and other types of corporations. The reason such institutions need some sort of "personhood" status is so they can engage in interactions with the rest of us—own and pay taxes on land, for example, or sue and be sued. From the seventh-century origins of British common law to the 1870s, nobody seriously challenged these two types of personhood, the need for each, and their clear and explicit differences.

But in the Reconstruction era following the Civil War, the most powerful corporations in America—the railroads—saw an opportunity to use the arguably sloppy construction of the language of the Fourteenth Amendment to radically grab more power for themselves. They and their attorneys began to argue that when the Fourteenth Amendment was written, its authors in Congress explicitly said "person" rather than "natural person" in the last part of Section 1 because they fully intended it to include both "natural persons" *and* "artificial persons," such as railroad corporations.

In plain language, they argued that the authors of the Fourteenth Amendment intended to free both the slaves *and* the corporations, giving to both full constitutional protections.

They sent these arguments up in the Ninth Circuit Court, then presided over by US Supreme Court Associate Justice Stephen J. Field (back then the SCOTUS Justices "rode the circuit" most of the year, and just met in Washington, DC, for a few months every year to convene as the Supreme Court). And Field was deeply in the pockets of at least one, and probably more, of the railroad barons.

When Field agreed with this argument that the Fourteenth Amendment freed the corporations along with the slaves in a Ninth Circuit Court case, which he then sent to the Supreme Court (on which he also sat), in 1873, Justice Samuel F. Miller minced no words in chastising corporations for trying to claim the rights of human beings.

The Fourteenth Amendment's "one pervading purpose," he wrote in the majority opinion, "was the freedom of the slave race, the security and firm establishment of that freedom, and the protection of the newly-made freeman and citizen from the oppression of those who had formerly exercised unlimited dominion over him."

The railroads, however, had a lot of money to pay for lawyers, and railroad lawyer S. W. Sanderson had the reputation of being a pit bull in the courtroom. Undeterred, the railroads again and again argued their corporations-are-persons position all the way to the Supreme Court. The peak year for their legal assault was 1877, with four different cases reaching the Supreme Court in which the railroads argued that governments could not regulate their fees or activities or tax them in differing ways because governments can't interfere to such an extent in the lives of "persons" and because different laws and taxes in different states and counties represented illegal discrimination against the persons of the railroads under the Fourteenth Amendment.

In 1882 the railroads' attorneys floated the claim in a Supreme Court pleading that when the Fourteenth Amendment was drafted, "a journal of the joint Congressional Committee which framed the amendment, secret and undisclosed up to that date, indicated the committee's desire to protect corporations by the use of the word 'person.'"

It was a complete fabrication, and they lost the 1882 case: Nobody took the "secret-journal theory" seriously except Justice Field, who had ruled in the railroad's favor in the Ninth Circuit Court.

Nonetheless, the railroad corporations were persistent, and in future cases the railroad attorneys were unable to produce or even prove legislative reference to the secret journal of the congressional committee.

In 1886, they received another chance while fighting another lawsuit for nonpayment of taxes from Santa Clara County, California. As usual, Justice Field had ruled in the railroads' favor, suggesting in his Ninth Circuit Court ruling that they were "persons" suffering unequal justice because different counties used different methods to compute the property taxes the railroad should pay.

From there it went to the Supreme Court, where the railroad's attorney, Sanderson, confronted an up-and-coming lawyer who would become internationally famous three decades later for his defense in a notorious murder case (the case was made into the movie *The Girl in the Red Velvet Swing*, starring Ray Milland). Delphin Delmas, while physically unimposing and certainly not the bear of a man Sanderson was, was one of the most brilliant orators of his day.

Delphin Delmas v. Corporate Personhood

In his pleadings before the Supreme Court in the *Santa Clara County v. Southern Pacific Railroad* case, Delmas said: "The defendant has been at pains to show that corporations are persons, and that being such they are entitled to the protection of the Fourteenth Amendment... The question is, Does that amendment place corporations on a footing of equality with individuals?"

He then quoted from the bible of legal scholars—the book that the framers of our Constitution had frequently cited and referenced in their deliberations in 1787 in Philadelphia—Sir William Blackstone's 1765 *Commentaries on the Laws of England*: "Blackstone says, 'Persons are divided by the law into either natural persons or artificial. Natural persons are such as the God of nature formed us; artificial are such as are created and devised by human laws for the purposes of society and government, which are called corporations or bodies politic.'"

Delmas then moved from quoting the core authority on law to pleading common sense. If a corporation was a "person" legally, why couldn't it make out a will or get married, for example?

"This definition suggests at once that it would seem unnecessary to dwell upon the idea that though a corporation is a 'person,' it is not the same kind of person as a human being, and need not, of necessity—nay, in the very nature of things, cannot—enjoy all the rights of such or be governed by the same laws. When the law says,

'Any person being of sound mind and of the age of discretion may make a will,' or 'any person having arrived at the age of majority may marry,' I presume the most ardent advocate of equality of protection would hardly contend that corporations must enjoy the right of testamentary disposition or of contracting matrimony."

The entire idea was beyond the pale, Delmas said. "The whole history of the Fourteenth Amendment," he told the court, "demonstrates beyond dispute that its whole scope and object was to establish equality between men—an attainable result—and not to establish equality between natural and artificial beings—an impossible result."

The purpose of the Fourteenth Amendment, passed just after the Civil War, was clear, Delmas said. "Its mission was to raise the humble, the down-trodden, and the oppressed to the level of the most exalted upon the broad plane of humanity—to make man the equal of man; but not to make the creature of the State—the bodiless, soulless, and mystic creature called a corporation—the equal of the creature of God."

He summarized his pleadings before the Supreme Court by saying, "Therefore, I venture to repeat that the Fourteenth Amendment does not command equality between human beings and corporations; that the state need not subject corporations to the same laws which govern natural persons; that it may, without infringing the rule of equality, confer upon corporations rights, privileges, and immunities which are not enjoyed by natural persons; that it may, for the same reasons, impose burdens upon a corporation, in the shape of taxation or otherwise, which are not imposed upon natural persons."

Delmas had every reason to assume the Court would agree with him—it already had in several similar cases. In an 1873 decision, Justice Samuel F. Miller wrote in the majority opinion that the Fourteenth Amendment's "one pervading purpose was the freedom of the slave race, the security and firm establishment of that freedom, and the protection of the newly-made freeman and citizen from the oppression of those who had formerly exercised unlimited dominion over him."

And, in fact, the court chose to stay with its previous precedent. It ruled on the tax aspects of the case, but explicitly avoided any decision on whether or not corporations were persons.

"There will be no occasion to consider the grave questions of constitutional law" raised by the railroad, the court ruled in its majority opinion. The case was about property taxes and not personhood, and "As the judgment can be sustained upon this ground, it is not necessary to consider any other questions raised by the pleadings."

In other words, corporations are not "persons" for purposes of constitutional protections.

While the court had *not* ruled in *Santa Clara* that corporations should have rights under the Fourteenth Amendment, which can be easily seen from a reading of the case itself, the clerk of the court had a different idea. John Chandler Bancroft Davis wrote in the decision's headnote that the chief justice had said that corporations were persons under the Fourteenth Amendment. It was published after the death of the chief justice, and although headnotes have no legal or precedential status, it was grabbed generations later by corporate lawyers to advance their own causes.

Indeed, as Justice Hugo Black noted in 1938, "Of the cases in this court in which the Fourteenth Amendment was applied during its first fifty years after its adoption, less than one half of one percent invoked it in protection of the Negro race, and more than fifty percent asked that its benefits be extended to corporations."

Thus began in a big way (it actually started a half century earlier in a much smaller way with a case involving Dartmouth University) the corruption of American democracy and the shift, over the 125 years since then, to our modern corporate oligarchy.

The Roberts Court Rules

On January 21, 2010, in another five-to-four decision with the Republican five Justices on the winning side, the Supreme Court ruled that it is unconstitutional for Congress to pass or the president to sign into law any restrictions on the "right" of a corporation to pour money into political campaigns so long as the money isn't directly given to the politicians, their campaigns, or their parties.

The majority decision, written by Justice Anthony Kennedy, was quite explicit in saying that the government has no right to limit corporate power or corporate "free speech."

Kennedy began this line of reasoning by positing, "Premised on mistrust of governmental power, the First Amendment stands against attempts to disfavor certain subjects or viewpoints."

He lays it out bluntly, writing, "The Court has recognized that First Amendment protection extends to corporations...Under that rationale of these precedents, political speech does not lose First Amendment protection 'simply because its source is a corporation.'"

Two sentences later he nails it home: "The Court has thus rejected the argument that political speech of corporations or other associations should be treated differently under the First Amendment simply because such associations are not 'natural persons.'"

Corporate executives and their lobbyists saw the value to them of this Supreme Court decision immediately. On February 7, 2010, the *New York Times* published an article by David D. Kirkpatrick titled "In a Message to Democrats, Wall St. Sends Cash to G.O.P." The article explicitly quoted banking-industry sources who said that now that they could use their considerable financial power politically, they were experiencing "buyer's remorse" over having given Obama's presidential campaign $89 million in 2008: "Republicans are rushing to capitalize on what they call Wall Street's 'buyer's remorse' with the Democrats. And industry executives and lobbyists are warning Democrats that if Mr. Obama keeps attacking Wall Street 'fat cats,' they may fight back by withholding their cash."

The article quoted several banking sources as saying they were outraged that the president had criticized their industry for the financial meltdown of 2008 and for their big bonuses. It wrapped up with a quote from Texas Republican John Cornyn, the senator tasked with raising money for the National Republican Senatorial Committee, noting that he was now making regular visits to Wall Street in New York City, because "I just don't know how long you can expect people to contribute money to a political party whose main plank of their platform is to punish you."

It was a loud shot across Obama's bow, and within two weeks Obama had, just like Clinton, changed his tune on a wide variety of initiatives, ranging from taxes on the wealthy to banking, insurance, and pharmaceutical industry reforms.

Our democracy died thanks to *Citizens United*. Justices John Paul Stevens, Ruth Bader Ginsburg, Stephen Breyer, and Sonia Sotomayor—all of whom dissented from the Roberts majority in the *Citizens United* case—knew it, too. Justice Stevens wrote the main dissent in the *Citizens United* case.

Calling the decision "misguided" in the first paragraph of his ninety-page dissent, Stevens (and colleagues) pointed out that the majority on the court had just handed our country over to any foreign interest willing to incorporate here and spend money on political TV ads.

"If taken seriously, our colleagues' assumption that the identity of a speaker has no relevance to the Government's ability to regulate political speech would lead to some remarkable conclusions," wrote Stevens. "Such an assumption would have accorded the propaganda broadcasts to our troops by 'Tokyo Rose' during World War II the same protection as speech by Allied commanders." Stevens then pointed out a dangerous consequence of John Roberts's ruling, writing, "More pertinently, it would appear to afford the same protection to multinational corporations controlled by foreigners as to individual Americans: To do otherwise, after all, could 'enhance the relative voice' of some (i.e., humans) over others (i.e., corporations)."

Justice Stevens further points out the absurdity of granting corporations what are essentially citizenship rights under the Constitution, suggesting that perhaps the next SCOTUS decision will be to give corporations the right to vote: "Under the majority's view, I suppose it may be a First Amendment problem that corporations are not permitted to vote, given that voting is, among other things, a form of speech."

Stevens recounted the history of the evolution of corporations in America, noting, "Corporations were created, supervised, and conceptualized as quasi-public entities, 'designed to serve a social function for the state.' It was 'assumed that [they] were legally privileged organizations that had to be closely scrutinized by the legislature because their purposes had to be made consistent with public welfare.'"

Quoting earlier Supreme Court cases and from the Founders, Stevens wrote, "The word 'soulless' constantly recurs in debates over corporations...Corporations, it was feared, could concentrate the worst urges of whole groups of men." Stevens was right: Thomas Jefferson famously fretted that corporations would subvert the republic.

In an incredible irony, Stevens even quoted Chief Justice John Marshall, the man who had first, in the 1803 *Marbury* case, given the court itself the power to overrule laws, such as McCain-Feingold, that had been passed by Congress: "A corporation is an artificial being, invisible, intangible, and existing only in contemplation of law. Being a mere creature of law, it possesses only those properties which the charter of its creation confers upon it."

This decision was a naked handoff of raw political power to corporate forces by five unelected judges. Indeed, with this decision in place and the law of the land, the First Amendment now protects the "free speech" rights of the presidents of Russia and China and Iran to form corporations in the United States and pour millions of dollars toward supporting or defeating the politicians of their choice.

It protects the "right" of the largest polluting corporations on earth to politically destroy any politician who wants to give any more authority to the Environmental Protection Agency. It protects their "right" to elevate to elected status any politician who is willing to dismantle the EPA—or any other government agency that protects or defends the people of America from Royalist predation.

The behavior of the Roberts court in *Citizens United* eerily parallels the day in 1936 when Roosevelt said about the Economic Royalists, "In vain they seek to hide behind the flag and the Constitution. In their blindness they forget what the flag and the Constitution stand for." Even before the *Citizens United* case blew open the doors to a corporate takeover of American politics, the corrosive influence of corporations' having "rights" was already evident. Now these "unequal consequences" have been put on steroids.

With the Supreme Court's *Citizens United* decision, President Obama's fledgling progressive agenda—already badly wounded by stimulus-act debate and the health reform debate—was dead. John Roberts killed it just one year after readministering the presidential oath in the Map Room.

From that point forward, corporations, with their newly acquired golden key to our democracy, jammed the airwaves with hundreds of millions of dollars in campaign advertising to send a message to Congress that there would be political consequences to any decisions made that year.

Only when the 2010 midterm elections finally did come around would the effects of this court decision really be known.

As a result of *Citizens United*, outside political spending skyrocketed from just $68 million in the 2006 midterms, to over $304 million in the 2010 midterms. That's a 400 percent increase in corporate cash influencing elections and buying politicians, just ten months after the *Citizens United* decision.

Royalist Republicans, this time calling themselves Tea Partiers, retook the majority in the House of Representatives, significantly cut into the Democrats' majority in the Senate, and most important turned a lot of blue state legislatures around the country—in states such as Wisconsin, Michigan, Ohio, and Pennsylvania—red.

Barack Obama's revolution was officially over after the 2010 midterm elections—the first national elections post-*Citizens United*.

This is when the Crash of 2016 was sealed.

Chapter 10

Masters of the Universe

What's happened is something that even Marx wasn't cynical enough to dream about. It's a financial war of Wall Street not only against labor but against industrial capitalism, it destroys the market.
                                                              —Michael Hudson

In 1981, I had a conversation with my friend Dick Gregory. We were on an airplane high above the Atlantic Ocean on our way to Uganda to do relief work, and our conversation turned to America's unfortunate wars abroad (mind you, this is twenty years before the start of our nation's most recent decade of military misadventures). It was during that conversation that Dick gave me one of the best insights I'd ever heard on democracy and human nature.

"I don't know why America always thinks she has to run all around the world forcing people to take democracy at the barrel of a gun," he said. He paused for a moment, and then added with a sly grin, "When you've got something really good, you don't have to force it on people. They will steal it!"

History proves Dick right. More than two hundred years ago, the American Revolution brought democratic government back to the world from a two-thousand-year exile, and ever since then people have been overthrowing kings, theocrats, and plutocrats across the planet—stealing back democracy. Most recently, it happened in 2011–12 in the Arab world.

During times of crisis, however, this happens in reverse—democracy is surrendered.

As mentioned in chapter 3, this happened in Chile when General Pinochet and the Chicago Boys took over and induced "shock treatment" economics that rapidly transformed Chile into a Royalist paradise.

Before that, it happened in Spain, Italy, and Germany during the last Great Crash. And it nearly happened in America, too, in 1935, had the Business Plot not been foiled.

After the Supreme Court's *Citizens United* decision in 2010, our nation, just a few years removed from the 2007–08 financial panic, and on the precipice of the Crash of 2016, was thrust into a fight for its democratic life.

Like a blitzkrieg, the Royalists launched an unprecedented assault on democracy around the globe.

In the United States, they'd learned what had happened after the last Great Crash, when they were banished to the political wilderness for two generations. So this time, they reasoned, if they seized power of the means to enact political and economic change, then nothing would get in their way as they completed their harvesting of the middle class and the entire wealth of the nation.

They would become Masters of the Universe.

First, Greece

In October 2011, Greece's democratically elected prime minister, George Papandreou, proposed a national referendum on the pending bailout package for his debt-ridden and bankster-conned nation.

Ten years earlier, Goldman Sachs secretly helped Greece hide billions of dollars of debt through the use of complex financial instruments such as credit default swaps.[127]

This allowed Greece to meet the baseline debt-to-GDP requirements to enter the Eurozone in the first place.[128]

Goldman made similar deals here in the United States, masking the true value of investments, then selling those worthless investments to customers while placing bets that those same investments would eventually fail. The most notorious example was the Timberwolf[129] deal, which brought down an Australian hedge fund, and which Goldman Sachs banksters e-mailed each other about, bragging, "Boy, that Timberwolf was one shitty deal."[130]

This sort of behavior by Goldman and other Royalist bankers through the "madness" period of the first decade of the twenty-first century helped inflate very profitable debt bubbles that all eventually popped, most notably the housing bubble in the United States.

The shock wave of the debt bubbles bursting then crossed the Atlantic, hitting Europe and turning Goldman's debt-masking deal with Greece years earlier sour, thus deepening the crisis.

Always looking ahead, Goldman protected itself from this debt bubble by betting against Greek bonds, expecting that they would eventually fail.

But the main crisis that Greece and other members of the Eurozone faced is that they can't print their own currency, unlike in the United States.

With only a finite amount of euros in the Greek economy, and hefty obligations to foreign and domestic bankers who'd saddled the Greek people with enormous amounts of debt, the government was facing a default crisis.

Some obligations simply could not be met. Greece either had to tell the bankers to take a hit or tell their own people—their public servants, their pensioners, and their most vulnerable—they have to pony up to pay off the debts run up by the bankers. This is known as "austerity" today, even though it's the exact same sort of harsh shock economics that the Chicago Boys were perfecting in the 1970s and 1980s.

Greek Prime Minister Papandreou wanted to leave it up to the Greek people to decide if staying in the Eurozone, in exchange for harsh austerity measures, was in their national best interest.

Global bankers panicked, and in less than a week, fearing that the Greek people would tell their creditors to go screw themselves, the bankers at the European Central Bank and the IMF took away democracy in Greece. They forced Papandreou to scrap the idea of a national referendum, and even kicked him out of office for good measure. He was replaced by the former vice president of the European Central Bank, Lucas Papademos.

Even Italian Prime Minister Silvio Berlusconi, whose enormous wealth and national media empire ensured his reelection over and over again despite endless frauds and scandals, was no match for the European technocrats. Berlusconi, too, was forced out of office in 2011 to make sure Italy's descent into austerity went off without any democratic hitches.

The people of Europe and the world were meant to believe that these nations faced a debt crisis and that radical measures needed to be taken to lower debt-to-GDP levels. However, in nearly every case study in Europe, nations that have endured austerity have actually seen debt-to-GDP ratios increase.

It's simple to understand why. When you take money out of the hands of working people, as austerity does, then they don't have as much money to spend in the economy, and everything slows down. When people have smaller paychecks, the government is then collecting even less revenue, thus making deficits worse.

The real reason why austerity was enacted is so that the finite number of euros left in places such as Greece and Italy, as well as in Spain and Portugal and others, would without a doubt wind up in the hands of the wealthy.

In Greece, they lost their health care system. In July 2011, the

Royalists in technocratic suits put up some of their demands. They said they'd give Greece a bailout to ward off complete collapse, but in return they wanted a big chunk of the money that was being used to treat sick Greek citizens.

And for the first time, unemployed Greeks who had lost their health benefits now had to pay out of their own pocket for any medical care they needed.

As Dr. Kostas Syrigos, the head of Greece's largest oncology department, told the *New York Times*, "We are moving to the same situation that the United States has been in, where when you lose your job and you are uninsured, you aren't covered."

Today, that's the case for roughly half of Greece's 1.2 million long-term unemployed workers.

One of those unemployed workers is a woman named Elena who was diagnosed with breast cancer a year ago, but under the new Greek law could not receive any medical care because her benefits had expired and she had no money. Without treatment, her tumor grew to the size of an orange and broke through her skin, leaving a gaping wound. At this point, any sort of medical treatment for Elena was hopeless.

After seeing Elena, Dr. Syrigos told the *Times*, "Things like that are described in textbooks, but you never see them because until now, anybody who got sick in this country could always get help… In Greece right now, to be unemployed means death."

And these death sentences are ordered by technocrats, who are coldly overseeing massive transfers of wealth from the hands of the people to the hands of the Economic Royalists. They won't settle until all of Greece is turned into Europe's Disney World and the Coliseum and Parthenon are Lloyd Blankfein's new mansions.

These events in Europe prompted *New York Times* editorialist Ross Douthat to make this observation about the theft of democracy in an op-ed in November 2011 titled, "Conspiracies, Coups and Currencies." He wrote, "[F]or the inhabitants of Italy and Greece, who have just watched democratically elected governments toppled by pressure from financiers, European Union bureaucrats and foreign heads of state, it evokes the cold reality of 21st-century politics. *Democracy may be nice in theory, but in a time of crisis it's the technocrats who really get to call the shots* [italics added]."[131]

It Spreads

When the people of Greece saw Papandreou ousted, most were unaware of the bigger picture of what was happening all around them.

Similarly, most of us in the United States were equally ignorant when, in 2008, despite the switchboards at the US Capitol crashing under the volume of phone calls from constituents urging a "no" vote, our elected representatives voted yes at the behest of Bush's treasury secretary, Henry Paulson, and jammed through the biggest bailout of Wall Street in our nation's history.

Steadily—and stealthily—Goldman Sachs and other banking elite were carrying out a global coup d'état.

There's one tie that binds Lucas Papademos (the man who replaced Papandreou in Greece in 2011), Henry Paulson in the United States, and other prominent technocrats in important financial posts around the world, and that's Goldman Sachs. All were former bankers and executives at the Wall Street giant, all assumed prominent positions of power, and all played a hand after the global financial meltdown of 2007–08, thus making sure Goldman Sachs and the rest of the Wall Street ilk weathered the storm and made significant profits in the process.

The British newspaper *The Independent* reported in early 2012 that conservative technocrats who are currently steering or who have steered postcrisis fiscal policy in Greece, Germany, Italy, Belgium, France, and now the United Kingdom all hail from Goldman Sachs. In fact, the head of the European Central Bank itself, Mario

Draghi, was the former managing director of Goldman Sachs International.

And here in the United States, after Treasury Secretary and former Goldman CEO Henry Paulson did his job in 2008 securing Goldman's multibillion-dollar bailout, he was replaced in the new Obama administration by Tim Geithner, who worked very closely with Goldman Sachs as head of the New York Fed and made sure Goldman received more than $14 billion from the bailout of failed insurance giant AIG.[132]

As the Daily Kos summed it up in November 2012, "The normal scenario usually involves helping a nation hide a problem and sell its debt until the problem blows up into a bubble that bursts in a spectacular way...Goldman Sachs then puts their 'man' into a position of power to direct the bailouts so that Goldman gets all its money back and more, while the nation's economy gets gutted."

We no longer have an economy that's geared to benefit working people around the world; we have an economy that's geared to exploit them for Wall Street profits.

Trader Alessio Rastani told the BBC[133] in September, before Goldman's Lucas Papademos was installed as Greece's prime minister, "We don't really care about having a fixed economy, having a fixed situation, our job is to make money from it...Personally, I've been dreaming of this moment for three years. I go to bed every night and I dream of another recession."

Rastani continued, "When the market crashes...if you know what to do, if you have the right plan set up, you can make a lot of money from this."

And as we've seen over the last decade, the bankers know exactly what to do. They've had the right plan set up, and it's nothing short of a global coup d'état.

As Rastani bluntly told the BBC, "This is not a time right now for wishful thinking that governments are going to sort things out. The governments don't rule the world, Goldman Sachs rules the world."

Little Dictators

The people of Michigan know very well what the people of Greece are going through.

What's disguised as technocracy in Europe is a shadow corporate government in the United States (described in chapter 8), steadily working to undermine our current democratic government. And, just like in Europe, making sure that whatever wealth is left post-crisis gets sucked up by the Royalists.

I was speaking to Reverend David Bullock, the president of the Rainbow/PUSH Coalition in Highland Park, Michigan, about what life is like under Governor Rick Snyder's new "Emergency Financial Managers" law.

The law—which has technically been on the books since the late 1980s, but was broadly expanded in 2011 when Republican Rick Snyder took over as governor—allows the governor of Michigan to appoint "financial managers" to take over cities that are struggling in the wake of the financial crisis.

These financial managers selected by Michigan's governor are typically paid six-figure salaries and have enormous power. They can fire local elected officials, stripping entire populations in places such as Highland Park of their voice, and their vote, to determine the best policies for their own community.

They can break contracts, especially union contracts with local police, firefighters, and teachers. They can sell off the city's assets—the commons—to corporate interests at a fire-sale price, such as what happened in the city of Benton Harbor. There, under the control of a "financial manager," a ninety-acre Lake Michigan waterfront park (a part of the commons that's enjoyed by mostly low-income kids in a minority neighborhood) was sold off to real estate developers, who wanted to build a golf course resort for the affluent white neighborhood across the river. And worse, Governor Snyder's managers can completely redo local budgets without any input from local elected officials.

In other words, they can do on a local level all the things austerity-obsessed technocrats can do in Europe.

"This is a state takeover," Reverend Bullock told me. "The vote does not count—it's null and void. We've got Michigan, the new Mississippi, where liberty is being lynched."[134]

Snyder's "financial managers" had been installed to replace democratically elected officials in the cities of Flint, Ecorse, Benton Harbor, Pontiac, and Reverend Bullock's Highland Park.

"What's it like to live under tyranny? What's it like to live under dictatorship?" Reverend Bullock asked rhetorically. "How about no police officers? How about limited firefighters? How about taking streetlights out of cities so that people are in the dark from five p.m. to roughly eight a.m.? How about living with low morale and despair?

"This is about dismantling democracy," Reverend Bullock concluded.[135]

In November 2012, organized people of Michigan gathered enough signatures to put Governor Snyder's little-dictators law on the ballot for repeal. And voters did indeed repeal the law in that election.

But at the beginning of 2013, the Republicans in the Michigan state legislature passed a carbon copy of the law, Snyder signed it, and it was again back on the books, against the people's will. Within months, Snyder announced he deemed the entire city of Detroit to be in a "financial emergency" and appointed one of his little dictators to oversee the city's deconstruction.

One-half of the entire black population in Michigan is now shut out of democracy and under the control of these "financial managers."

Reporter Andy Kroll at *Mother Jones* magazine traces the origins of this law to the Mackinac Center for Public Policy, noting, "the free-market-loving center published four recommendations, including granting emergency managers the power to override elected officials (such as a mayor or school board member) and toss out union contracts. All four ended up in Snyder's legislation."[136]

The Mackinac Center is affiliated with the Heritage Foundation, one of the many Royalist think tanks spawned from the Powell Memo, and the Center has received tens of thousands of dollars in funding, that we know of, from the Koch brothers.

When corporate-funded think tanks are doing the work of our democratically elected lawmakers, there's something seriously wrong.

The ALEC Shadow Government

For more than a decade, Marc Pocan (now a member of the US House of Representatives) was regularly elected every two years by his constituents in the Seventy-Eighth District of Wisconsin to represent their interests in the Wisconsin State Assembly. In fact, he won 93 percent of the vote in his first bid back in 1998.

But, Representative Pocan soon learned, in Royalist America, there's no place for him, or his constituents, in government anymore.

Pocan realized this when he attended the annual convention of the American Legislative Exchange Council, better known as ALEC, down in New Orleans back in August 2011.

Established in 1973, ALEC claims on its website that its mission is "to advance the Jeffersonian principles of free markets, limited government, federalism, and individual liberty, through a nonpartisan public-private partnership of America's state legislators, members of the private sector, the federal government, and general public."[137]

But Representative Pocan had a different take on ALEC. "Literally, it's a dating service setting up corporate lobbyists and state legislators," he told me. "The culmination is the passing of special-interest legislation."[138]

Over the past few decades, the job of writing and passing legislation, which used to take place in the halls of state governments across the nation and in Congress by lawmakers who were elected by the people, has been outsourced to—or hijacked by—ALEC.

And contrary to any definitions of democracy we were taught in school, less than half of the policy makers of ALEC are actually elected officials. The majority are very, very wealthy corporate interests residing in the top 1 percent who are trying to occupy the thrones once belonging to feudal lords.

State representatives such as Mark Pocan and other members of Congress can join ALEC for an annual membership fee of $50. Currently there are about two thousand members of ALEC who are elected officials and they make up less than 2 percent of the organization's annual funding, which in 2009 was nearly $7 million.[139]

The majority of policy makers within ALEC are corporate executives and lobbyists, who pay a membership fee of between a few thousand dollars and as much as a couple hundred thousand dollars, depending on how much influence they want within ALEC, plus annual dues. That's where ALEC gets roughly 98 percent of its funding, along with stand-alone, hefty corporate, foundation, and personal contributions. For example, at the 2011 convention, BP—fresh from its oil catastrophe in the Gulf—was at the top of the list of donors to ALEC, likely dishing out as much as $100,000.[140] Other donors included ExxonMobil (the most profitable corporation in the history of the world), Shell, Chevron, Wal-Mart, Visa, and a name Americans have increasingly come to know: Koch Industries.[141]

All that money dished out by all the corporations buys them equal standing in the ALEC "democracy."

In the same way state and federal governments divide their work into committees (such as the House Energy and Commerce Committee in Congress, or the Public Health and Public Safety Committee in the Wisconsin State Assembly), ALEC also breaks up into committees—or what it calls "task forces." There are seven of them in total, involving all the same areas congressional committees cover:

- Commerce, Insurance, and Economic Development
- Communications and Technology
- Education
- Energy, Environment, and Agriculture
- Health and Human Services
- International Relations
- Tax and Fiscal Policy

Within each ALEC "task force," both elected legislators and corporate lobbyists are represented equally—fifty-fifty. The two sides sit together and then discuss and mark up what they aim to one day make actual legislation, based in large part on what was taught in earlier workshops.

Walking around an ALEC convention, you'd probably feel like you were at a high school civics fair or a Model UN Conference. There're a few thousand men and women in suits milling about, attending corporate-funded workshops, all with one central theme: profitization.

From ways corporations can make a profit from our public education system, to ways corporations can skim more and more off the top of Medicare, to ways corporations can avoid pollution regulations—it all comes down to finding new ways to convert the public good and the public trust into the private profit, just as the Goldman Sachs–trained technocrats in Europe are doing.

And, like attentive students, state lawmakers sit quietly and are spoon-fed by faux, corporate-funded climate change "scientists," speakers who twist the words of Jefferson and other Founders to unintelligibility, and free-market "economists."

"They literally referred to the legislators as the football team," Pocan said, "and the corporate lobbyists making presentations were our coaches. Those were their words."[142]

It's the ultimate culmination of the Powell Memo.

As Pocan put it, the legislators were "being given their game plans" before they were shuffled off to the next phase of the ALEC convention—the "task force" meetings.

"You need a majority vote from each group for something to advance," Pocan told me, referring to the corporations on the ALEC task forces.[143] "So not only do they write the legislation but then they vote on the legislation for it to move forward."

Once the ALEC task force approves legislation, it's then handed off to the legislators to take back home and introduce in their respective state governments.

Florida State Representative Rachel Burgin didn't even bother to remove the ALEC mission statement from the top of the "model legislation" that she introduced in the Florida House of Representatives back in February 2012. Right below the header of her bill, "urging Congress to cut the federal corporate tax rate," were the words "Whereas it is the mission of the American Legislative Exchange Council..."[144]

She realized her mistake the next day and immediately withdrew the bill.

ALEC, however, makes no secret of its legislation-writing wing, bragging on its website, "ALEC's Task Forces have considered, written and approved hundreds of model bills on a wide range of issues, model legislation that will frame the debate today and far into the future. Each year, close to 1,000 bills, based at least in part on ALEC Model Legislation, are introduced in the states. Of these, an average of 20 percent become law."[145]

But in states where Republicans control both chambers of the state legislature as well as the governor's mansion, such as Wisconsin, the success rate is much higher.

I asked Representative Pocan how much of the legislation he's seeing introduced in the state legislature in Wisconsin is coming out of ALEC.

"The vast majority," he said. "All the attacks on collective-bargaining rights, all the changes to pension law, all of the cuts and 'reforms' to education, all of these are part and parcel of workshops and task forces that I've been to."[146]

Nine different states have passed ALEC-written legislation to reject efforts to bring transparency to our elections by requiring shareholders to approve corporate election spending. Those states include Massachusetts, Michigan, Minnesota, New Hampshire, North Carolina, Ohio, South Dakota, West Virginia, and Wisconsin.

Coincidentally, ALEC's leading corporate contributors have funneled more than $16 million into state political campaigns since 2001.[147]

The group Common Cause identified several pieces of legislation that are virtual carbon copies of model ALEC legislation (minus the mission statement), introduced by at least nineteen members of the Republican-controlled Minnesota state legislature, giving tax breaks to tobacco companies, striking down greenhouse-gas-emissions regulations, and taking away the rights of people to vote.[148]

After the ALEC members in the Minnesota legislature passed four bills that would have given corporations more protections from lawsuits, Democratic governor Mark Dayton vetoed them and then called out his state's Republican legislators for copying ALEC's "boot camp manual."

"I've found that Minnesotans do not want their laws written by the lobbyists of big corporations," he said.

"Since these Republican bills so closely follow ALEC's instructions on tort reform and since ALEC's opinion on these subjects are evidently more important to Republican legislators than mine, their fellow DFL legislators or the Minnesota Supreme Court's, perhaps they would share with us all of the other ALEC boot camp manuals so we can know in advance what to expect from them for the rest of the session."[149]

The democracy-stealing agenda of ALEC is most evident in the spate of voter ID laws that have been passed in Republican-controlled state legislatures around the nation. These new laws, virtual carbon copies of ALEC's model legislation, will dispropor- tionately affect low-income, minority, elderly, and college-age voters (people who usually vote for Democrats). According to a Brennan Center for Justice study, as many as five million people will be disen- franchised by voter ID laws.

Ironically, ALEC's founder was conservative strategist Paul Weyrich, who, according to Republican Speaker of the House John Boehner, is a "giant of the Conservative movement."[150]

Weyrich was instrumental in organizing this corporate takeover of our democracy, funding the politically powerful "Moral Major- ity" as well as the right-wing think tank the Heritage Foundation. In 1980, Weyrich revealed a key conservative strategy and the game plan for ALEC thirty years later, saying in a speech, "I don't want everybody to vote. Elections are not won by a majority of people. They never have been from the beginning of our country and they are not now. As a matter of fact, our leverage in the elections goes up as the voting populace goes down."[151]

Kick more voters off the rolls, and let corporations have more of an influence in who wins them—that's ALEC's strategy.

Democracy Defamed

As organized people's access to democracy disappears, the for- mal institutions of government devolve into dysfunction.

Lawmakers are no longer listening to their constituencies but instead to the technocrats on Wall Street and the Royalist shadow government manifested in "think tanks" such as the Mackinac Cen- ter and ALEC.

The 112th session of Congress (2011–12) earned the low- est approval rating ever. It was the least productive since the 80th "Do-Nothing" Congress (1947–48). Filibustering and obstruction in the Senate reached unprecedented levels.

It's not a coincidence that this was the first Congress elected post-*Citizens United*.

All that money that the Supreme Court allowed Royalists to spend elected one of the most corporate-friendly House of Representatives since the Gilded Age.

The members of Congress they owned went to work on Capitol Hill in the 2011 session fiercely defending the interests of America's superrich, protecting everything from the Bush tax cuts, to taxpayer subsidies for transnational oil corporations, to bonuses and malfeasance on Wall Street.

An early warning came from Standard & Poor's, when they noted that the effectiveness of Congress is in question.

"The downgrade"—referring to the credit downgrade of the United States from AAA to AA+—the report states, "reflects our view that the effectiveness, stability, and predictability of American policymaking and political institutions have weakened at a time of ongoing fiscal and economic challenges to a degree more than we envisioned when we assigned a negative outlook to the rating on April 18, 2011."

Yes, America still *looks* like a democracy. One in which we still vote (or about half of all registered people do), we have big election-night specials on major news networks. We all embrace the idea of American democracy at work. But deep down it's been rotted by greed and corruption.

On average, a member of the House of Representatives must raise $5,000 a week for his or her campaign. That means that every morning, Monday through Friday, they must wake up not thinking about governing but about fund-raising—how to scrounge up a thousand bucks that day. In the Senate it's even worse, at an average of $14,000 a week.[152]

And those numbers were compiled by PBS before the *Citizens United* decision—today's numbers are significantly higher.

No other developed nation in the world ties its democracy to endless fund-raising and unlimited corporate spending like we do in the United States.

Each year, total election spending increases. Curiously, spending on lobbying Congress went down in 2011 for the first time in a decade.[153] One reason could be the recession. But more likely, spending on lobbying is down because, since *Citizens United,* Royalists can now invest in whichever politician they want *before* an election, so their guy is already bought and paid for by the time he is sworn into office—no need to lobby later.

It's no wonder that the American people have played into the hands of the Royalists and, as a result, have very little trust in government. After all, there is no reason why they should, because democratic government, as we once knew it, no longer exists—the Royalists stole it.

Now the Royalist Masters of the Universe reign.

In just over three decades, the Royalists have crept into power, destroyed the fundamentals that supported a strong middle class, allowed Wall Street and corporate psychopaths to devour working people and transform the economy into a massive get-rich-quick scheme, and nearly crashed everything, only to rise again and promise to do the same thing all over again.

And this time, the Masters of the Universe are completely unresponsive to any democratic controls. They want to see this drastic transformation of America to its bitter, feudal end.

This development brings us to the final stage of this crisis.

Cancer Stage

A Great Crash is a painful event, often too terrible for its citizens even to contemplate.

History tells us that when the foundations collapse, and a society's cultural core is hollowed out and the "madness" takes hold, its members will pretend all is well. Life seems to go on as average citizens try to get by, while the very rich, who understand what's happening, consolidate their power and wealth before the final crash.

This is the cancer stage of capitalism—the point at which the Royalists have fully contaminated the body economic and politic, making the crash inevitable.

This is where we are today.

One of the foremost chroniclers of the rise of these Royalists and the consequences they bring is journalist and author Chris Hedges. He described how he views this current cancer stage in America.

"We have powerful corporate interests that have commodified everything," he told me, including human labor, which means, according to Hedges, "human beings no longer have any intrinsic value in the ethics of corporations."

He added, "They are commodities to exploit until exhaustion or collapse. The same is true of the natural world—we exploit the natural world until exhaustion or collapse."

In the next section, we'll see exactly what collapse looks like.

PART 4

The Great Crash

Chapter 11

This Is the End

I think historians when they look at this time, they're going to wonder why the wealthy overplayed their hand like this. Why would they, when they had it so good? They had the middle class voting for the politicians that the wealthy bought, everything was running just fine, they were posting profits of a billion a year, but that wasn't enough for them. What they did was started to ruin the lives of the very people who voted for their politicians and supported them all these years, the middle class.

Michael Moore, October 2011

If you want to know which way the wind is blowing, keep an eye on the billionaires.

So what are the billionaires telling us just ahead of the Crash of 2016?

Well, in 2012, four years before the Crash of 2016, Moody's Investors Service noted something peculiar. It noticed American companies are hoarding record amounts of cash.

For example, in 2012 Apple was discovered to be sitting on $137 billion worth of cash. Investors actually sued the company to make it pass some of that wealth down to shareholders.

But what Apple was doing was comparatively minor. Altogether, US companies stashed away $1.45 trillion in cash in 2012, a 10 percent increase from 2011.

They aren't investing it, they aren't expanding their businesses with it, they aren't hiring more workers. They're just sitting on it. They aren't even paying taxes on it, since, as Moody's discovered, 68 percent of all that cash is stashed overseas.

Wall Street is also hoarding enormous amounts of money. Dan Froomkin at the *Huffington Post* explained in July 2012, "The latest report from the Federal Reserve shows that big banks' cash reserves peaked in the third quarter of 2011, but are still near their all-time high at just under $1.6 trillion—an astonishing 80 times the $20 billion they held in reserve in 2007."[154]

But it's not just in the United States; it's all around the world.

The *Wall Street Journal* wrote on Europe's banks holding cash at the end of 2012: "A dozen of Europe's largest banks reported holding a total of $1.43 trillion of cash on deposit at various central banks."

It adds, "That represents at least the sixth consecutive quarter that the banks have increased their overall central-bank deposits. Since the end of 2010, the banks have boosted the amount they are stockpiling at central banks by 84%."[155]

The Institute of International Finance, a Washington-based organization, calculated that companies in the United States, United Kingdom, Eurozone, and Japan were sitting on nearly $8 trillion worth of cash.[156]

Altogether, the wealthiest people on the planet have as much as $32 trillion stashed away in overseas financial institutions, according to a study by the Tax Justice Center in 2012.

All of this is taking place just as the stock market was reaching historic new levels, and profits in corporate America reached the highest levels as a percent-of-GDP ever recorded. Yet, in early 2013, *Money News* reported that "a handful of billionaires are quietly dumping their American stocks," including Warren Buffett, John Paulson, and George Soros.

Senator Elizabeth Warren spoke about another Wall Street quirk during a 2013 Senate Banking Committee meeting.

She noted that while most major corporations trade well above book value, all the large banks are actually being traded well below book value. She concluded there are two possible explanations for this.

"One," she said, "because nobody believes that the banks' books are honest." In other words, the banks are actually still teetering on the edge, and the banks themselves know it.

"Or the second," she added, "nobody believes that the banks are really manageable. They are too complex for their own institutions or the regulators to manage them."[157]

If the economy really is doing so well, then why are the wealthy giving signs of the opposite, quietly leaving markets and just sitting on the sidelines?

The answer is they know what's coming. They know 2008 was just the precursor, and 2016 will be the real catastrophe.

The billionaires are preparing for a series of economic shocks on the horizon, probably beginning in Europe and spreading across the planet, eventually toppling the United States.

Germany Finally Wins World War II

After the 2007–08 global financial panic, the three main monetary institutions of Europe: the European Central Bank, the European Commission, and the International Monetary Fund—together known as the "Troika"—imposed a strict austerity regime on debt-saddled nations such as Greece, Ireland, Spain, and Portugal, nations that suddenly found themselves in a fiscal crisis and yet had no control over their own money supplies thanks to the structural flaws of the Eurozone.

This austerity has produced devastating effects.

Since the Troika's takeover of Greece began in 2009, a quarter of all Greek businesses have closed their doors, half of all small businesses can't meet their payroll, nearly half of all young workers under twenty-five are unemployed, the total unemployment rate is around 20 percent, suicide rates have shot up 40 percent, radical political parties gain traction, and the streets of Athens are routinely set on fire in violent riots.[158]

This is what the Crash of 2016, in its early stages, looks like.

Driving the Troika's austerity agenda is Germany, one of the few nations in Europe that found itself on the other side of the financial panic and not in a debt crisis.

That's because Germany acted like America did after World War II (and even outdid us). They built up an enormous manufacturing base, shielded it from low-wage nations, and nurtured a strong middle class with labor protections and a social safety net guaranteeing health care as a basic human right.

They became an export machine. In 2011, they held the second largest trade surplus in the world, over $200 billion (the United States was in debt $800 billion). And they turned into Europe's primary manufacturing plant, supplying most of the European continent with its goods.

While Germany boasted one of the largest trade surpluses in the world, other European nations were driven into trade deficits. The United Kingdom, France, Spain, Italy, Greece, and Portugal all have some of the largest trade deficits in the world.

Greece's trade deficit with Germany is startling. In 2009, Greece sold 1.8 billion euros of exports to Germany. But that same year, it bought 6.7 billion euros of imports from Germany.

What all of this meant is that wealth was flying out of indebted European nations such as Greece, Italy, and Spain and accumulating in German banks. And those German banks, flush with cash, became epicenters of lending throughout Europe, since they were able to offer better interest rates than most other nations.

This Is the End

This export machine makes up 40 percent of the German economy today, and has catapulted them to the fourth largest economy in the world in terms of nominal dollars, despite having a significantly smaller population than the top three nations of Japan, China, and the United States.

So, when the financial panic blew a hole in their economy, the Germans were able to recover quickly. Their enormous manufacturing base immediately went to work recouping lost wealth. In 2012, unemployment dropped to just three million people, the lowest level in twenty years.

Meanwhile their bankers and Economic Royalists went to work recouping the rest.

As the biggest economy in Europe, and with the most cash on hand to help ailing nations, Germany has been driving the Troika's agenda across Europe. It helps, too, that the European Central Bank is headquartered in Frankfurt.

The people of Germany may have kept their own Economic Royalists shackled and incapable of feasting on the middle class the way they've done in the United States.* Meanwhile, the German people have quietly endorsed the pillaging of fellow European nations through austerity.

Germany could have endorsed a plan to have the European Central Bank print more euros, and fund stimulus programs in indebted nations to put people in Greece and Spain back to work growing their respective economies (similar to what FDR did in the 1930s and what Germany did domestically after the 2007–08 financial panic).

But instead, German bankers exploited the debt crisis to turn the rest of Europe into indebted slaves. They funneled hundreds of billions of dollars in loans through bailout programs across Europe to

---

* In a later chapter, we'll examine a lot of lessons we can learn from Germany after the crash.

ensure that foreign depositors (many of whom were Germans) are repaid by debtor nations. And in return for those bailouts, Germany demanded that Greece, Spain, Portugal, and Ireland carry out painful spending cuts that crippled working people in those nations who were employed by or relied on the government.

Despite the intended purpose of austerity, research from the United Kingdom's National Institute of Economic and Social Research found, in October 2012, that debt-to-GDP ratios increased significantly higher and faster under austerity than if no austerity had been imposed at all.[159]

But reducing the debt-to-GDP ratios was never the intent of the Royalists allied with Germany and the technocrats at the Troika. Instead, their goal was to harvest Europe in the same way Bain Capital would have done to an American business. Bulldoze the economy and working class, sell off the commons, and then prime Greece to be sold off to foreign investors (many of them German) at fire-sale prices.

With the entire continent still racked by economic turmoil five years into the austerity era, Germany has profited immensely.

Since it is the only stable economy left, investors actually pay Germany to take a loan from them. In 2012, Germany was paying a 0.01 percent interest rate on about $5 billion worth of debt. As *Der Spiegel* notes, "Amid the ongoing euro crisis, Germany is one of the few borrowers that are still regarded as a safe haven. Many investors would rather lend the government money at bargain-basement rates than risk losses."[160]

Der Spiegel goes on to say, "It has become a rule of the euro crisis: While a number of Eurozone countries suffer, Germany profits. The crisis may slow economic growth in Germany, but there are also a raft of crisis-related mechanisms that help the country profit at the expense of other nations."

As of 2013, Germany has spent or committed to spend nearly $400 billion on these "crisis-related mechanisms" aimed at saving the Eurozone in a way that ensures German dominance over the continent on a scale not seen since Hitler toppled Paris.

George Soros criticized the German response to the euro crisis, saying, "Germany did the minimum that was necessary to preserve the euro but no more! And that is what maintained the crisis conditions which are now four years old."[161]

He remarked on what Europe looks like now under German financial rule, "I am afraid Europe is in an existential crisis. The debtor countries are subordinate to the dictates of the creditor countries and have effectively been relegated to second-class memberships."[162]

In fact, in January 2012, when it looked like Greece might reject a bailout and leave the euro, Germany proposed ousting the democratically elected government of Greece and installing a European commissioner (think Detroit financial manager) with the power to rewrite the national budget and make sure that Greece takes its medicine prescribed by Germany.

Economist Richard Wolff remarked to me on the Greece situation, in which Royalists are squeezing whatever they can out of the population, "The irony is, when you look back at the history of empires, it has been that narrowness, that failure to look at the long-term, that absorbed self-interest, that has been the final end of those empires."[163]

Germany Goes Too Far

The question asked in 2013 in Europe was just how far were Germany and the Troika willing to go? Not only how much more money are they willing to spend keeping the Eurozone intact but just how ruthless will they be in their continuing demands for austerity as governments in Greece and Spain unwind into austerity death spirals, thus deepening the debt crisis?

After all, if Germany destroys Europe's economy, won't they destroy their own consumer base?

Not necessarily. Based on the way they're structuring their trade relations, Germany is able to see the Eurozone out to its bitter end.

Like the Economic Royalists in America who've sold out the middle class to capture emerging markets in the developing world, the Germans are preparing for a post-Europe export economy.

As the BBC reported in late 2012, "German businesses are becoming less and less reliant on selling to Eurozone countries and are becoming more and more successful in selling to China and the leading emerging markets."[164]

Since 2000, Germany's trade to European partners has dropped significantly from over 45 percent to 38 percent in 2012, and it is projected to be 34 percent by 2020.

Meanwhile trade to the BRIC nations—Brazil, Russia, India, and China—is surging from 3.9 percent in 2000 to almost 12 percent in 2012, and projected to be 24 percent in 2020.

The BBC notes the significance of China in Germany's trade strategy, reporting, "What is particularly striking is that in eight years German trade with China alone is projected to be 15.6 percent of the total, according to the trends, or not far off double the share represented by Germany's most important Eurozone trading partner, France."

So just as the European continent is becoming more and more reliant on Germany, Germany is gearing up to cut the strings loose. Pegging the emergence of China in Germany's trade relations, the BBC notes, "To put it another way, by 2015 it will be so obvious to the German people that it is business with China that is making them richer that their incentive to show fiscal solidarity with Spain and Italy—to use German wealth to underpin the recovery of weaker Eurozone economies—will be even less than it is today."

And that's when the Eurozone crisis will hit a critical turning point. Up until now, Germany has spent a lot of money keeping the Eurozone together, not only to enrich its own economy but also to protect its economy from the damage that would ensue if the Euro-zone breaks apart.

But sometime in the next few years, German policy makers will deem the collapse of the Eurozone as a necessary road bump in their transition to new developing economies. And they just might be willing to go through a recession, knowing that their structurally sound economy will leave them in better shape on the other side of it.

At this point, without fear of a Eurozone collapse, Germany and the Troika will demand even more radical austerity.

The world got a glimpse of what happens when austerity goes too far when the tiny Mediterranean member of the Eurozone, Cyprus, became the fifth country in need of a euro bailout.

With little fear of the consequences of a Cyprus exit from the euro, Germany and the European Central Bank demanded a first-of-its-kind austerity on savers, average people who had money deposited in banking accounts in the nation.

Initially the European Central Bank demanded, as collateral for a 10-billion-euro bailout package, a percentage of all banking deposits in Cyprus.

This had an expected result: People rushed to the banks to pull their money out before it could be taxed. Cyprus had to shut down all their banks for over a week, and to set withdrawal limits. Just floating the idea of confiscating banking accounts shattered faith in the Cypriot banking institutions.

Whether or not Germany and the Troika take this aggressive posture toward other bailouts in the future doesn't matter all that much. The damage has already been done. The already fragile European banking system received another loss of confidence.

These fears were encapsulated in an op-ed that ran in the *Irish Examiner* during the Cyprus crisis, in March 2013. "The raid on Cypriot banks deposits," the authors noted, "held in the name of ordinary people, businesses, institutions, communities, and prudent savers, breaks one of the fundamental trust-based relationships that has sustained western societies for centuries."

It goes on, "It sets a precedent that will reverberate across Europe and find particular resonance in other supplicant countries dependent on external finance."

Of course, Ireland knows this situation as well, being a victim itself of Germany's austerity.

Then the op-ed asks the expected question: "If bank deposits can be raided by a government in one bankrupt Eurozone country, then why not in another?"

Columnist Henry Blodget for *Business Insider* noted the Continental shock wave from Cyprus. He wrote, "Other depositors at weak banks all over Europe, in places like Spain, Italy, and Greece, will rightly wonder whether this is the beginning of a new era of bank bailouts."

He goes on to ask, "What do you think those other depositors in Spain, Italy, Greece, etc., are going to feel like doing when they realize that, if their banks ever need a bailout, they might have their deposits seized?"

Nearing the Crash of 2016, Eurozone nations crippled by austerity and unable to print their own currencies will ask for more and more bailouts. This will spark runs on the banks across Europe, leading to a series of terrific failures and economic shocks across Europe.

Germany and the Troika will not have nearly enough money, or support, to reach into the bailout coffers anymore. Country by country the Eurozone will disintegrate.

In the United Kingdom, officials have been planning for another Great Crash for years. As a November 2011 article in the *Telegraph* exposed, "Diplomats are preparing to help Britons abroad through a banking collapse and even riots arising from the debt crisis."[165]

The article goes on to say that the United Kingdom believes "that a euro collapse is now just a matter of time ... [and] planning for extreme scenarios including rioting and social unrest" are under way.

Referring to the failure of Lehman Brothers bank, which shocked the financial system in 2008, the chief economist at the European Central Bank warned in July 2012 that the "Eurozone crisis is now much more profound and fundamental than at the time of Lehman."

By inflicting economic pain on working people across Europe, Germany is playing with fire on a continent that saw the bloodiest war in human history. A war that people are just now forgetting about.

The Divergence and War

It's hard to imagine that the European Union, after winning a Nobel Peace Prize in 2012, would descend into war in 2016.

But prior to the French Revolution, people thought things were going great, too. As de Tocqueville writes: "No one in 1780 had any idea that France was on the decline; on the contrary, there seemed to be no bounds to its progress. It was then that the theory of the continual and indefinite perfectibility of man took its rise. Twenty years before, nothing was hoped from the future; in 1780 nothing was feared. Imagination anticipated a coming era of unheard-of felicity, diverted attention from present blessings, and concentrated it upon novelties."

And, indeed, there had been a bubble prosperity. As de Tocqueville notes, "Public prosperity began to develop with unexampled strides. This is shown by all sorts of evidence. Population increased rapidly; wealth more rapidly still."

To prove his point, he cites numerous sources: An official of the time states that in 1774 "industrial progress had been so rapid that the amount of taxable articles had largely increased. On comparing the various contracts made between the state and the companies to which the taxes were farmed out, at different periods during the reign of Louis XVI, one perceives that the yield was increasing with astonishing rapidity. The lease of 1786 yielded fourteen millions more than that of 1780. Necker, in his report of 1781, estimated that 'the produce of taxes on articles of consumption increased at the rate of two millions a year.'"

British writer Arthur Young (1741–1820) wrote in his auto-biography[166] that when he visited France in 1788, the commerce of Bordeaux was greater than that of Liverpool, and adds that "of late years maritime trade has made more progress in France than in England; the whole trade of France has doubled in the last twenty years. Due allowance made for the difference of the times, it may be asserted that at no period since the Revolution has public prosperity made such progress as it did during the twenty years prior to the Revolution."

Thus, while "bread lines" and "bread shortages" and "bread riots"—juxtaposed with mind-boggling excesses including lavish parties at the court of Louis XVI—are often cited as a simplistic explanation for the French Revolution (egged on by the example of the Americans), the real cause, de Tocqueville suggests, was a rapid reversal of fortunes. While people will tolerate terrible poverty—and do, daily, all over the world (and did in his day, too) without revolution or war—they will not tolerate a rapid change from economic circumstances they expect to those they don't.

This is not, of course, an idea unique to de Tocqueville, although he highlighted it in a way that lit up dialogue in the mid-nineteenth century about the American Civil War and other wars around the world. More recently, here in the United States, in 1977, Harold E. Davis wrote a brilliant monograph for the Georgia Historical Society titled *The Scissors Thesis, or Frustrated Expectations as the Cause of the Revolution in Georgia*. Paraphrasing the work of earlier social scientists and historians Professors R. R. Palmer and James Chowning Davies, he wrote: "Revolutions are most likely to occur when a prolonged period of objective economic and social development is followed by a short period of sharp reversal." Revolution occurs when "reality breaks away from anticipated reality."

While both de Tocqueville's and Davis's observations have to do with internal wars—revolutions—it's easy to build a strong and historically grounded case for wars breaking out when a nation has Davis's break from anticipated reality and then blames it on another nation-state.

In a more contemporary commentary, this logic was extended by *Business Insider*'s Ricky Kreitner in an article whose title says it all: "Serious People Are Starting to Realize That We May Be Looking at World War III."

Similarly, the *New Republic*'s John Judis wrote in August 2011 that "in the U.S. and Europe, the downturn has already inspired unsavory, right-wing populist movements. It could also bring about trade wars and intense competition over natural resources, and the eventual breakdown of important institutions like European Union and the World Trade Organization. Even a shooting war is possible."

War following a Great Crash that blew out people's expectations of continued prosperity was unimaginable in the 1920s. Similarly, nobody seriously considered it in the early 1850s. And even Thomas Jefferson, in the late 1760s, was writing tracts about how American colonists could be "good citizens" of the United Kingdom.

But then came the divergence.

The China Syndrome

While America declines and Europe convulses, in China, huge cities are being constructed at breakneck speed, complete with brand-new high-rise condominiums, office buildings, and infrastructure such as roads and bridges.

Only, no one lives there. They are ghost cities. As *60 Minutes* correspondent Leslie Stahl noted in March 2013, "We discovered that the most populated nation on earth is building houses, districts and cities with no one in them...desolate condos and vacant subdivisions uninhabited for miles and miles and miles and miles."

The Chinese economy is growing at speeds not seen at any other time in world history. It's estimated that as many as 200 million Chinese will undergo the urbanization process and move into the cities. That means more housing needs to be built, about ten million new units a year.

Build the cities and the people will come.

But construction is far outpacing projected demand.

As *Forbes* contributor Gordon Chang reported in March 2013, the Chinese put up 11 million new units in 2012, but in five years they will be building 19 million units every single year—far more than is needed to keep up with demand for housing.

What's really happening in China is a housing bubble, even worse than the one that popped in the United States. And, like in the United States before it, the housing bubble is being driven in large part by a debt bubble.

This expectation of limitless demand is driving an enormous construction boom in China, which accounts for about half of the entire Chinese economy.

And expecting that property values will continue rising dramatically, the emerging Chinese upper and middle classes are investing everything they have, and leveraging their wealth with bank debt, buying up property in these ghost cities as investments for the future.

Chang explains, "The rich buy apartments and often leave them empty, treating them as a store of value. It's not uncommon to find a single owner with as many as 20 vacant flats."

But what happens if, under pressure from economies that buy from them, the Chinese economy slows down?

Chang writes, "When the underlying economy erodes—as it is showing signs of doing now—owners will dump units either to raise cash or to avoid taking even bigger losses. Most unsold apartments are in smaller urban areas, which is where a panic could start."

The panic may already be under way. In 2012, unsold Chinese apartments increased by 40 percent, as measured by floor space.

China has done unprecedented things in its rise to becoming an economic powerhouse. But that doesn't mean it's immune from the dangers of Royalist capitalism.

Chang adds, "Analysts like to say China is different. Yet we hear a variation of this line just before every economic collapse. Beijing's technocrats can postpone a reckoning, but they have not repealed the laws of economics. There will be a crash."[167]

And this crash could come sooner than projected.

Economist Richard Wolff argued in 2010 that the Chinese economy is secretly making a huge gamble on the global economy.

With exports making up nearly a third of the entire Chinese economy, a slowdown all around the world means big trouble for the Chinese domestic economy.

Yet in 2009 the Chinese economy grew by 8.7 percent, only slightly lower than in 2008, and then in 2010 it grew by more than 10 percent.

"How are they doing this?" Wolff asks. "How are they employing all of these people, keeping people out of the streets? They are an export economy, and the exports have dried up!"

Wolff explains what's going on: "They are keeping everybody working. They are literally holding, stockpiling, warehousing unspeakable quantities of output in the hope that the world economy will correct itself soon enough that they can unload all that stuff."

But they can't do this indefinitely.

"This is the biggest gamble any country we know of has ever taken," Wolff adds.

By 2012, it began to look like the gamble might not pay off. That year, the Chinese growth rate drastically slowed to 7.8 percent, its lowest rate in thirteen years.

With their consumer base drying up around the world, the internal problems in the Chinese economy will only worsen. By 2016, as the masses that moved in to the cities start losing their jobs, unrest will sweep the country.

The faster the domestic Chinese economy shrinks, the quicker the real estate bubble will burst, dragging upper-income Chinese citizens into the economic crisis, too.

Suddenly, the primary cheap-labor source the Western economies, in particular the United States, rely on will be wiped out.

Wolff warned what happens if the Chinese gamble doesn't pay off: "The kind of economic downturn we had [in 2008] will look like a picnic."

Those emerging markets that the Economic Royalists in Germany and the United States were betting will still be there after the Great Crash will, instead, be swept up into the global catastrophe.

The Oil Shock

Assuming the Eurozone holds it together, and assuming the technocrats in China are able to stave off the pitfalls of rapid economic growth, there's still another potential shock lurking that can bring down the entire system: *oil*.

The entire world's economy is lubricated by oil. We rely on oil for energy, to grow and transport food, for construction, for our military, and as a raw material for fertilizers, pesticides/herbicides, and pharmaceuticals, just to name a few.

So when the price of oil goes up, then the price of everything goes up, the economy grinds to a halt.

This happened in the United States during the oil shocks of the 1970s, when OPEC cut off oil exports to the United States in October 1974. The price of a barrel of oil doubled in one year, and a deep economic recession hit the nation that cracked open the door for the Economic Royalists.

Similarly, while the 2007–08 financial panic was certainly caused by bad behavior on Wall Street, it was preceded by another drastic spike in oil prices. Between 2004 and 2008, the price of oil climbed from the $40-a-barrel range to a peak of $147 a barrel in 2008.

Economist Jeremy Rifkin, author of the book *The Third Industrial Revolution*, argues that the root cause of the 2007–08 financial panic was the surge in oil prices. And ultimately, there will be several more shocks as the Industrial Revolution, which has been based on fossil fuels, reaches its inevitable conclusion—the point at which we run out of oil.

Rifkin said in 2012, "When oil hit $147 a barrel on world markets," then "the other prices across the supply chain went through the roof because so much in this civilization is made out of fossil fuels."

The effects were catastrophic.

"We had food riots in twenty-two countries," Rifkin said. "The price on basic commodities, rice, wheat, and other basic foodstuffs was doubling and tripling. We had a billion people in harm's way in terms of hunger and starvation. People stopped buying everywhere."

Finally, Rifkin argued, "The entire economic engine—the growing economy—shut down, and purchasing went plummeting... that was an economic earthquake. The collapse of the financial market sixty days later—that was the aftershock."[168]

As oil becomes more and more scarce, and developing economies such as China and India demand more and more oil, then the prices will inevitably increase, producing a vicious cycle of oil shocks every time the world economy starts to grow again.

Rifkin notes, "[W]ithin the last ten years, China and India made a bid to bring a third of the human race into a second industrial revolution. The aggregate demand was so great, it dramatically spiked prices for oil. All the other goods and services went up, and per capita purchasing powers shut down.

"This is an endgame," Rifkin says. Referring to the coming oil-shock cycles, he adds, "Every time we try to restart the economy at the same rate it was growing before July 2008, this process repeats itself… [When] India and China started moving, Europe and America started moving, and immediately oil prices shot up over a hundred [dollars] a barrel, all the other prices went up, and purchasing power shut down again.

"We're likely to see these gyration cycles: wild gyration cycles of four to five years of growth and then collapse," Rifkin added.

To protect our supplies of oil around the world, the United States has built up an enormous military, which could get dragged into the Great Crash scenario.

Military Misadventure

The father of our Constitution and fourth president of the United States, James Madison, would be horrified. He knew just how dangerous never-ending war is to a nation.

"Of all the enemies of true liberty, war is, perhaps, the most to be dreaded, because it comprises and develops the germ of every other," wrote Madison in 1795.[169]

"No nation could preserve its freedom in the midst of continual warfare," he concluded.*

Yet, after Jimmy Carter's four years of relative peace, every single American president has started his own military conflict: Reagan invaded Grenada, Bush senior went to war against Iraq, Clinton launched strikes against Kosovo and Iraq. And we know well of

---

* Madison arrived at this conclusion by giving the following explanation from his book *Political Observations*: "War is the parent of armies; from these proceed debts and taxes; and armies, and debts, and taxes are the known instruments for bringing the many under the domination of the few. In war, too, the discretionary power of the Executive is extended; its influence in dealing out offices, honors, and emoluments is multiplied; and all the means of seducing the minds, are added to those of subduing the force, of the people. The same malignant aspect in republicanism may be traced in the inequality of fortunes, and the opportunities of fraud, growing out of a state of war, and in the degeneracy of manners and of morals engendered by both."

Bush junior's military exploits. All the while the mansions belonging to defense contractors that ring Washington, DC—making the DC suburbs the most affluent zip codes in the nation—just kept adding more and more floors and wings, while missile makers and private-security CEOs became multimillionaire war profiteers.

Today, our military is scattered across the Arab world, throwing trillions of dollars into known and unknown wars in Afghanistan, Iraq, Yemen, Libya, Somalia, Pakistan, and who-knows-where-else. These military misadventures have swelled the Pentagon budget to nearly half the entire federal budget: Fifty cents of every single dollar you pay in taxes goes to war.

And you can see the damage of war, not just in our economy but also in the broken spirits and traumatized minds of the soldiers we send off to tour after tour of military duty in some of the most violent regions of the world. Thousands are coming back to the United States every year maimed both physically and mentally. In 2012, a record number of men and women in our armed forces committed suicide.[170]

The burdens of war also manifest themselves in atrocities in the theaters of war—from service members going rogue and joining "kill squads," to institutionalized torture in military prisons such as Abu Ghraib and Gitmo, to the desecration of enemy bodies.

Even the most powerful men in our nation have been seduced by war. On television and in their memoirs, both President George W. Bush and Vice President Dick Cheney confessed to authorizing "enhanced interrogation" such as waterboarding, which is considered a form of torture under international law. The most frightening part about all of this militarism is if we were to instantly scale our military back to where it was in 1997—with one-third the budget it has today—our economy would disintegrate. We've made such a Faustian deal with the Gods of War that our economic survival, at least over the short term, depends on continually feeding the war machine.

And feed it well we have. Between 1997 and 2012, our "defense" budget *tripled*.

The double whammy of this is that when our manufacturing base is military, we produce things that don't produce any lasting benefit for our society.

When we build a school or a bridge or a high-speed rail system, years, decades, sometimes even centuries of use and value come from it. They produce for us, over time, far more than they cost us. Even consumer goods—from homes to washing machines to computers—increase our personal ability to be productive, thus producing a return on investment (albeit not so visible in GDP as are infrastructure investments).

But when we spend $100 million on a bunker-buster bomb, and that bomb is dropped somewhere, that $100 million just went up in smoke, never to be seen again. As the Romans and the Soviets and so many other empires before ours have found out, military spending is the least productive and sustainable way to build an economy.

In fact, a quick inspection of previous world superpowers reveals that they all met their demise by economic collapse following binges of military adventurism—often after a desperate campaign was launched to protect the last vestiges of their empire.

It's what happened to the Romans and it's also what happened to the Soviet Union, the last great economic superpower to collapse. After a nine-year military quagmire in Afghanistan, the Soviets found themselves so drained of resources that they had to withdraw their troops to tend to their own collapsing economy. Only a few years after the Afghan war, as Osama Bin Laden proudly proclaimed, the Soviet Union was in full meltdown.

We didn't get the memo. And today, at the behest of the Royalists, our nation is still fighting a more-than-decade-long war in Afghanistan that's producing the same empire-destroying consequences that befell the Soviet Union.

This Is the End

$1,200,000,000,000,000

So, what does the United States look like when one, or all, of these shocks converge by 2016, or sooner?

Well, to begin with, whatever cash the major banks and corporations have stashed away heading into the Great Crash won't be nearly enough to cover the subsequent losses that come with the collapse of the global banking system.

According to the Bank of International Settlements, the global derivatives market is now $1.2 quadrillion, or $1,200 trillion.

As economist Steve Keen explains in chapter 6, the financial sector inherently wants to produce more and more debt in an economy, since its primary way of making profit is through interest on that debt and fees to service that debt.

The financial sector received a huge stimulus when, thanks to Reaganomics, working people's wages stopped growing even as productivity and inflation increased.

As a result of declining wages, the only way the middle class could maintain their American lifestyle was by taking on loads and loads of debt in the form of home mortgages, credit card loans, and student loans.

Richard Wolff notes that during the 150-year period from 1820 until the 1970s, Americans saw a steadily rising standard of living.[171] He notes that around the time of the Great Depression the average American family owed about one-third of their annual income in debt.

But by 2008, the average American family was in debt to the tune of 130 percent of their average annual income. These are debt levels never before seen in history, and the middle class now has nowhere else to go. They're tapped out. They're not going to start spending and, thus, "save" the economy the way they did in the middle of the twentieth century.

Credit card debt in America has reached over $860 billion. Student loan debt is at just under $1 trillion. Mortgage debt is at over $10 trillion.[172]

But this is just the beginning. Wall Street can only make so much money through traditional lending, but through complex derivatives that banks can sell back and forth to one another, then an endless amount of profits, unlike any the world has seen before, can be made.

So Wall Street went nuts buying and selling derivatives to and from each other. That derivative market grew 1,000 percent since 1996.

Sensing that something bad is happening, Warren Buffett told Berkshire Hathaway shareholders, "The derivatives genie is now well out of the bottle, and these instruments will almost certainly multiply in variety and number until some event makes their toxicity clear… [They] are financial weapons of mass destruction, carrying dangers that while not latent, are potentially lethal."[173]

We learned the dangers of the derivatives market in 2008, when the world's largest insurance corporation, AIG, failed because of bad bets on derivatives. Today, the derivatives market is even larger, and banks and sovereign economies have mind-bogglingly dangerous exposure to these derivatives.

Columnist Thomas Kostigen explains the scope of this problem in a 2009 *MarketWatch* article, writing, "Try as we might to salvage the residential real estate market, it's at best worth $23 trillion in the U.S. We're struggling to save the stock market, but that's valued at less than $15 trillion. And we hope to keep the entire U.S. economy from collapsing, yet gross domestic product stands at $14.2 trillion."[174]

He adds, "Compare any of these to the derivatives market and you can easily see that we are just closing the windows as a tsunami crashes to shore."

At $1.2 quadrillion, the derivatives market is roughly twenty-one times the size of the *global* GDP. To say that all the money in the world can't stop the derivatives market from imploding wouldn't be an exaggeration. In fact, it'd be a gross understatement.

The biggest American banks stand to lose the most as the derivatives market begins unwinding as a result of the economic shocks in Europe and China.

JPMorgan Chase, with total assets of just over $1.8 trillion, has more than $69 trillion exposed in derivatives.

Bank of America, with total assets of $1.4 trillion, is exposed to $44 trillion in derivatives.

And Goldman Sachs, with $114 billion in assets, is exposed to more than $41 trillion in derivatives.

Should the massive derivatives market get destabilized (as it appears the Royalists are preparing for), then there's no amount of money that can prevent the coming crisis.

So with no other choice, the Royalists have to keep the scheme going at all costs. More than five years removed from the last burst of the housing bubble, it's increasingly obvious that another housing bubble is being inflated with low-interest-rate money.

Major cities such as Los Angeles, New York, and Washington, DC, are seeing their real estate sectors boom once again despite the internal problems with the economy.

In April 2013, house-flipping in California reached its highest level since 2005, fueled by rapidly increasing real estate prices. In fact, median home prices in the Bay Area have returned to pre-2007–08 housing-crash levels. In San Francisco, the median home price is more than $1 million.[175]

But this endless boom-bust cycle in real estate can sustain itself only for so long. Eventually the Crash of 2016 will spread from disaster zones such as Camden, New Jersey, and Flint, Michigan, to the centers of affluence in America.

When this starts to happen, there will be European-style runs on the banks in America. One by one, the major banking institutions in

America will dissolve, taking with them the credit lines to businesses large and small. Companies won't be able to meet their payrolls. There will be massive layoffs.

The American economy, the largest empire that has ever graced the planet, will collapse spectacularly in front of our eyes.

PART 5

Out of the Ashes

Chapter 12

Organized People *v.*
Organized Money

*It seemed but a few short days until more than fifty [tents] were set up,
and then our troubles began. Business houses in the district did not know
us. They considered us a bunch of ne'er-do-well undesirables and wanted
to be rid of us... [H]ealth officials decided our shacks were unfit for
human habitation and a menace to health conditions in the city, and
posted official notices... informing us of the fact and giving us seven days
in which to vacate them... [A]t the expiration of the seven-day notice,
at 5 a.m., just as daylight was breaking, in one of the heaviest down-
pours... a regiment of uniformed officers of law and order swooped down
upon us, with cans of kerosene and applied the torch.*
—Jesse Jackson, Mayor of Seattle's "Hooverville," 1930

Jesse Jackson tried to find cover from the rain, but his makeshift
home, cobbled together with scrap wood, canvas, and tin sheets,
provided little cover. He waited with trepidation, knowing that as
soon as the sun broke the horizon in the East, then all hell would
break loose around him.

He was surrounded by several hundred others just like him, people who had come to the shores of Elliott Bay in Seattle, Washington, flanked by a steel-manufacturing plant, shipping crates, and the Seattle Transfer Company warehouse, to find a new start while the American economy went into a tailspin.

There were no jobs, no social safety net, and little charity to be found in the city, so the unemployed and desperate began occupying a nine-acre space of land in between the bay and a line of railroad tracks to the east, building shacks and tents for shelter and setting up a community to help one another survive.

But their occupation didn't sit too well with nearby businesses. The "occupiers" were considered riffraff troublemakers and criminals. Health officials dropped by and decided the occupation was a health risk that threatened the city of Seattle. Soon, Jackson noticed official warnings posted around the various dwellings informing the occupiers that they had seven days to pack up and get out.

The notices were ignored, and on that seventh night, as their encampments were sinking into the mud in the relentless downpour, Jackson and the other occupiers waited for what might happen in the morning.

Then, just as they feared, at five o'clock in the morning, when the sun breached the railroad tracks, a cavalry of police officers swooped down upon Jackson and the others. Armed with cans of kerosene, they doused the makeshift city and applied the torch, thus putting an end to the occupation.

Just replace the kerosene and torches with less-lethal rubber bullets and pepper spray, and this sounds like a story from 2011, when the Occupy Movement flared up and began setting up tents in public parks all around the nation, from New York City to Chicago to Seattle. But it actually happened exactly eighty years earlier, when the nation was drowning in President Hoover's Great Depression, and not President Bush's Great Recession. These settlements weren't called "occupations" at the time, they were called "Hoovervilles."

When those Hoovervilles spread around the country in the early 1930s, and then became bastions for progressive organization and action, FDR had no choice but to be a revolutionary president, fundamentally change America, and wage war on the Royalists.

The Crash of 2016, like previous Great Crashes, will be a time of great opportunity to reclaim much of the ground lost to the Economic Royalists since the 1970s.

But it will also be time of great danger, as history has proven. In the period after the last Great Crash Germany had Hitler and we had FDR, and our nations took very different directions in response to the crash. An awakened citizenry and honorable leadership will determine whether we succeed or fail.

We do know that no matter how bad things get during the Crash of 2016, organized people will always find one another and begin building the movements necessary to take on the Economic Royalists. It happened in the 1930s, and it will happen again following the Crash of 2016. We must rely on them.

Move to Amend

First things first: We need to tip the scales of power away from organized money and back to organized people. And the way to do that is to get rid of this whole idea of corporate personhood.

The Supreme Court gave us corporate personhood, and there are only three ways to undo a bad Supreme Court decision. All three have been used at various times.

The first is to wait until the composition of the court changes, which can only happen when one or more of the bad judges retires or dies and is replaced by others more competent. Then the court takes on a case that involves the same issues and, as with the *Brown v. Board of Education* or *Roe v. Wade* decisions, pushes the court in a new direction.

The second is for the American people, the president, and

Congress to understand the consequences of *Citizens United,* and break with the court.

Arguably this happened with the *Dred Scott* decision in 1857, which ruled that black *persons* were actually *property,* and thus led us directly into the Civil War. That Supreme Court decision led to Abraham Lincoln's Emancipation Proclamation and the passage of legislation clarifying the rights of African Americans, although it ultimately took a war and the passage of the Thirteenth, Fourteenth, and Fifteenth Amendments to purge slavery from our laws and from our Constitution.

Ironically, the *Citizens United* case is the mirror opposite of *Dred Scott* in that it ruled that *property*—a corporation—is now a *person.* And, rhetoric from some on the fringes of both the Tea Party and the Occupy Wall Street movements notwithstanding, few Americans have any desire to see a second Civil War or American Revolution.

The third way to undo—or supersede—a Supreme Court decision is to amend the Constitution itself so the Court can no longer play word games with ambiguous or broadly worded language. We did this, for example, to both institute and then to repeal the prohibition, manufacture, and sale of alcohol.

The constitutional-amendment route seems the most practical and long lasting, even though it may be the most challenging. But post-crash, the urgency will be there to make it happen.

Over 29,000 amendments to our Constitution have been put forth in Congress since the founding of our republic, and only 27 have passed the hurdle of approval by two-thirds of the members of Congress and three-fourths of the states. Nonetheless, successful amendments are driven by a widespread sense that the change is absolutely essential for the good of the nation.

An example of this is the Twenty-Sixth Amendment to drop the voting age from twenty-one to eighteen. It was largely brought about by the rage and impotence young people felt in America during the Vietnam War era (as expressed in the protest song "Eve of Destruction": "You're old enough to kill, but not for votin'...."). The need for young people to participate in a political process that could lead them to war was so clear that the Twenty-Sixth Amendment passed the Senate in March 1971 and was completely ratified by the states on July 1, 1971.

On December 6, 2011, Los Angeles became the first major city in the United States to call for a constitutional amendment to end corporate personhood. The Los Angeles City Council voted unanimously to say that money is not the same as free speech, thus asserting a basis to overturn the *Citizens United* decision.

There have been similar resolutions passed in Boulder, Colorado, and Missoula, Montana, that say corporations are not people and money is not speech.

A group of Democratic senators introduced a new constitutional amendment to overturn the Supreme Court's *Citizens United* decision. The senators who signed on to this amendment include Tom Udall, Michael Bennet, Tom Harkin, Dick Durbin, Chuck Schumer, Sheldon Whitehouse, and Jeff Merkley.

Representative Ted Deutch, a Democrat on the House Judiciary Committee, introduced another constitutional amendment in November 2011, the "Outlawing Corporate Cash Undermining the Public Interest in Our Elections" Amendment. Robert Weissman, president of Public Citizen, applauded Representative Deutch's amendment, saying, "It would clarify that constitutional rights are intended for real, live, breathing human beings. It would end corporate spending on elections. And it would give Congress authority to adopt a sensible campaign finance system. It would make America stronger, more democratic and more just."

Senator Bernie Sanders proposed, in December 2011, the "Saving American Democracy" Amendment, which would overturn *Citizens United* and make it clear that corporations are not people. In a statement Senator Sanders said, "There comes a time when an issue is so important that the only way to address it is by a constitutional amendment." Sanders said in the effort to override the court decision that he labeled it "a complete undermining of democracy." Senator Sanders's "Saving American Democracy" Amendment has an interesting component that makes it different from all of the other proposed amendments and remedies: Section 4 of the amendment challenges the basis for every other Supreme Court decision related to campaign finance. He takes aim at the 1976 *Buckley v. Valeo* decision, in which the Supreme Court ruled that spending money to influence elections was a form of protected free speech, and struck down limits on expenditures.

There are groups all over America bringing forth resolutions in cities large and small to say the same. These are the training grounds for a constitutional amendment.

Several proposals are on the table, but I particularly recommend the model put forth by David Cobb at MoveToAmend.org. This proposed amendment is more explicit than simply inserting the word "natural" before the word "person" in the Fourteenth Amendment and could seriously begin the process of turning the United States into a democratic republic that is once again responsive and responsible to its citizens instead of to its most powerful corporations. The proposed amendment states the following:

Section 1
***[A corporation is not a person
and can be regulated]***

The rights protected by the Constitution of the United States are the rights of natural persons only.

Artificial entities, such as corporations, limited liability companies, and other entities, established by the laws of any State, the United States, or any foreign state shall have no rights under this Constitution and are subject to regulation by the People, through Federal, State, or local law.

The privileges of artificial entities shall be determined by the People, through Federal, State, or local law, and shall not be construed to be inherent or inalienable.

Section 2
[Money is not speech and can be regulated]

Federal, State and local government shall regulate, limit, or prohibit contributions and expenditures, including a candidate's own contributions and expenditures, for the purpose of influencing in any way the election of any candidate for public office or any ballot measure.

Federal, State and local government shall require that any permissible contributions and expenditures be publicly disclosed.

The judiciary shall not construe the spending of money to influence elections to be speech under the First Amendment.

Section 3

Nothing contained in this amendment shall be construed to abridge the freedom of the press.

Section 4

Congress shall have power to implement this article by appropriate legislation.

Other variations on this amendment, some simpler and some more complex, can be found at MoveToAmend.org. The elegance of explicitly denying constitutional rights to anything except "living human beings" is that it will not only roll back *Citizens United* but it will also allow future legislatures to challenge corporate claims to "rights" of privacy (Fourth Amendment), protection from self-incrimination (Fifth Amendment), and the power to force themselves on communities that don't want them because to do otherwise is "discrimination" (Fourteenth Amendment).

We must be very careful that any amendment put forth isn't just limited to giving Congress the power to regulate campaign spending; to do so would leave a wide swath of other Bill of Rights powers in the hands of corporations. Instead, an amendment must explicitly overturn the headnote to the *Santa Clara County* 1886 decision that asserted corporations are the same as natural persons in terms of constitutional protections.

By doing this, we can begin the transition back from a Royalist state to the constitutionally limited representative democratic republic our Founders envisioned.

Even before the *Citizens United* case blew open the doors to a corporate takeover of American politics, the corrosive influence of corporations having "rights" was already evident. After the crash, "we the people" must once again assert our right to do what's best for the common good and, through the mechanism of a constitutional amendment, relegate corporations to their rightful place—as legal fictions and not natural persons.

Take On the Court

To ensure that the Supreme Court is never able to overturn the will of organized people again, we must also reconsider the role of the high court itself after the Crash of 2016.

Ever since taking on the power to strike down laws passed by Congress and signed by the president, the Supreme Court has been behind a series of radical decisions that have provoked previous Great Crashes and wars.

On June 16, 1858, Abraham Lincoln—shortly after he'd been nominated by the newly minted Republican Party as their candidate for the US Senate—denounced the Supreme Court's decision in his famous "House Divided" speech in Springfield, Illinois. "We shall lie down pleasantly dreaming that the people of Missouri are on the verge of making their State free," he said, "and we shall awake to the reality instead, that the Supreme Court has made Illinois a slave State."

Lincoln went on to lose the Senate campaign to Stephen Douglas, but after the loss his party nominated him for president, and he won that election in November 1860. During the four months between then and March 4, 1861, when he was sworn into office, seven southern states had organized and announced their intention to secede from the United States and form their own nation, the Confederate States of America. Lame-duck president James Buchanan declared their secession illegal, but could or would do little else. Lincoln was alarmed, but he was not yet president.

On the day of his inauguration, Monday, March 4, 1861, Lincoln spoke explicitly and gravely to the seven secessionist states, and to another eight that were considering joining them. He didn't want a war, and was willing to give in to the slave owners to avoid it.

"I have no purpose, directly or indirectly, to interfere with the institution of slavery in the States where it exists," Lincoln said in his inaugural address. "I believe I have no lawful right to do so, and I have no inclination to do so."

But knowing, also, that if the Supreme Court had not ruled the way they had in *Dred Scott v. Sandford*, the drums of war probably wouldn't be beating, Lincoln let his inner lawyer loose and said right out loud:

> [T]he candid citizen must confess that if the policy of the Government upon vital questions affecting the whole people is to be irrevocably fixed by decisions of the Supreme Court, the instant they are made in ordinary litigation between parties in personal actions the people

will have ceased to be their own rulers, having to that extent practically resigned their Government into the hands of that eminent tribunal.

Although he'd sugar-coated the statement, there it was.

Lincoln knew that the entire concept that the Supreme Court could strike down laws passed by Congress and signed by the president was not one of the powers given to it by the Constitution.

The Constitution, in Section 2 of Article 3, which establishes the judiciary branch, gives Congress the power to define and limit what the Supreme Court can and can't do.

Here's part of the exact language: "[T]he Supreme Court shall have appellate jurisdiction both as to law and fact, with such exceptions, and under such regulations as the Congress shall make."

The Congress can control the terms and conditions under which the Supreme Court can rule? Yes, according to the Constitution.

The framers of the Constitution wanted the greatest power to be closest to "We the People"—and that's why the entire House of Representatives and a third of the Senate is up for election every two years. Congress is the body in our representative democratic republic that is closest to the people, so that's where they wanted most of the power. That's also why Congress is defined in Article 1 of the Constitution, establishing it as the first among equals.

As Thomas Jefferson wrote in an 1820 letter to William Charles Jarvis, who thought Supreme Court justices should have the power to strike down laws: "You seem to consider the judges the ultimate arbiters of all constitutional questions; a very dangerous doctrine indeed, and one which would place us under the despotism of an oligarchy... The Constitution has erected no such single tribunal... I know of no safe depository of the ultimate powers of the society, but the people themselves."

Nowhere in the Constitution does it say that the Supreme Court can strike down laws passed by Congress and signed by the president. Nowhere.

And for the first fourteen years of our republic, the court, under Chief Justice John Jay (who coauthored *The Federalist Papers* with Hamilton and Madison, wrote New York State's constitution, and was a president of the Continental Congress), Chief Justice John Rutledge (who helped write the Constitution and signed it), and Chief Justice Oliver Ellsworth (who helped write the Constitution and signed it), never even considered the idea.

When he and James Madison were selling the Constitution in 1878, Alexander Hamilton wrote a newspaper article, now known as "Federalist No. 78," stating:

> [T]he judiciary, from the nature of its functions, will always be the least dangerous to the political rights of the Constitution; because it will be least in a capacity to annoy or injure them. The Executive not only dispenses the honors, but holds the sword of the community. The legislature not only commands the purse, but prescribes the rules by which the duties and rights of every citizen are to be regulated. The judiciary, on the contrary, has no influence over either the sword or the purse; no direction either of the strength or of the wealth of the society; and can take no active resolution whatever...It proves incontestably, that the judiciary is beyond comparison the weakest of the three departments of power; that it can never attack with success either of the other two.

The Court Takes the Power

But in 1803, a hard-right-wing (Federalist) chief justice named John Marshall (who'd been only eleven years old when the

Declaration of Independence was written and signed) ruled, in the case of *Marbury v. Madison*, that the Supreme Court could strike down laws as "unconstitutional."

Although the power of "judicial supremacy" over the other two branches had been discussed extensively in the early days of the republic and debated in the constitutional convention, it had been rejected and does not appear in the Constitution.

But Marshall took it onto himself and his court, instantly transforming the Supreme Court from "the weakest of the three" to the absolute overlord tribunal.

John Marshall had, in effect, turned himself into a king, along with his colleagues on the Supreme Court. No matter what Congress and the president—the other two branches of government—did, the Supreme Court could overturn them. A tiny group of unelected lawyers who, like kings of old, had jobs for life, now controlled the fate and destiny of the United States.

President Thomas Jefferson went apoplectic.

He wrote that if that decision wasn't challenged by Congress: "[T]hen indeed is our Constitution a complete felo-de-se [a suicide pact]...The Constitution, on this hypothesis, is a mere thing of wax in the hands of the judiciary, which they may twist and shape into any form they may please."[176]

Marshall and the court backed down, at least in appearance. For as long as Jefferson was alive, Marshall never again ruled a law unconstitutional. He never again said that a few unelected judges were the kings of America, with nobody else having the power to undo their decisions.

Nonetheless, Jefferson saw the direction of the future. Several decades later (while Marshall was still the chief justice, as he remained for nine years after Jefferson died), Jefferson wrote: "The judiciary of the United States is the subtle corps of sappers and miners constantly working underground to undermine our Constitution...I will say, that 'against this every man should raise his voice,' and, more, should uplift his arm."

Because, Jefferson said, "For judges to usurp the powers of the legislature is unconstitutional judicial tyranny... One single object... will entitle you to the endless gratitude of society; that of restraining judges from usurping legislation."

But as much as he tried, Jefferson was not able to stir up enough outrage in Congress to pass a law limiting the Supreme Court from continuing its new "judicial supremacy" doctrine of "judicial review" of laws in the context of the Constitution. Jefferson had actually won in the *Marbury* ruling, which somewhat deflated the outrage he might have been able to otherwise marshal from politicians in his Democratic Republican Party (today's Democratic Party).

And most politicians weren't seeing the long view—they never, in their wildest dreams, imagined that the court would become the final hurdle over which every single law passed by Congress and signed by the president must leap.

As mentioned, the Supreme Court was very wary about using judicial review in its first century. Mostly it just did what the Constitution says it should do—be the final court of appeals in legal disputes and criminal prosecutions, and in issues between the states. The buck has to stop somewhere, and that's the Supreme Court.

But striking down laws? That's a power only kings have, and in the modern era even most kings in constitutional monarchies don't have that power. In the United Kingdom, for example, not only does the king (or queen) not have the power to strike down laws, neither does the United Kingdom's own supreme court. Ditto for the royal family and the supreme court of The Netherlands.

Depose the Kings!

The Supreme Court was beyond their constitutional power when they handed George W. Bush the victory in 2000 by ruling that if all the votes were counted in Florida, as that state's supreme court had ordered, it would "cause irreparable harm to petitioner [George W. Bush]."

They were beyond their constitutional power every single time they struck down a law passed by Congress and signed by the president over the years.

And most important, the Supreme Court was way beyond their constitutional authority every single time they created out of whole cloth new legal doctrines, such as "separate but equal" in *Plessy v. Ferguson*, "privacy" in *Roe v. Wade*, or "corporations are people" in *Citizens United v. Federal Election Commission*.

But in the fine tradition of John Marshall, today's Supreme Court wants you to believe that they are the über-overlords of our nation. They can make George W. Bush president, without any appeal. They can make money into speech, they can turn corporations into people, and the rest of us have no say in it.

And they're wrong.

It's not what the Constitution says, and it's not what most of our Founders said.

Which raises the question: If the Supreme Court can't decide what is and what isn't constitutional, then what is its purpose? What's it really supposed to be doing?

The answer to that is laid out in the Constitution in plain black-and-white. It's the first court where the nation goes for cases involving disputes about treaties, ambassadors, controversies between two or more states, between a state and citizen of another state, between citizens of different states, and between our country and foreign states. Read Article 3, Section 2 of the Constitution—it's all there.

Not a word in there about "judicial supremacy" or "judicial review"—the supposed powers of the court to strike down (or write) laws by deciding what is and what isn't constitutional.

President Thomas Jefferson was pretty clear about that—as were most of the Founders—and the court didn't start seriously deciding "constitutionality" until after all of them were dead. But back in the day, here's what Jefferson had to say:

Organized People v. Organized Money

> *The Constitution has erected no such single tribunal, knowing that to whatever hands confided, with the corruptions of time and party, its members would become despots. It has more wisely made all the departments co-equal and co-sovereign within themselves ... When the legislative or executive functionaries act unconstitutionally, they are responsible to the people in their elective capacity.*[177]

Their elective capacity? That's a fancy presidential-founder way of saying that the people can toss out on their butts any member of Congress or any president who behaves in a way that's unconstitutional. The ultimate remedy is with the people—it's the ballot box. If we don't like the laws being passed, then we elect new legislators and a new president. It's pretty simple.

But without the Supreme Court, some say, we never would have had *Brown v. Board of Education* in 1954, which ended apartheid in America, or *Roe v. Wade*, which ended restrictions on abortion in 1973.

Maybe.

Brown v. Board was mostly the Supreme Court reversing itself from its own 1886 *Plessy v. Ferguson* decision, which is what established legal apartheid in America. And if the Supreme Court hadn't decided *Roe v. Wade*—remember, the birth control pill had just been invented and brought to market thirteen years earlier and the women's movement in 1973 was in full bloom—then it would have been just a matter of a few years before Congress took care of it.

The fact of the matter is that the Supreme Court has never found eternal truths in the Constitution—they just reflect current popular view, and they usually do that with about a twenty-year lag time.

The power of "We the People" should be with us and the officials we elect, not nine lawyers who have claimed the illegitimate right to rule over every other branch of our government.

After the crash, we must address the Supreme Court's power grab and strengthen our system of checks and balances in our government to empower organized people over organized money.

Chapter 13

Repair the Fundamentals

The most perfect political community must be among those who are in the middle rank, and those states are best instituted wherein these are a larger and more respectable part, if possible, than both the other; or, if that cannot be, at least than either of them separate.
—Aristotle, *A Treatise on Government*, 322 BC

Amending the Constitution and putting an end to corporate personhood could take years. In the meantime, post-crash, we need to get to work repairing the fundamentals that sustained a middle class after the last Great Crash.

That means making our social safety net stronger, reclaiming our commons, taking on Wall Street, investing in working people again, and rolling back Ronald Reagan's disastrous tax cuts.

Medicare Part E

A 2009 study by Harvard University found that 45,000 Americans die every single year because they lack health insurance.[178] After the last Great Crash, while Europe began rebuilding, several nations adopted single-payer health care systems. After the Crash of 2016, the United States should do the same.

The way we do that is by building off the single-payer system we already have in place that's worked perfectly for generation after generation of senior citizens and never missed a payment—Medicare. I've long advocated what former Congressman Dennis Kucinich calls "Medicare Part E"—"E" as in "for Everybody"—and I still think it's the right way to go.

Just like in the Occupy Wall Street encampments that sprang up across America at the end of 2011, where doctors volunteered to man tents where people received basic health care for free, our nation should make a commitment to healing the sick without consideration of who or what will make a profit off of it.

This won't be done overnight, but we can look north toward Canada for a strategy on exactly how to do it.

The Canadian government didn't just one day say, "It's time for a single-payer system," and then poof everyone was covered. Instead, it was a process. It was a process that started locally.

It began in 1946, when Saskatchewan became the first province in Canada to say that everyone should be able to get medical care when they are sick by passing the Saskatchewan Hospitalization Act.

While that was a big step forward, the province wanted to do more. It wanted universal health care for all its citizens, but it just didn't have the money yet. Then, a few years later, in 1950, Alberta saw what was happening in Saskatchewan and thought it was a good idea. They passed their own plan, which gave health coverage to 90 percent of the population.

In 1957, the federal government saw what was happening around the nation and passed the Hospital Insurance and Diagnostic Services Act, which paid for half of all the costs of any single-payer system passed by the provinces.

After that, by 1961, fifteen years after Saskatchewan started the process, all ten provinces had similar single-payer programs.

Today, Canada has one of the highest life expectancies in the world and spends almost a third less a year on health care than we do in the United States.

That process is already starting in the United States. Vermont and Montana are looking into setting up their own single-payer health care systems based on the Canadian model.

And the largest state in the nation, California, has twice passed a single-payer health care law, only to see it vetoed by Republican governor Arnold Schwarzenegger. Then, with a Democrat in the governor's mansion in Sacramento, the state legislature came just two votes shy of passing a single-payer law. We're getting very close to that "Saskatchewan moment" in America.

After the Crash of 2016, we'll get there, and our nation will be fundamentally changed for the better.

We'll be a nation where people can start a new business or pursue a new career field without having to worry about losing their insurance. A nation where a mother or father can get sick without it affecting whether their child can afford to go to college. And a nation that's not drowning in debt because for-profit health insurance CEOs need another mansion.

Look anywhere you want and you'll never see a successful nation with a sick population or a nation where the sick have to go to prison just to get the care they need. Most of the developed nations in the world that have universal health care, such as Canada and the United Kingdom, created their systems following crises like World War II and the Great Depression. Now we'll have our chance to do the same.

As Occupy has demonstrated, health care is sacred. We *are* our brothers' keepers.

Reclaim the Commons

When the Royal Dutch Shell rig *Kulluk* got stuck on the rocky shores of Alaska on New Year's Eve in 2013, the people of that state paid close attention—not just because they worried about the potential for another environmental disaster in their backyard but because they pay close attention to their state's oil industry in general since they each make a lot of money off of it.

Alaska is unique in that it has something called the Alaska Permanent Fund.[179]

Believing that all residents of the state should profit off the resources that are naturally below their feet, Alaska takes the money that big oil corporations pay them in oil leases and royalties, invests that money, and then distributes the returns on those investments to each and every resident of the state.

It works out to between $1,000 and $2,000 for every man, woman, and child in Alaska every single year.[180] So if you're a husband and wife with two kids, you could earn as much as $8,000 at the end of the year—and that's not pocket change for a working family trying to make it by.

Thanks to this supplemental income to each resident of Alaska, the state enjoys the third highest median income in the nation, and is also the second most equal state in the nation.

It's a system that works, and it's been embraced by both Democrats and Republicans—even Sarah Palin.

Before the Crash of 2016, this system was applied to the rest of the country, but only the Economic Royalists enjoyed it.

Under their reign, our entire economic model, largely controlled by this billionaire class, depends on enriching the lives of shareholders and business owners—but not average working-class Americans.

From Wall Street, to Big Oil, to the for-profit health insurance industry, business decisions are geared to increasing the wealth of shareholders. Take a gander at the Forbes 400 Richest Americans list and you'll see a slew of billionaires who collect most of their money in the form of nonlabor dividend income from things they "own," such as businesses, land, and infrastructure.

Paris Hilton collects a steady stream of dividend checks from her family's businesses. The Koch brothers get their regular checks in the mail courtesy of the massive energy conglomerate their dad built up known as Koch Industries. Mitt Romney continues to cash his checks from Bain Capital.

It's good to be a shareholder or corporate owner in capitalist America. And that's all well and good.

But aren't we all shareholders in our commons, just like Alaskans? And being such, shouldn't we all share the dividends every time our commons turns a profit for others, just like Alaskans?

In Alaska, the money oil corporations pay to lease and extract oil on public lands is distributed to all Alaskans equally. So, nationwide, all the money oil corporations pay to lease and extract oil on public lands could be distributed to all Americans equally, too.

In 2007, the US government collected $9 billion in royalty payments from Big Oil on just the drilling done in the Gulf of Mexico.[181] In reality, we taxpayers should have earned a lot more, but the United States ranks ninety-third in the world in how much revenue it extracts from oil and gas extraction compared with the profits these industries enjoy.[182]

That has something to do with Ronald Reagan. Between 1954 and 1983, the average lease for federal land was $2,224 per acre. But after Reagan, between 1983 and 2008, the average lease was just $263 an acre.

But still, $9 billion in royalties from just the Gulf of Mexico is a considerable chunk of change. And if we were to distribute that money equally to all Americans, as they do in Alaska, then it works out to about $30 a person. Not too much money, but when you throw in the leases and royalties paid everywhere else around the nation for oil, gas, and coal—from the East Coast drilling platforms, to the fracking wells and coal mines in Appalachia, to the oil derricks in the Midwest and Texas, we're talking serious money.

Not only that, think of how much money is put into our common military to defend the interests of Big Oil abroad to make sure the shipping lanes stay open and the oil spigot keeps flowing. Big Oil should contribute a small fee for this service, which can also be added to this common "permanent fund" to be shared by all Americans.

And what about making Big Oil pay for their pollution of the commons? A cap-and-trade system, which forces polluters to pay for how much carbon they dump into the atmosphere, is a good start and could raise even more money for our commons permanent fund to be shared by all of us.

The point is, our commons belong to all of us and should be enriching all of us, and not just the billionaires who've put a flag in the ground.

And it shouldn't stop at just oil.

Wall Street relies heavily on the commons, too. Our markets are regulated by common government, enforced through common courts, and fueled by workers who were educated in our commons.

As entrepreneur and cofounder of On the Commons, Peter Barnes proposes that we should all get a cut every time a company goes public. Barnes argues, "When a company like Facebook or Google goes public, its value rises dramatically... Experts call this a 'liquidity premium,' and it's generated not by the company but by society. This socially created wealth now flows mostly to a small number of Americans... Let's say we required public companies to deposit 1 percent of their shares in the [common fund] for ten years, up to a total of 10 percent. In due time, the [common fund] would have a diversified portfolio worth trillions of dollars."[183]

Now consider the enormous profits that radio, television, and entertainment companies receive by using our common air and infrastructure and our common copyright laws for basically no charge. They, too, should be paying into the common fund.

Add together all of these "rents" for using our commons, and "We the People" have a raised quite a bit of money for our common permanent fund, money that could go a long way to supplementing the annual incomes of millions of Americans who desperately need a bit more cash.

Somehow, as Royalists were left to run amok in America over the last few decades, we forgot the important role our commons can play in enriching all of our lives. Rather than billionaire CEOs paying us to use our commons, pollute our air and water, dictate our military missions, exploit our markets, and hijack our radio and TV airwaves, it's all been flipped on its head and *we* end up paying *them*. We give them subsidies, generous tax breaks, free usage, and no requirement that they have to share with the rest of us, who actually own those commons, any of the wealth our commons have produced for them.

So in the end, they make billions off what should belong to all of us while we make squat. This makes no sense. And with pressing concerns about wealth inequality, economic insecurity, and environmental disasters, we need to move away from this corporate-exploitation model, and embrace a new universal-shareholder model.

Cure Wall Street's Madness

One of the ways to put a check on Wall Street's madness that's caused the last Great Crashes is through something called a Robin Hood tax—or a financial transaction tax, as it's technically called.

It's pretty simple; every single security that's bought and sold comes with a tiny tax—usually less than 1 percent. In 2012, then French president Nicolas Sarkozy announced a new financial-transaction tax on banking institutions in France—charging a tiny one-tenth-of-one-percent tax on all stock trades.

It's called a Robin Hood tax, because it's a tax that only affects banks and wealthy traders, and it generates a lot of much-needed revenue to tackle issues such as poverty, health care, and infrastructure rebuilding.

Repair the Fundamentals

That tiny, little just one-tenth-of-one-percent tax on only the banks and other stock traders will generate massive revenue for the rest of the nation—upward of 12 billion euros a year.

And if the whole debt-ridden European continent were to go the way of France and put in place a Robin Hood tax on stock trades, that'd be an additional 50 billion euros flowing in.

Not only would a Robin Hood tax raise much-needed revenue, it would also discourage bad behavior, such as excessive financial speculation and high-frequency trading—triggers of economic crises.

As one of the main proponents of the Robin Hood tax in France, an organization called Friends of the Earth Europe argued, "European banks, pension funds and insurance companies are increasing global hunger and poverty by speculating on food prices and financing land grabs in poorer countries... Food speculation, with billions of euros flooding in and out of financial products... causes price volatility. These rapid and unpredictable price swings hit the most vulnerable hardest, threatening their right to food, and making it more difficult for farmers to maintain an income—creating instability, hunger and poverty."

And they were just talking about European banks, not even American banks. It's been proven that Goldman Sachs—which opened up the market for speculation on everything from oil to food to gold—played an integral role in the 2008 food shortages around the planet as well as the housing crash.

This is what the banks are doing with all that untaxed money: speculating and creating instability around the planet. But a Robin Hood tax would change all that. And it would put an end to the high-speed machines that account for most of the trades made on Wall Street—machines that make tens of thousands of trades a second based solely on some computer formula.

After the Crash of 2016, it'll be time to put an end to fraud and theft on Wall Street and make banksters pay their fair share again.

Reinvest

There's something that every single American family understands—something that Royalists don't want us to talk about—and that's the difference between spending and investing.

Let's assume that the typical American family collects its paycheck at the end of the month and decides to go out to eat for a fancy dinner. A couple of glasses of wine, an appetizer, four entrees, and a few desserts later, the waiter brings the check and that family is now out about $150. Do that once a month as a special treat, and you're pushing $2,000 a year. That money is not coming back. It was spent and is now gone.

Now let's assume that same family decides to skip the fancy dinners all year. Instead they take their $2,000 and put it into home repairs, such as a new air conditioner, improved insulation, or a new rooftop deck. Unlike spending it on a fancy dinner, that money doesn't just disappear. It will actually create more wealth in the long run through lower energy bills and an increase in the value of their home. That's an investment.

Or let's assume that same family uses a chunk of their paycheck to start a prepaid college fund for their kids. Again, that money doesn't disappear. Instead, it was invested in the future for their kids to earn a college degree.

Or maybe, they just buy $150 worth of stocks every month like many other people. Again, the money doesn't disappear. In fact, in a year it might be worth $2,500.

That's another investment.

American families know the difference between spending and investing. And they know that when times are tough, they need to cut back on their spending but not on their investments. That means fewer fancy dinners out, but no cuts to their kids' college fund or mortgage payments on their home.

However, since the Royalists took over, this same logic isn't applied to our government.

Like a family, our government is capable of spending and investing.

Money put into our wars is the perfect example of spending. As a nation, we can spend a trillion dollars deploying troops in Iraq and Afghanistan, manufacturing and detonating bunker-busting bombs, and refueling aircraft carriers in the Gulf. Guess what happens to all of that money? It's obliterated.

War spending is just that—spending. It doesn't create more wealth in the future. The shards of a Predator drone's Tomahawk missile in northern Pakistan will not create one dime of lasting wealth for our nation. Our military might as well have gone out for a few million big fancy steak dinners.

No question about it, our government spends a lot of money. And when it comes to reducing our deficits, there's certainly a lot of waste, fraud, and abuse within that spending that can be cut—particularly in the Defense Department, which seems to have lost $2 trillion they can't account for.

But let's not confuse spending with investing, which our government also does a lot of.

For example, money put into Pell Grants so more kids can go to college is an investment that will create lasting wealth for our entire nation when those kids graduate and become a productive part of the economy. Our experience with the GI Bill indicates that every $1 spent will return at least $7—and maybe as much as $50—back to government coffers in the form of income taxes from more productive and higher-paid workers.

Money put toward green-energy projects such as wind farms, solar plants, and electric cars are investments that will create a boatload of jobs, reduce our demand for foreign oil, and make our environment cleaner.

Money put toward infrastructure such as new roads, bridges, and high-speed rail systems are investments that will make it cheaper and easier for businesses to ship goods across the country or for Americans to travel and go on vacation.

Money put into health care research is an investment that will cut down on the costs diseases inflict on our economy and, as a bonus, give us a healthier, more productive workforce.

Even money put toward social welfare programs such as food stamps and unemployment benefits are investments. Moody's did research into this and found that for every dollar invested in expanding the food stamp program, the economy generates an additional $1.73.[184] And for every dollar invested in unemployment benefits, the economy generates an additional $1.64. That's a pretty good return on investment.

Ever since Ronald Reagan said, "The nine most terrifying words in the English language are, 'I'm from the government and I'm here to help,'"[185] conservatives have been hell-bent on convincing all of us that government can't do anything right. That all it can do is spend—or waste—money.

But this ridiculous talking point ignores an entire national history of worthwhile investments—from Jefferson's Louisiana Purchase, to Lincoln's land-grant colleges, to FDR's New Deal, to Eisenhower's interstate highway system. All were investments made by our government that created enormous wealth in the long term for the nation in the form of new jobs, better education, and more efficient transportation. And they all more than paid for themselves by the increase in tax revenues that comes with increased economic activity.

After the crash, we must recapture this spirit of investment in the people.

Card Check

It's no coincidence that the rise of the oligarchs and the corporate state has coincided with the decimation of organized labor.

Repair the Fundamentals

As the rates of unionization have steadily declined over the last thirty-plus years, so, too, has the share of national income held by the middle class. And as union rates have declined, the share of wealth in the hands of the superrich has increased.

There is a direct correlation between the wealth inequality that pushed us to the Crash of 2016 and plummeting union rates.

With unionization rates at historic lows for modern America, it's clear labor needs a new weapon to fight back against the Royalists. They need what's called "card check."[186]

Under current law, if some workers want to form a union, then 35 percent of the workforce has to sign a petition or a card stating they agree to be unionized. From there the National Labor Relations Board will set up an election, and if half of the workforce votes to unionize, then they have a union.

Under this current procedure, employers have several tools— both legal and illegal—to disrupt the organizing process, including intimidating or firing employees, spreading lies and misinformation about unions, threatening to close down stores, delaying union elections, and so on. Organizing is an uphill battle, which is why union busters have been so successful breaking up unions while organizers have had so much trouble starting new unions.

But card check would level the playing field. With card check, there is no election and employers never have to catch wind of what's going on. Basically, if 50 percent of all the workers sign a petition or card indicating they support forming a union, then that union is immediately recognized by the NLRB without the extra, added step of an election and without an opportunity for employers to twist arms.

With card check, unions can reverse the tide in the war against labor and actually start chipping away at the corporate state. They can start demanding better wages and benefits, limiting political coercion in the workplace, and funding political candidates who will continue the fight in the halls of Congress.

In 2008, when Democrats took control of Congress, there was a huge push by labor to have card check passed. It was part of the Employee Free Choice Act, known as EFCA. Unfortunately, those efforts failed, and ever since then, card check has been absent from the national debate—a testament to how successful the Royalists have been in crushing organized labor.

But now is as good a time as ever to bring card check back.

Printing Money

FDR famously said, "The best welfare program is a job." And then he set about creating the WPA and the CCC and dozens of other institutions that put millions back to work.

Putting people back to work is always the best way to recover from an economic disaster. Jobs programs not only transformed people from being consumers of government resources (unemployment benefits and welfare) to being taxpayers but also produced goods and services that increased the overall value of the economy and the wealth of the nation.

The argument against government jobs programs during a time of recession is that they require deficit spending. Government deficits, it is said, are bad things that ultimately do bad things to economies.

Let's face it, however: That's a simple fallacy. When governments borrow money, they issue bonds. People in the private sector want a place to put their money that will return a reasonable interest rate on their investment and is supersafe. Government bonds fill that need. In fact, it would be safe to say that government deficits, in large part, simply represent private-sector savings. And the private sector needs a safe place to put its money.

Another strategy to produce the revenue for governments to become the employer of last resort is to simply issue the money. Our Constitution gives Congress this power. And a growing number of economists, led by Professor Stephanie Kelton, at the University of Missouri in Saint Louis, and Dr. Steve Keen, in Australia, are suggesting that during times of severe economic crisis a government should do just that.

The main argument against simply printing money is that it would depreciate the country's money supply, thus producing inflation. But this type of devaluation of currency inflation is extremely rare. So long as the government is only printing enough money to get employment up to full employment, or something close to it, these modern monetary theorists say there will be no inflation.

Instead, they say that inflation is caused by shortages. In the 1970s in the United States there was a shortage of oil caused by the Arab oil embargoes. Because oil is so intrinsic to so many parts of our economy, that caused shortages, and the resulting increase in the price of oil led to inflation.

Similarly, in Zimbabwe, when President Robert Mugabe took away farmland from farmers and passed it out to his cronies, most of them had no farming expertise. Because they didn't know how to farm, the crops failed, and there was a countrywide food shortage. The shortage of food drove up the price of food, which produced a general inflation, which devastated their economy.

In fact, the United States regularly brings money into being from nothing. During the banking crisis of 2008–09, the Federal Reserve created tens of trillions of dollars out of thin air, and distributed it to banks, corporations, and even wealthy individuals worldwide. It produced no inflation.

In general, with fiat currencies like we have here in the United States, the money supply should expand or contract to reflect the overall size of the economy. So when money is brought into being to put people back to work, and when those working people are now expanding the economy, that "printed" money is not inflationary. And by putting people back to work, the government ends the depression.

Jubilee

The largest of the economic dislocations of the post-Reaganomics era has been in the area of debt. As productivity has climbed since 1980, wages have remained flat, and enormous profits have gone to corporations, with fat paychecks going to their CEOs and stockholders. But workers have seen no gains, so they've had to turn their homes into ATMs, rely on their credit cards, and have their children take out student loans. Debt has exploded.

While government debt in the United States is in the neighborhood of $15 trillion, private-sector debt is over $40 trillion. This is absolutely unprecedented for our nation, and will make it very difficult to climb out of the hole that the Great Crash of 2016 will cause.

Unwinding this debt will be one of the largest challenges our government will confront. And one tried-and-true method to unwind debt is called a "debt jubilee."

The biblical jubilee happened every fifty years, when all the wealth was distributed evenly to everybody, and all the slaves were freed. A debt jubilee would have to be much more selective.

For example, we currently have over $1 trillion in student loan debt in the United States. Arguably, none of this debt should ever have been run up. College education is free in most developed countries, and it used to be free in much of the United States. So if the government were to simply take that $1 trillion in debt and wipe it out, it would go a long way toward saving working-class America and our economy.

Housing debt is a bit more complex, but FDR created what was, in effect, a housing-debt jubilee in the 1930s. He created a government agency that bought up people's distressed mortgages, and rolled them over into thirty-year, low-interest, fixed-rate loans. By the time the last of these loans were paid off in the 1960s, the federal government had actually shown a profit on the program. And while it didn't much help the banksters, it saved millions of American homeowners.

Repair the Fundamentals

Since the banking crisis of 2008, our federal government has been largely playing the same role, only for the mortgage companies instead of the consumers. Over 95 percent of all new mortgage debt in that time has been backstopped by the federal government. It would be much more efficient to take the bankers out of the equation, and for the government to simply become the *lender* of last resort for its citizens, just like it should be the *employer* of last resort.

No Billionaires!

And finally, after the Crash of 2016, it's time we as a nation have a serious discussion about outlawing billionaires.

Just ahead of the Great Crash, the wealthiest one hundred people in the world had a combined net worth of $1.9 trillion—making them wealthier than the entire GDP of nations such as Italy, Mexico, Spain, Canada, Australia, and about 170 other nations.

This is the economy we got when Ronald Reagan and the Royalists drastically slashed taxes on the superrich in the early 1980s.

But just as we learned during the Gilded Age and the Crash of 2016, it's impossible to build a healthy, stable economy on the backs of a few billionaires.

That's because billionaires are not job creators; they are somewhere between symbionts and parasites. That's not meant as a personal insult against billionaires, many of whom are decent people. But it's meant as a statement of common sense. If vast fortunes are being hoarded in the hands of very few people who can't possibly spend that much money in their lifetime or their kids' lifetime or even their kids' kids' kids' kids' lifetime, then it's essentially being wasted.

This is the point billionaire Nick Hanauer was making in his recent TED talk[187] explaining why rich people aren't job creators. As he said, "There can never be enough superrich Americans to power a great economy. The annual earnings of people like me are hundreds, if not thousands, of times greater than those of the median American, but we don't buy hundreds or thousands of times more stuff."

If the four hundred richest billionaires in America could generate just as much economic activity alone as the rest of us can, then maybe there'd be an argument for such vast wealth. But they can't. The typical billionaire doesn't buy thousands more pairs of pants, or dine out thousands more times, or buy thousands more cars than the typical working-class American.

Hanauer concludes, "I can't buy enough of anything to make up for the fact that millions of unemployed and underemployed Americans can't buy any new clothes or cars or enjoy any meals out. Or to make up for the decreasing consumption of the vast majority of American families that are barely squeaking by, buried by spiraling costs and trapped by stagnant or declining wages."

Imagine walking into a classroom of kindergarteners and finding that just one kid is in possession of nearly all the toys. Just one kid has thousands of toy cars, army men, and building blocks piled up like Scrooge's money bin, filling half the classroom; one or two of the kids have a dozen or so toys; and the rest of the class of kids have to share just one dinky, old rag doll. No one could possibly think that's a healthy way of distributing toys to a kindergarten class. That one kid couldn't even play with all his toys.

Would we call that kid a toy creator? Would we tell all the other kindergarteners that they can only play with toys when that one student decides to share them?

Of course not. Yet that's exactly what we do with billionaires in our economy. Billionaires who can't spend all the money they have, and are more and more reluctant to invest that money in their workers, their businesses, or their communities.

So what good are they?

It's time to put in place a new wealth tax in America, one that prevents the accumulation of all wealth over $1 billion. If you can't get by on $1,000 million, then you probably shouldn't have access to that much money in the first place. There's nobody who can't make it on $1 billion. So any wealth over $1 billion, 100 percent of it goes to helping the rest of the country have a decent life.

That money can lift 49 million Americans out of poverty and move the 46 million Americans on food stamps into the middle class. They will—by the "invisible hand" of human instinct and need—better know how to spend the money and generate economic activity than the billionaire class, which currently has its excess trillions stashed in off-shore bank accounts.

This wealth tax would also break up giant monopolies and open up the market for small businesses. We shouldn't rely just on the Bain Capitals and the Koch brothers to start or buy up new businesses. If the riches of the billionaire class were redistributed (a word progressives should embrace), then more and more Americans could have access to start-up capital and earn a living as entrepreneurs.

Trust me, the billionaires can spare it. The total wealth of the average American family is $57,000.[188] Convert that into hundred-dollar bills, and it's a stack about two inches tall. The one-percenters, at an income of around $300,000 a year, earn a stack every year that's about a foot high. But the average wealth of the billionaires on the Forbes 400 list is $4.2 billion. Convert that into a stack of hundred-dollar bills and it would reach over two miles into the sky. It would be a navigation risk to aircraft.

It's time to start funneling the riches produced by the American economy to the real job creators: working-class people who are spending money. And the best way to do that is to roll back the Bush and Reagan tax cuts, and reinstitute as much as a 90 percent top marginal income tax rate on the Royalists—where it was throughout the middle part of the twentieth century, America's golden age of the middle class.

Chapter 14

Green Revolution

[F]or the sake of our children and our future, we must do more to combat climate change… [T]he fact is the twelve hottest years on record have all come in the last fifteen. Heat waves, droughts, wildfires, floods—all are now more frequent and more intense. We can choose to believe that Superstorm Sandy, and the most severe drought in decades, and the worst wildfires some states have ever seen were all just a freak coincidence. Or we can choose to believe in the overwhelming judgment of science—and act before it's too late.
—President Barack Obama, 2013
State of the Union Address

One of the biggest challenges we face when it comes to ending wars is what President Dwight D. Eisenhower termed the "military-industrial complex."

When you drive out to the wealthy Virginia suburbs just a few miles from the Pentagon, you can find communities—both gated and open (but with private security patrolling the streets)—with mile after mile of mansions. Ten-, twenty-, thirty-bedroom affairs, with six- or ten-car garages, and a house in the back where the butlers, maids, cooks, nannies, gardeners, pool man, and other servants live.

These are the homes of the CEOs and senior executives and lob-byists for the military-industrial complex (which, since 9/11, has added "security" to its name). Missiles, drones, and tanks; nerve gas, weaponized anthrax, and biological weapons; nuclear bombs, X-ray body/truck/building scanners, and electronics to spy on everybody from the Chinese to you and me—all built these homes. And the people who live in them get richer and richer whenever we march off to war.

While there are—literally—millions of people who make their living off the war machine central to the American Empire, the really big bucks are concentrated in the hands of a few dozen corpora-tions and their suppliers. That consolidation makes them very, very powerful when it comes time to decide how much money to spend with phony Astroturf "Citizens for a Better America" type of adver-tisements to either build up or tear down any particular member of Congress or candidate for president.

Similarly, our power industries are concentrated in only a few hundred hands nationwide. Hub-and-spoke centralized power gen-eration is how this country started, with George Westinghouse and Thomas Edison competing to see who would ultimately build the giant power plants from which tendrils of high-tension lines would supply entire cities with electricity. (Westinghouse won the com-petition, by the way, because Edison stubbornly held on to direct current—DC—power when the advantages of alternating current—AC—were so manifold.)

So there is only one power line going into your home, and it's coming from one power substation for your neighborhood, which is supplied by one giant power plant that's feeding a large chunk of your town.

Grids and smart grids allow various power companies to share capacity and load, buying and selling electricity back and forth on the fly and by the second when necessary, but at the end of the day you and I write a check to one company.

That company is your local entry point into—or handcuff to—the power-industrial complex.

They like big. Big nuclear plants. Big coal plants. Big dams. Big oil- or gas-fired plants.

By keeping things centralized and big, they're able to ensure they can always, forever and ever, skim a few dollars out of your wallet every day for your electricity.

Which is why it's such a good idea to decentralize our power systems.

Decentralization

Big Power is jumping on Big Solar and Big Wind projects like there's no tomorrow—they already have a business model that works for it. And to some extent this isn't a bad thing: We have to make a transition from Big Coal and nuclear plants to something, and with the existing grid and distribution systems in place, these companies are ideally situated to be agents of that change.

But what happens when a critical mass of people figure out they can live, like my friend Hal Cohen, without ever having to send a penny to a power company?

Hal and Shelley live just outside Montpelier, Vermont—about as northern and mountainous a place as you'll find in America. They have a beautiful, spacious house, with all the modern appliances and amenities. And there is no electric power wire coming to their house, and never has been.

Hal's house is a more modern version of thousands built nation-wide back in the late 1970s, when President Jimmy Carter had pushed through Congress a series of bills that made it profitable to build off-the-grid houses. He explicitly said, in an address to the nation in 1979, that his goal was to have 20 percent of the nation's power produced by solar energy by the year 2000. And with the programs he put into place, we would have easily reached it.

Every time Louise and I move (which has been about every five years for the past forty-plus that we've been married), be it in Georgia, New Hampshire, Oregon, or Vermont, the realtors have always either had or known of off-the-grid houses for sale. And these houses were almost always either very recent or built between 1978 and 1982, when Ronald Reagan killed off the programs in a nod to his big-energy financial supporters.

The Tipping Point

If you type "solar power rooftop shingles" into a search engine, over three million hits come back. At the top is a 2010 video review that *Consumer Reports* did of Dow's new "Powerhouse Solar Shingles," which the company was just then rolling out. They require no wires or wiring—and so can be installed by a normal roofer using normal roofing nails. They look pretty much like asphalt shingles, and protect the roof of the house the same or better. And they can generate "from forty to sixty percent" of all the electricity a home needs (and that's assuming the home hasn't been superinsulated and appliances haven't been upgraded to low-power-consumption types).

At the moment, according to *Consumer Reports*, it costs about $25,000 to cover your roof with Dow's new photovoltaic shingles, but federal tax advantages can cut that price by a third, and state tax incentives can drop it even further.

Meanwhile, a new technology was announced in late 2011 that allows solar-electric-generating panels to be created using an ink-jet printing technique to apply the light-catching/electricity-producing material, rather than the now-current "gas diffusion" method, which requires large machines, lots of heat, and wastes much of the material. The cost of solar panels is dropping like a stone, pretty much following Moore's Law—every year or two the price drops by half, while the capability doubles. As of this writing, solar panels are competitive with any other form of electricity generation, and far cheaper than coal or nuclear when you monetize the externalities such as fly ash, smoke/mercury, and nuclear waste. Wind is even cheaper. Both solar and wind will become so inexpensive soon—perhaps even by the time you read these words—that the tipping point will have been reached and most all of the investment, development, and research money and effort will be there.

As will people's homes.

Just as America now faces an unsustainable thirst for energy, so, too, was Germany faced with a power crisis in the late 1990s. Growing demands for electricity collided with the reality that the country has no oil reserves and a strong bias among its people against building new nuclear power plants in the wake of the nearby Chernobyl meltdown.

Yet the government knew that the country needed the electricity equivalent of at least one or two nuclear power plants over the next decade. So, how to generate that much electricity without nuclear power?

In 1999, progressives in Germany passed the 100,000 Roofs Program,[189] which mandated that banks had to provide low-interest ten-year loans to homeowners sufficient for them to put solar panels on their houses. They then passed the Renewable Energy Law and integrated the 100,000 Roofs Program into it in 2004.[190] The REL mandated that for the next ten years, the power company had to buy power back from those homeowners at a level substantially above the going rate so that the homeowners' income from the solar panels would equal their loan payment on the panels and would also represent the actual cost to the power company to generate that amount of power by building a new nuclear power plant.

At the end of the ten years, the power company gets to buy solar power at its regular rate, and it now has a new source of power without having to pay to maintain (and eventually dismantle) a nuclear reactor. In fact, while the reactor would have a twenty-to-thirty-year life span, the solar panels typically last fifty years.

For the homeowners, it was a no-brainer: They were getting low-interest loans from banks for the solar panels, and the power companies were paying for the power generated from those panels at a rate high enough to pay off the loans. It was like getting solar-power panels for free.

If anything, the government underestimated how rapidly Germans would embrace the program, and thus how much power would be produced by the program, and how quickly. By 2007, Germany accounted for about half of the entire world's solar market. Just that one year, 2007, saw 1,300 megawatts (millions of watts) of solar-generating capacity brought on line across the country.[191]

For comparison, consider that the average generating capacity of each of the last five nuclear power plants brought on line in the United States is 1,160 megawatts.[192]

In 2008, Germany added 2,000 megawatts of solar power to their grid, and in 2009 homeowners and businesses put onto their roofs enough solar panels to glean an additional 2,500 megawatts. Although the goal for the first decade of this century was to generate around 3,000 megawatts, eliminating the need to build two new nuclear power plants, this simple, no-risk program had instead added over 8,500 megawatts of power.

And, because the generation sources were scattered across the country, there was no need to run new high-tension power lines from central generating stations, making it more efficient and less expensive. Meanwhile, as dozens of German companies got into the business of manufacturing and installing solar-power systems, the cost dropped by more than half between 1997 and 2007, and continues to plummet.[193]

The Germans expect that by 2050 more than a quarter of all their electricity will come from solar (it's now just over 1 percent), adding to the roughly 12.5 percent of all German energy currently being produced by renewable energy sources (mostly hydro, but also including wind, biomass, and geothermal).[194]

The solar-panel program has been so successful that the German government is now thinking that it's time to back off and leave this to the marketplace. As the *New York Times* noted in May 2008:

> Thanks to its aggressive push into renewable energies, cloud-wreathed Germany has become an unlikely leader in the race to harness the sun's energy. It has by far the largest market for photovoltaic systems, which convert sunlight into electricity, with roughly half of the world's total installations...
>
> Now, though, with so many solar panels on so many rooftops, critics say Germany has too much of a good thing—even in a time of record oil prices. Conservative lawmakers, in particular, want to pare back generous government incentives that support solar development. They say solar generation is growing so fast that it threatens to overburden consumers with high electricity bills.[195]

Translation: The solar-panel manufacturers want the subsidies to stop so they can catch up with demand and then bump up the price, and profits. Because of the subsidies, prices have been dropping faster than manufacturing costs.

Germany is now considering incentives to its world-famous domestic auto industry to manufacture flex-fuel plug-in hybrid automobiles that can get over 500 miles per gallon of (strategic) gasoline (boosted by domestically produced rooftop solar) with existing technology.

Meanwhile, Denmark has invested billions into having more than half of its entire auto fleet using only electricity by 2030.

And China is no slouch when it comes to renewable energy. Although the Chinese continue to bring another dirty coal-fired power plant on line about once a week, they surpassed every other nation in the world in 2010 in direct investment in the production of solar and wind power. As the *Los Angeles Times* reported in March 2010:

> U.S. clean energy investments hit $18.6 billion last year, a report from the Pew Charitable Trusts said, a little more than half the Chinese total of $34.6 billion. Five years ago, China's investments in clean energy totaled just $2.5 billion. The United States also slipped behind 10 other countries, including Canada and Mexico, in clean energy investments as a share of the national economy...
>
> [T]he Pew report pointed to another factor constraining U.S. competitiveness: a lack of national mandates for renewable energy production or a surcharge on greenhouse gas emissions that would make fossil fuels more expensive.[196]

The ultimate "power to the people" is for homes to have their own solar roofs, no longer needing power lines from distant power plants owned by big transnational corporations.

A few countries are pushing this solar tipping point, like China and Germany. Jimmy Carter started us in this direction a generation ago, but Reagan and the Bushes paused it, and we've never recovered. Ironically, if our government doesn't participate in bringing along the tipping point to solar and other renewable-energy systems, it'll happen anyway because of the strong demand in other nations that is driving the technology to be cheaper and more easily accessed. The only downside for us will be that, like with our clothes and computers and TVs and pretty much everything else except weaponry, we'll be buying our solar panels from overseas.

The final point, which I also noted in my book *Rebooting the American Dream*, is that if we don't strip oil of its strategic value, we will continue to be at the mercy of OPEC—which comprises more than a few nations that don't much like us.

Stripping Oil of Its Strategic Value

Two hundred years ago, and for a thousand years before that, one of the most strategic substances on earth was salt. It was "strategic" because no army could travel without it—salt was necessary to preserve food in a prerefrigeration era. Wars were fought over it, and countries that had lots of salt made out well, while landlocked countries with no salt reserves were forced to sell their natural resources in exchange for it.

Oil is the new salt. It is now the planet's number one strategic resource. And as has been noted by numerous commentators since the first Gulf War, in 1990–91, if the primary export of Iraq was broccoli, we wouldn't have given a damn that Saddam Hussein was a tin-pot tyrant.

The unfortunate reality is that we have within and around our national boundaries about 3 percent of the world's oil, but we consume about 24 percent of the world's produced oil. So we buy what we don't produce. This dependence represents a massive transfer of wealth from us to oil-producing countries. It's a strategic blunder that would have horrified Julius Caesar, who expanded the Roman Empire all the way to central Europe when he ran out of fuel—wood—by deforesting virtually all of Italy,* and then paid the price as his empire began to collapse from overexpansion.

---

* The most conspicuous consequence of the deforestation of Italy during the early years of Caesar's rule was the "currency crisis," in which the cost of refining the silver used in Roman coins doubled—because the cost of the wood used to fire the smelters more than doubled. Some historians argue that this moment—when Rome could no longer supply its own energy needs—was the first signal of the beginning of the end of the Roman Empire. Interestingly, 1970 is widely accepted as the "peak oil" year for the United States, when our domestic oil supplies began an irreversible slide and our imports began to shoot up from 10 to 20 percent into the 50 to 60 percent range, where they are today. Then president Richard Nixon called for an alternative-energy strategy to get us off oil, and President Jimmy Carter actually put one in place in 1978, but Ronald Reagan rolled it back in 1981, leading directly to a dramatic increase in our imports of foreign oil.

Countries like Saudi Arabia rake in billions from oil-dependent countries like the United States, and oil revenues fuel their economies. In 2008, for instance, Saudi oil revenues spiked to $281 billion, a quadrupling of revenues from 2002. In 2009, those fell sharply to $115 billion, still nothing to sneeze at.[197] Oil revenues fund much of the fundamentalist Wahhabi movement within Saudi Arabia, and it's out of this movement that come the most virulent anti-American and anti-Semitic rhetoric, textbooks, and television and radio programming.

Thirty years ago, the OPEC nations were producing around 30 million barrels a day, nearly half of the world oil consumption. Regardless of how much we buy from them or instead buy from Mexico, because oil is a fungible commodity, their production will continue and just go to others who are no longer buying from whomever we choose to buy from. The proof of this is that today OPEC production is still around 30 million barrels—even though world oil consumption has gone up and is now around 85 million barrels a day. The OPEC nations don't adjust production to meet demand; they maintain it to control prices so they have relatively stable income.

Thus, the only way we can change this situation is to reduce the amount of oil we use. Oil is a strategic commodity, and we need to strip it of its strategic value.

So what do we use all that oil for that makes it a strategic resource? We certainly don't use it to produce electricity—only 2 percent of our electricity is generated by oil, because we have huge domestic supplies of coal, which produce over half of our electricity. Pretty much nobody is producing electricity with oil except the oil-rich countries of the Middle East—even rapidly-growing countries like China and India, for example, are not producing oil-fired power plants.

Thus, moving to solar, wind, biomass, or even nuclear power to generate electricity in the United States will help tremendously with our CO_2 output and all the pollution "externalities" associated with coal—but it will not make us less oil dependent or strip oil of its strategic significance.

The simple fact is that oil accounts for roughly 95 percent of the energy used for transportation in the United States (our military is the world's single largest consumer of oil), and that's what makes it "strategic." If we want to strip oil of its strategic value so it can't be used as a weapon against us and so we can use our remaining oil supplies for rational things, such as producing plastics and medicines, we need to shift our transportation sector away from oil, and do so quickly.

This has been the essence of T. Boone Pickens's rant, although the eccentric oil billionaire is now a natural-gas billionaire, and he's suggesting that we convert our truck fleet in this country from oil to natural gas, which is nearly as bad a source of greenhouse gases as is oil. He's right that such a change would make us stronger and safer, both militarily and strategically, but he misses the global-warming part of the equation (which is also increasingly becoming a strategic issue, as global climate deterioration leads to crises both at home and abroad).

Europe, Japan, and China are moving fast to shift their transportation sectors from oil to electricity, mostly through the use of trains. Brazil did it over the past twenty years by mandating that all cars and trucks sold would have to be "flex fuel"—capable of burning gasoline or ethanol, diesel or biodiesel. The result is that Brazil now provides nearly half of their transportation needs with domestically grown ethanol made from sugarcane (over 80 percent of their cars and trucks are now flex-fuel). And the added cost to Brazilian drivers to buy a flex-fuel car instead of gasoline or diesel-only car? About $100.

China is similarly moving in the direction of flex-fuel cars, and doubling every year their methanol production (mostly derived from domestically produced coal).

Flex-fuel cars can also burn part-ethanol, part-gasoline. If, for example, we were to shift to only 20 percent of the fuel being used by a car being gasoline (the remainder being ethanol or methanol), then a single gallon of gas would go five times as far. A 40-mpg car would become a 200-mpg vehicle in terms of the strategic resource of oil-derived gasoline.

Most significantly, in the United States, fully half of all automobiles are driven fewer than twenty miles in any given day. This is an easy range for an electric-only or a plug-in hybrid car, and by moving to the latter immediately—mandating them—we could shift the entire US auto fleet to consuming 50 percent or more electricity instead of gas/diesel in less than a decade, stripping oil of half its strategic importance.

And our trade policies are really stupid on this. We have no import tariff whatsoever on oil, so there is nothing to discourage American drivers from using foreign-produced oil products to fuel their cars and trucks. But we charge an import tariff of over a half a dollar a gallon on ethanol, discouraging Americans from using the fuel and discouraging the more than one hundred countries in the world where there's enough intense sunlight and where sugarcane grows well from becoming net fuel exporters. And while we offer billions in tax breaks and incentives to oil, gas, and coal companies in the United States, we don't subsidize or support with tax subsidies (as the Danes are doing) electric or part-electric cars, either in their production or on the consumer end.

If we add to all of this some good scientific innovation in developing a mix of low-carbon energy resources (biomass, geothermal, wind, tidal power, and so on), and can figure out a way to strip the carbon dioxide out of our power-plant smokestacks (and our atmosphere) and turn it into a solid (calcium carbonate—which you can buy at the store under the brand name Tums—is a good candidate for a desirable product produced by binding carbon, in this case to calcium), it's not inconceivable that by 2050 we could cut our CO_2 emissions by over 80 percent. And perhaps even decades sooner, if we begin now.[198] Plus we could strip oil of its strategic value and make our nation independent of Middle Eastern dictatorships.

Tipping Point Reached

A new study by the research firm Bloomberg New Energy Finance has found that unsubsidized renewable energy is now cheaper than fossil fuels such as coal and gas.

In fact, it's a lot cheaper.

Data show that wind farms in Australia can produce energy at AU\$80/MWh (megawatt hour). Meanwhile, coal plants are producing energy at AU\$143/MWh and gas at AU\$116/MWh.

Unlike the United States, where energy companies can pollute and have the costs (from illness to environmental degradation) picked up by the taxpayers, Australia has a carbon tax, which partially explains why renewables have a price advantage. But the data show that even without the cost of the carbon tax factored in, wind energy is still 14 cents cheaper than coal and 18 cents cheaper than gas.

And this is in a nation that relies more heavily on coal than any other industrialized nation in the world. But that coal reliance will soon change, because companies in Australia are quickly adopting new, cheaper, renewable energies. As the study found, banks and lending institutions in Australia are now less and less likely to finance new coal plants, because they've simply become a bad investment.

And while Australian wind is cheapest now, by 2020—and maybe sooner—solar power will also be cheaper than coal and gas in Australia. The energy game is rapidly changing in that country.

Michael Liebreich, the chief executive of Bloomberg New Energy

Finance, noted, "The perception that fossil fuels are cheap and renewables are expensive is now out of date."

Well, here's a news flash: That perception has been out of date for a while now—even right here in the United States.

According to the Energy Information Administration,[199] looking ahead to 2016, natural gas is the cheapest energy in the United States at roughly \$66/MWh. Coal comes in second at \$94/MWh. But right behind coal is renewable wind at \$97/MWh, which in large part accounts for why US wind energy production has tripled since 2000.

And, unlike in Australia, none of those US prices account for the externalities associated with fossil fuels, consequences such as pollution, cancers, the need for military protection, or global warming. In America, the fossil-fuel industry has made sure those externalities are paid for not by the coal and gas energy producers but instead by you and me.

The fossil-fuel industry doesn't pay a penny of the cost of rapidly accelerating climate change. Or the health care costs from exhaust- and refinery-driven diseases and deaths from air, water, and other pollution. Not to mention the community costs of decreasing property values when a coal plant is put in your backyard. Nor do they put a cent toward the cost of our navy keeping the oil-shipping lanes open or of our soldiers "protecting" the countries that "produce" all that oil.

All of these externalities come with fossil-fuel production, but pretty much don't exist with renewable-energy production. And those externality costs are not only not paid for by the fossil-fuel industry—they're never even mentioned in the corporate-run "news" media in America.

Research from the *Annals of the New York Academy of Sciences* concludes that the total cost of these externalities, if paid by the polluters themselves, would raise US fossil-fuel prices by as much as nearly

$3/MWh.[200] And that's an extremely conservative estimate. Which puts wind power on parity with coal in America.

The trend lines here are pretty clear: Buggywhip, meet automobile!

Renewables are getting cheaper, and fossil fuels are getting more expensive.

Which is why we as a nation need to throw everything we have at making renewable energies our primary way of powering America into the twenty-first century.

Think of it as a new Apollo Project. We need green energy, local energy, and a twenty-first-century smart grid to handle it all.

Over time, the marketplace could do this. But markets are reactive, not active. With just about every developed country in the world ahead of us, and our dependence on oil making us more and more tightly bound to Middle Eastern dictators and radicals, to wait and hope that big transnational corporations will help birth a new America is both naive and stupid. Instead of depending on them, we should be recovering from them the cost of their externalities with a carbon tax that can be used to build that new energy infrastructure for America.

Let's take a lesson from Australia and the Eurozone, which have both set up carbon taxes to make nineteenth-century energy barons pay for at least some of the damage they've done. And then use that revenue for a green-energy revolution here in America.

The way to get there is known. The products are available. The pressure is growing, from climate change–induced disasters to a growing recognition that transferring $1 billion a day to other countries (and big transnational corporations) to buy oil is no way to live.

In January 2013, in Chattanooga, Tennessee, a massive solar-power facility comprising over 33,600 individual solar modules capable of producing 13.1 gigawatt hours of electricity every year was turned on.[201] It's big enough to power 1,200 homes, but will be used to power a Volkswagen manufacturing plant. And it's the biggest solar installation ever built in the state of Tennessee.

Green Revolution

Also, the United States just surpassed Germany as the number two country in the world when it comes to producing wind power. The largest wind farm in the world, the Alta Wind Energy Center,[202] is located right here in the United States in Kern County, California. The Department of Energy estimates that 20 percent of our national energy could be produced by wind come 2030.[203]

After the Crash of 2016, we must move forward with new energy.

Chapter 15

Democratize the Economy

The few own the many because they possess the means of livelihood of all... The country is governed for the richest, for the corporations, the bankers, the land speculators, and for the exploiters of labor. The majority of mankind are working people. So long as their fair demands—the ownership and control of their livelihoods—are set at naught, we can have neither men's rights nor women's rights. The majority of mankind is ground down by industrial oppression in order that the small remnant may live in ease.

—Helen Keller, 1911

I got picked up in a cab by a lawyer.

I was in Madison, Wisconsin, to speak, for the second year in a row, at the "Fighting Bob Fest," where about ten thousand progressives from the upper Midwest have gotten together every year for the past decade (at the suggestion of Jim Hightower, and organized by Ed Garvey) to celebrate the memory of progressive Republican "Fighting Bob" La Follette. I gave one of several keynote addresses along with Senator Bernie Sanders, Cornel West, and Greg Palast, among others.

Democratize the Economy

But this year was different from previous years at Fighting Bob Fest. The new governor, Scott Walker, had launched his attack on unions, sparking hundreds of thousands of Wisconsinites and other supporters of unions from across America to gather on the lawns of the capitol in Madison in protest. With the unions mobilized, recall elections were launched against several Republican state senators, and were successful against two, nearly tipping the balance of power in the state senate back to the Democrats. Soon, a recall campaign would be launched against Governor Scott Walker himself.

So there was an incredible energy among progressives in Wisconsin that year, one that was most palpable at the Fighting Bob Fest. But it was when I was being shuffled around the Badger State by taxicab that I caught a whiff of true progressivism at work. It was on a ride back to my hotel that I encountered an economic model that could be our nation's savior after the Great Crash of 2016.

The Silent Revolution

There's something just below the surface that most of us are unaware of in America.

While the all-powerful profit motive dominates the global economy, there's a new and very far-reaching economy that's sprung up in just the last few decades that's trying something different. It's the cooperative economy.

Currently, one billion people around the world are members of cooperatives.

While each cooperative is run differently, they all have the same characteristic: democracy in the workplace. There is no all-powerful CEO determining the pay for himself and his workers, there is no secret board of directors looking out for the best interest of unknown shareholders.

A cooperative is managed and owned by its workers. Usually through a small fee, an employee can buy a stake in the co-op and be part of the decision-making process—one person, one vote. As business gets better, the profits don't go to the very top, they are spread among the workers, incentivizing everyone to work harder and sell more together—hence the name "cooperative."

In communism everything is owned by the entire state, by everybody. That is a profound and radical difference from co-ops. Worker-owned co-ops are arguably a form of capitalism, where workers hold the capital in individual companies. With communism, the state controls the means of both supply and distribution.

And a billion people around the world rely on cooperatives—from people banking at credit unions to farmers joining together to sell their crops as a cooperative enterprise. Not only that, the United Nations estimates that 3 billion people, nearly half the global population, has been positively affected by a cooperative enterprise. It's no coincidence that cooperatives are popping up so frequently and having such an impact around the world at this particular moment.

In his book *America Beyond Capitalism*, historian and author Gar Alperovitz refers to the emerging cooperative model as the new way forward in a global economy that has witnessed state socialism fail and is now witnessing corporate capitalism fail.

I had a conversation with Gar and he told me, warning about the impending failure of corporate capitalism, "There's either another way forward over the long haul or I think we're in for real trouble and decay—and decay is what we're seeing."

The rest of the world has already seen that decay and has moved toward co-ops.

In 2001, Argentina went into an economic crisis after it told the IMF to get off its back and defaulted on its $132 billion foreign debt. Suddenly, the world's seventh largest economy at the time collapsed. A quarter of the population was unemployed; the middle class disappeared into the working-poor class. People went hungry and turned desperate, leading to a surge in violence and crime. And many of the 1 percent fled or moved their money and assets offshore.

Democratize the Economy

I was in the nation's capital, Buenos Aires, in September 2002 to give a speech. I was staying with friends in an upper-middle-class part of town (Palermo), and the crash was beginning to resolve. The looting of the previous year was over, the new president was stabilizing the country, the peso was becoming stable, but the unemployment crisis was still very, very real.

One of the clearest memories I have of that time and that visit was of driving down the streets of this nice neighborhood and seeing, in front of every third or fourth house, a pile of furniture or TVs or tools with a for-sale sign and price. People were selling their belongings just to pay for food and rent.

With no one able to buy their goods, factory owners in Argentina had shut down in search of new consumers and new workers elsewhere. Collapses aren't good for business. This was a nation that had seen its social democracy overthrown and replaced by a corporate capitalist system; and that system had just imploded and hit rock bottom. The country was now desperately searching for a new way forward.

And they found it right in front of their eyes.

In the weeks after the crash, the people began returning to the now-empty and gutted factories that they had worked in before the crash. Initially, they just started sleeping there, hoping they'd be first in line to work should the CEOs ever return and open up shop again. But that never happened.

And then they just started working on their own. They fixed up the machines, elected a small commission of people to coordinate the work, and went right back to manufacturing stuff. Through democratic procedures, the workers decided how they would spend the profits, first paying off the debts the factory owed to get it back on its feet, then spreading the rest out in salary among themselves.

Since then, the cooperative model has flourished, and Argentina is again a thriving economy less than a decade after the crash. Today, there are 16,000 cooperatives in Argentina, employing

300,000 people and making up 10 percent of the nation's GDP. One out of every four Argentinians does business with a cooperative and thus has some sort of say in how money is spent in the economy.

Gar calls this "democratizing capital," which is taking the flow of money—whether it's workers' wages, reinvestment, or profits—and putting it up to a vote among those who are most affected by that money, such as the workers themselves, the customers, and the community. That's different from corporate capitalism, in which the CEO or a small board of directors and shareholders exclusively makes the decisions about capital.

For decades, our economy has felt the pain of corporations deciding to close millions of factories and send tens of millions of jobs offshore. It has been polluted by millions of tons of toxic gas into the atmosphere and ground and water that have poisoned entire cities. And it has been victimized by theft, as 100 percent of the excess profits made thanks to forty years of automation and increased efficiency have gone to corporate executives rather than paid to workers through higher wages and more leisure time. Given all of this, democratizing capital sure seems like a damn good idea.

Not only that, cooperatives can be just as competitive in the global market as transnational corporations.

The Dragon's Mountain

There's a small town in Spain, nestled away in the shadow of a mountain that used to house a vicious dragon. It's called Mondragón—and it's home to the largest cooperative federation in the entire world.

That dragon—now long extinct—was likely a brutal lord or local king who terrorized the people of the small town during the feudal dark ages. But now, as the United States and other Western economies descend into a form of neofeudalism with predatory transnational corporations terrorizing labor around the world, Mondragón is a beacon of hope for a new capitalism.

Back in 2009, Louise and I visited the town that lies in the shadow of the mountain, as well as the Mondragon Cooperative, which employs more than ninety thousand people in more than 250 different companies focused on retail, finance, industry, and knowledge. In 2008, Mondragon's revenue was $24.2 billion—and every single penny of profit was either reinvested back in the business, given to charity, or paid as dividends to Mondragon's worker-owners.

Unlike the top-down nature of most capitalistic businesses—and even communism—Mondragon and other cooperatives have flipped the pyramid upside-down. There are no CEOs making two thousand times more than the average worker, there is no board demanding higher and higher profits and pushing for offshoring, there is no contract with an outside acquisition firm, such as Mitt Romney's Bain Capital, to "trim the fat." The workers are trusted to determine the best direction for their company, for themselves, and for the economy.

I saw firsthand how decisions are made at Mondragon as I stood on the spotless factory floor of a washing-machine manufacturing plant within Mondragon. All around me, worker-owners at the state-of-the-art industrial facility were converting sheet metal into finished washing-machine parts and assembling electronics to go in those washing machines on a U-shaped assembly line. That's when a "manager" walked up asking for everyone's attention. He notified his colleagues that the following Thursday there needed to be a schedule change due to a local event and therefore a different number of units would have to be produced.

Rather than giving new orders regarding how the workers were supposed to deal with the change, he ceded his authority to those on the assembly line and asked, "How do you think we should do this?"

Then a conversation took place. The workers offered suggestions, critiquing the strengths and weaknesses of each idea. There was no arguing or complaining or fighting; it was an exchange of ideas, with the "manager" listening attentively as though he was actually the one who was being told how things would change next Thursday.

Ten minutes or so passed and a consensus was reached on how the factory would adjust; the "manager" thanked everyone and walked off; and the machine and conveyor belts were turned back on. It was true democracy in the workplace.

But cooperatives are just one way of "democratizing capital." Germany has another way.

The Mercedes and the Labor Union

When the American auto companies were on the verge of failure following the financial crisis of 2008, the Obama administration moved to bail them out.

Conservatives were outraged. Mitt Romney in particular called for letting the American auto industry go bankrupt. Since most of the American auto plants employed unionized workers, a bankruptcy would have allowed the companies to renegotiate union contracts and pensions, thus continuing the right-wing assault on unions.

At the time, the Economic Royalists argued that American auto companies were failing not because they were getting destroyed in the market by better-quality cars made overseas or by irresponsible free-trade policies but instead because they were paying unionized workers far too much. In today's global economy, the Royalists insisted, workers had to take pay cuts so that the corporation they worked for could be more profitable and more competitive in the global market. You can call it the growing pains of globalization.

But is it true? Do American workers really need to lose wages for the sake of our economy?

Not if we just do what Germany is doing. In 2010, Germany

manufactured 5.5 million cars. The United States manufactured less than half that—just 2.7 million cars. So according to the logic of the Economic Royalist—Germany must pay their autoworkers jack, right?

Actually, Germany paid their autoworkers about $67 an hour (including wages and benefits). But the United States paid its average worker only $33 an hour (also including wages and benefits). On top of that, German car manufacturers were highly profitable, despite the comparatively large paychecks of their workers. BMW earned a before-tax profit of 3.8 billion euros, and Mercedes-Benz hauled in profits of 4.6 billion euros.

So how did Germany just completely blow up the Royalist myth that car companies have to pay their workers less to be more profitable and manufacture more cars? How can Germany do the opposite: pay their workers more, be more profitable, and make more cars?

The answer: democracy.

First, Germans have completely democratized the auto plant by unionizing nearly every single autoworker in the country—under IG Metall, the German autoworkers union. With such a high union membership rate, autoworkers hold a lot of sway when they threaten to go on strike. That's how workers have been able to keep wages high and working conditions satisfactory. But as Horst Mund, the head of the International Department of the German autoworkers union, pointed out, unions hardly ever go on strike in Germany, "because there is an elaborate system of conflict resolution that regularly is used to come to some sort of compromise that is acceptable to all parties."

One reason for the more collaborative relationship between CEOs and workers is that, unlike in the United States, unions aren't under attack and there aren't any "right to work for less" zones in Germany to which car manufacturers can flee so they can ignore the voice of organized labor.

Another and perhaps more powerful reason is that there is a constitutional amendment in Germany that forces corporate executives to listen to labor unions. The Works Constitution Act requires every factory to set up a works council that gives representatives of the workers a seat at the table in every decision-making process at the factory. That is the democratization of capitalism, expanding the decision-making process to not just the corporate elite but the entirety of the company, from the bottom up.

This, according to Mund, is the real reason why the autoworkers union has a loud voice in the German economy. Pointing to the adversarial relationship between employers and labor unions in America, Mund says, "The accusation that American unions are more radical and destructive...definitely has to do with the hostile environment in which the unions have to act. How can they be constructive and friendly if their asses are kicked all the time?" He goes on to say that without the Works Constitution Act in Germany, "employers would not talk to us either if they had the choice."

But intentions aside, the empowerment of labor unions in Germany and the democratization of the workplace through an enforced constitutional amendment has been an economic boon for Germany, as demonstrated by car sales, employee wages, and profitability.

As Mund concludes, "We have strong unions, we have strong social security systems, we have high wages. So, if I believed what the neo-liberals are arguing, we would have to be bankrupt, but apparently this is not the case...the economy is working well in Germany."

So how do we democratize capital in the United States and give workers more of a say in how our economy is run? And why, if a $24 billion cooperative venture can be successfully established in the remote Basque region of northern Spain, can't such a massive venture take hold here in the big cities of the world's wealthiest nation?

The Seeds

Compared to the rest of the world, we're falling behind.

As Rebecca Kemble, the president of the US Federation of

Worker Cooperatives, told me, "The US is probably the smallest and most insignificant part of this international movement."

But the seeds are there.

Madison, Wisconsin, seems like any other midwestern town at first glance. It's the state capital and a college town, so, having grown up in Lansing and East Lansing, Michigan, I figured it was pretty much like home.

Until I got into the cab. A couple of times.

The company is called Union Cab, and one of my drivers used to be a lawyer; another used to teach college. Another was a high school graduate who loved what he was doing and considered driving a cab an art form—he was also a pretty good tour guide! And these people had actually worked to get out of their old jobs and into driving a cab.

Why is that? Why the heck would people leave seemingly very lucrative jobs to sit behind the wheel of a cab all day?

So I asked the general manager, a guy named John McNamara, exactly what makes his cab company different from all the rest. The answer is that they all belonged to a cooperative.

"The basic story," he told me, "really goes back to the late sixties, with both the antiwar and the social justice and civil rights movements." Cabdrivers were organizing into unions in response to the political climate of the day, but weren't making any headway to better wages and working conditions with their bosses. When the unions went on strike, the owners just shut down the companies.

After one strike in particular, and subsequent shutdown, in 1978 against the Checker Cab company, the drivers decided to give starting their own cooperative cab company a shot. "It was a lot of hard work, and the first winter was really bleak," McNamara told me. But around the same time, the bus drivers union went on strike, and the fledgling co-op lent out a few cabs to the out-of-work bus drivers. "It really helped launch our company," he said, and business has been good ever since.

McNamara himself ditched going to graduate school in 1988 to join the Union Cab co-op. "I was bartending in a bar where a bunch of cabdrivers would stop by, and I heard about Union Cab. I wanted to see what it was like to work in a worker-owned company," he told me. "It was a great fit with my worldview. To find a company whose culture and worldview matches my own, especially since I was coming from totally left of center, was really amazing—it was like being home."

When I visited in 2010, Union Cab had about 220 people working for it. That's 180 drivers plus mechanics, a call-center staff, an IT department for dispatching, and an administrative staff. The entire operation runs a bit over $6 million a year. It's the only cab company in the state that gives health insurance to its drivers, who are some of the best paid in the country.

"We have drivers who've come to this company literally homeless and have managed to buy homes," McNamara told me. "One of those homeless people is now driving a BMW...We're head and shoulders above our competitors in how we treat our workers, and that translates into the service we give our customers."

I talked with one of the drivers, Fred Schepartz, about how Union Cab is different from the rest. "The industry as a whole is exploitative and corrupt, and it's getting worse," Fred said. "The cab industry in Milwaukee is more and more like a sweatshop, with a lot of immigrant drivers, who are more desperate than we are for work."

Unlike Union Cab, the rest of the cab industry isn't set up for the drivers to make money; it's set up for the owners to make money, Fred told me. He gave me an example of one of the other cab companies in town that uses the standard sole-proprietorship model, in which the owner is in the business of making as much money for himself as he can and he does it by exploiting the hard work of his drivers. He takes $1.50 off the top of every ride a driver does. He pays his drivers a commission, but that $1.50 is not commissionable. He presumably makes that choice because it makes his company more money.

Democratize the Economy

But at Union Cab, "You don't have to work sixty or eighty hours like so many other cabdrivers have to do. You don't leave work with your soul sucked out so badly that you can't do anything else afterward," Fred told me. "I get a fifty-two percent commission, I have health insurance, and my wife is on the policy and that's literally been a lifesaver, as she's had major and minor surgery over the past few years. Working in a workplace where every single person has a say and every single person is a vital piece of the whole company is a totally different experience."

With fewer hours and better pay, most of the drivers at Union Cab can pursue their other interests. While working as a driver, Fred has published several short stories, with his first novel published four years ago entitled *Vampire Cabby*, about a 1,000-year-old vampire who loses his money in the stock market crash of '87. At the time I talked to him, he was working on another book, "Solidarity Moon," about a labor struggle on the first colony in a star system.

"I ended up living it instead of writing about it," he told me.

"We have a number of musicians who have put together two-CD compilations of their music, we have artists, we have three published authors, so people are able to pursue other things in their lives because we do allow people to make enough in a normal forty-hour workweek that they can also do other things."

Unlike the big banks on Wall Street and the same transnational corporations that line Main Streets across America, Union Cab isn't run by the profit motive. As John McNamara told me, "We don't want a huge profit at the end of the year, because that means you didn't pay your workers enough."

But can a company not exclusively motivated by profit be able to compete and do well in the market? Absolutely. Union Cab is the largest of the four cab companies in Madison; it has the largest fleet and the best service. It has an employee retention rate of 85 percent and most workers stay there beyond five years.

In fact, Union isn't alone. There are nine other successful cooperatives—from bakeries, to engineering companies, to pharmacies—within five miles of the state capital, employing over four hundred people and doing more than $30 million in business a year.[204]

In fact, a lot of Americans have endorsed cooperatives in recent decades, thus laying the foundation for an entirely new economy to replace the one that will be in tatters following the Crash of 2016.

We think that giant transnational energy corporations dominate the energy market, but in reality cooperatives do. More than nine hundred rural electric cooperatives deliver electricity to more than 42 million people in forty-seven states.

There are roughly thirty thousand cooperatives in the United States, running 73,000 businesses and owning more than $3 trillion in assets. They bring in $500 billion in revenue and pay $25 billion in wages to 2 million workers in every sector of the economy.

Despite falling behind the rest of the world, Rebecca told me, "It feels like we're on the edge of a huge explosion in the sector, and we're working to build the capacity to support that."

The crash will be the trigger.

Chapter 16

Epilogue–A Letter to
My Great-Grandchildren

The test of our progress is not whether we add more to the abundance of those who have much; it is whether we provide enough for those who have too little.

—President Franklin D. Roosevelt, 1937
Second Inaugural Address

In 2090, you live in an "interesting" time, much like the one I'm alive in right now and my children are experiencing with some ferocity.

After the Progressive Revolution that followed the Crash of 2016, the conservative/neoliberal laissez-faire economics championed by Reagan, Greenspan, and Milton and Tom Friedman was so discredited that, like the last time it was discredited in 1929, it pretty much went underground. Ayn Rand and her bizarre writings were viewed as crackpot and ignored.

The "Democratic Socialism"—which had already been largely adopted by Japan, South Korea, Australia/New Zealand, and many South and Central American countries by 2016—was finally accepted by Americans as the only viable way to have both a vibrant—and, perhaps most important, stable—economy and at the same time have an uncorrupted democratic form of governance.

Semiprotectionist trade and manufacturing policies were adopted, energy independence was achieved during the first few decades after the crash, and taxes were raised on the Economic Royalists—and their behaviors in the political arena were restricted by constitutional amendment—so for another few generations (much like in the era of 1935–80) their ability to control governance was limited and their ability to crash the economy again was stopped.

That lasted from roughly 2016 through about 2066—much like the fifty-year period after the crash of 1929.

But then your generation's Lewis Powell, Jude Wanniski, Milton Friedman, and—ultimately—Ronald Reagan emerged. Your generation's very wealthy—your equivalent of our Koch brothers and Walton heirs—found people to draft policy papers, invent institutions, write novels, and busy themselves in the political arena.

Your Federalist Party, which grew out of the ashes of our Republican Party after its internecine wars with its billionaire-funded Tea Party faction, began to convince people that the social safety net that had kept our nation stable and secure for two generations was a terrible thing. They argued that too much money was going to the lower rungs of society, particularly those they suggested oh-so-subtly were genetically and intellectually inferior. Those people should know their place, and it was ridiculous, they said in the 2060s, that *everybody* should enjoy basic levels of safety and security in society. After all, they said, without the threat of homelessness and illness, why would they ever bother to get out and work?

Of course, what all that rhetoric hid was the Federalists' efforts to shift wealth—and power, particularly political power—from the "rabble" (as Federalist John Adams called the working classes) to the Economic Royalists themselves. Steadily, steadily, through the

Epilogue

2070s and 2080s, they cut away at the social safety net. And just like Warren Harding in 1921 and Ronald Reagan in 1981, your Federalist politicians put in place policies—from huge tax cuts on the Economic Royalists to dilution of the anticorruption laws passed in 2016–17—that cut the economic and political power of average working people and shifted it to the corporate and inherited-wealth elite.

If you'd looked back at our history, from the eras of the Cotton Kings in the 1850s to those of the Robber Barons of the 1900s, the Economic Royalists of the 1930s, and the Republicans of the 1980s, you'd have seen the beginnings of the process. The front men for the Economic Royalists—you call them the Federalists, we called them the Republicans, during Lincoln's era he called them Secessionists— were busy as termites gnawing holes through the policies that had kept them in check for two generations.

Through that third generation of the 2060s and 2070s, nobody much noticed, although the political rhetoric had taken on a harder edge. By the 2080s, they had pretty much seized control of most state and federal legislative and judicial bodies. And they had the economy roaring white-hot, making the top 1 percent richer than any kings of old, before the crash that happened in 2090.

Learn from history.

With the invention of the cotton gin and other steam-operated machinery, our economy in the American South had exploded in the 1840s and 1850s. Same with the banking industry in the American North. And then they all collapsed in the Great Crash of 1856, which led to the Civil War.

While our economy had been largely based on slavery before the Civil War, we built our way out of it with the Industrial Revolution and the use of coal and oil for power instead of the muscles of slaves. But that, too, got taken over by the Economic Royalists in the 1920s, leading to the Great Crash of 1929.

Out of the ashes of that crash, America was rebuilt by the New

Deal, whose cornerstones were high tax rates on the Royalists, unions for the workers, and a well-informed electorate thanks to the Fairness Doctrine, which required radio and TV stations to give free time to political candidates. All three of those pillars began to disintegrate during the 1980s with Reagan, leading to a generation of "hot-bubble" economies, just like you were experiencing before your crash.

After our Crash of 2016, we built our way back to prosperity by using alternative energies, building a national transportation and energy infrastructure, and stripping the Economic Royalists of their ability to pursue so-called "free trade" policies that not only decimated our nation but those we traded with as well. We shifted from Reagan's laissez-faire economics to the regulated economics of the Founders, of Lincoln, of FDR. And we built large community- and national-based cooperatives as alternatives to raw capitalism, with workers having ownership stakes in the businesses for which they worked.

You, too, are now facing an economy in ruins and a world in turmoil. Climate change has altered the face and economy of every nation on the planet, and your generation of Economic Royalists figured out how to profit from it, watching the trends and carefully buying and selling lands and businesses as people were forced to move from areas where deserts were on the march into areas that had become more habitable than before. But they overreached, ended up owning too much in too few hands, and so—just like in all the cycles before, you and your children are paying for their greed.

Learn from our mistakes, and from what we got right.

You won't have novel new power and economic stimulants such as steam, the way Lincoln's generation did. You won't have oil as a new resource, the way Teddy Roosevelt's generation did. You won't have unions, the way Eisenhower's generation did. And you won't have the explosion of an alternative-energy economy, the way my children's generation did in the years after the Obama administration and the recovery from the Great Crash of 2016.

Epilogue

But there will be something new in each of those areas.

Looking forward from 2013, as I am now, I don't know what it will be. But the one thing history—over ten thousand years of the history of civilization—tells us is that it will be *something*.

Use it. But be very, very careful that, in doing so, you don't hand your generation of Economic Royalists another tool they can use to once again rise up like lords and kings to take control. Keep it decentralized. As Thomas Jefferson urged at the founding of our nation, keep both power *and* economic strength local and broadly based. That will keep political power local and broadly based as well, which is the surest way to have stability going forward into the future.

A pyramid standing on its base is stable, although unlike the Egyptian pyramids, the pyramids of economies and political systems are made of stuff that changes from generation to generation: agriculture and human/animal power, coal and steam power, oil and industrial power, solar and cooperative power.

As you make the transition into a new world and a new economy, rising out of the ashes of the crash your generation of Economic Royalists brought you, always remember that they will still be there. They'll be watching and planning and grasping for the levers that will bring them back on top. Be careful and—as Dwight Eisenhower warned my generation in his Farewell Address—be "ever vigilant" against that "misplaced power" that they are seeking.

It's unlikely that you'll be able to stop altogether the rise of the Economic Royalists during the lifetimes of your children and grandchildren. They've always figured out a way to pull it off, all the way back to the era of Gilgamesh, seven thousand years ago in Uruk (what we now call Iraq).

But please do your best to send a warning to your future generations. Don't do like we did with Reaganomics and blow up the protections for your working people. Don't jump into the equivalent of our Clinton/Gingrich/Greenspan experiment of deregulating the institutions owned by the Economic Royalists.

Tell *your* children, and ask them to tell theirs.

Maybe, just maybe, you and your peers can break these cycles of history, stop the boom-bust-war merry-go-round that this nation (and the world) has endured for more than half a millennium since Elizabeth I chartered the East India Company in 1601.

Because, just as democracies will always have Economic Royalists looking for ways to subvert them to their own ends, they will also always have people who remember the lessons of history. People who know the possibility of a stable world at peace. People willing to sacrifice and work and put themselves on the front lines of history to build a better world.

Find them. Celebrate them. Become one of them.

Tag, you're "It."

ABOUT THE AUTHOR

Thom Hartmann is a progressive national and internationally syndicated radio and TV talk show host whose shows are available every weekday in more than a half-billion homes in 104 countries worldwide. He's the *New York Times* best-selling, four-time Project Censored Award–winning author of twenty-four books in print in seventeen languages on five continents.

Thom has written extensively about culture, ecology, psychology, politics, and economics. His most well-known book on the intersection of ecology and anthropology, *The Last Hours of Ancient Sunlight*, inspired Leonardo DiCaprio to make the movie *The 11th Hour* (in which Thom appears). His book *Attention Deficit Disorder: A Different Perception* sparked a national debate, both in the psychology/psychiatry community and among the general public, on ADD/ADHD and neurological differences ranging from giftedness to autism. His book *Rebooting the American Dream* so inspired Senator Bernie Sanders that he wrote a cover letter to accompany the delivery of the book to his ninety-nine colleagues in the United States Senate and he read from it extensively on the floor of the Senate during his famous filibuster.

In addition to being an accomplished writer, Thom and his wife, Louise, have also started a number of successful businesses and a community and school for abused children. Thom's also helped start programs ranging from famine relief to medical centers to schools on four continents.

He and Louise live on a boat in Washington, DC, with their attack cat, Higgins.

NOTES

1 Statement of Secretary of Labor Robert B. Reich before the Subcommittee on Deficits, Debt Management and Long-Term Growth, Senate Committee on Finance, December 7, 1994, http://www.dol.gov/oasam/programs/history/reich/congress/120794rr.htm.
2 http://www.cbsnews.com/2100-500395_162-1293943.html.
3 Thomas Jefferson, Letter to William Pinkney, September 30, 1820, in *The Declaration of Independence and Letters*, Richard S. Poppen, ed. (University of Virginia, 1904).
4 Asher Price, "Suicide Pilot Joe Stack Had History of Shutting Doors on People," March 7, 2010, Statesman.com, http://www.statesman.com/news/news/local/suicide-pilot-joe-stack-had-history-of-shutting-do/nRq6N/.
5 Ibid.
6 From a web posting authorities believed to be written by Joe Stack, http://www.foxnews.com/story/0,2933,586627,00.html.
7 CBS Los Angeles, "Newbury Park Woman Faces Eviction After Husband's Suicide," May 16, 2012, http://losangeles.cbslocal.com/2012/05/16/newbury-park-woman-faces-eviction-after-husbands-suicide/.
8 Katie Moisse, "James Verone: The Medical Motive for his $1 Bank Robbery," June 23, 2011, ABC News, http://abcnews.go.com/Health/Wellness/james-verone-medical-motive-bank-robbery/story?id=13895584#.UaMiNY6hDzI.
9 From press release: "New Pollution Report Measures Global Health Impact Across 49 Countries; Reveals Pollution to Be Critical Threat on Par with Malaria, TB; Identifies Top Ten Toxic Industries Responsible," http://www.blacksmithinstitute.org/press-release-2012-world-s-worst-pollution-problems-report.html.

Notes

10 From Bill Moyers interview, July 20, 2012, http://billmoyers.com/segment /chris-hedges-on-capitalism's-'sacrifice-zones'/.

11 Ibid.

12 Ibid.

13 Dean Reynolds, "Chicago police sergeant: 'Tribal warfare' on the streets," CBS News report, July 11, 2012, http://www.cbsnews.com/8301-18563_162 -57470618/chicago-police-sergeant-tribal-warfare-on-the-streets/.

14 Franklin Delano Roosevelt, First Inaugural Address, March 4, 1933, Washington, DC.

15 William Strauss and Neil Howe, *The Fourth Turning* (New York: Broadway Books, 1997).

16 http://research.stlouisfed.org/fred2/series/HOUST. http://www.econbrowser.com/archives/2006/11/housing_stats_l.html.

17 Barack Obama, First Inaugural Address, January 20, 2009, Washington, DC.

18 Daniel Sisson, *The American Revolution of 1800* (New York: Knopf, 1974).

19 Thomas Jefferson, Letter to John Adams, October 28, 1813, in *Memoirs, Correspondence and Private Papers of Thomas Jefferson, Late President of the United States*, Volume 2 (London: Colburn and Bentley, 1829).

20 Thomas Jefferson, *Memoirs, Correspondence and Private Papers of Thomas Jefferson, Late President of the United States*, Volume 2 (London: Colburn and Bentley, 1829).

21 Andrew Jackson, Veto Message, July 10, 1832, The Founders' Constitution, Document 20, University of Chicago, http://press-pubs.uchicago.edu /founders/documents/a1_8_18s20.html.

22 I.C.R.R. Co. notice published in the New York papers and signed by the railroad's treasurer, J. N. Perkins.

23 Grover Cleveland, 1888 State of the Union Address, December 3, 1888, Washington, DC.

24 Frederick Lewis Allen, *Only Yesterday: An Informal History of the 1920's* (New York: HarperCollins, 2000).

25 Warren Harding's campaign slogan was "Less government in business and more business in government," http://www.whitehouse.gov/about/presidents /warrenharding.

26 Paul Krugman, "The Mellon Doctrine," *New York Times*, March 31, 2011, http://www.nytimes.com/2011/04/01/opinion/01krugman.html?_r=0.

27 Franklin Delano Roosevelt, 1936 Democratic National Convention speech, June 27, 1936, Philadelphia, Pennsylvania.

28 Morris Berman, *The Twilight of American Cluture* (New York: Norton & Co., 2000).

29 http://en.wikipedia.org/wiki/1960s, accessed September 5, 2011.

30 Hyrum S. Lewis, *Sacralizing the Right: William F. Buckley Jr., Whittaker Chambers, Will Herberg and the Transformation of Intellectual Conservatism* (ProQuest, 2007), http://books.google.com/books?id=QviaoxgkmFwC&pg=PA227&lpg=

Notes

PA227&dq=%22russell+kirk%22+%22social+unrest%22&source=bl&ots
=6Ds8B9XwZq&sig=QTd_BdnI6lCEM8cafJ6_SouuOe0&hl=en&ei=
6fdjTrz-OuLc0QHcq5i3Cg&sa=X&oi=book_result&ct=result&resnum
=1&ved=0CBoQ6AEwAA#v=onepage&q=%22russell%20kirk%22%20
%22social%20unrest%22&f=false.

31 Jack Anderson, "Powell's Lesson to Business Aired," *Washington Post*, September 28, 1972.

32 Ibid.

33 Ibid.

34 "The Powell Memo," ReclaimDemocracy.org, http://reclaimdemocracy .org/powell_memo_lewis/.

35 Ibid.

36 Ibid.

37 Ibid.

38 Ibid.

39 Ibid.

40 Ibid.

41 Ibid.

42 Tom Dickinson, "How Roger Ailes Built the Fox News Fear Factory," *Rolling Stone*, May 25, 2011, http://www.rollingstone.com/politics/news/how -roger-ailes-built-the-fox-news-fear-factory-20110525.

43 John Cook, "Roger Ailes' Secret Nixon-Era Blueprint for Fox News," Gawker, June 30, 2011, http://gawker.com/5814150/roger-ailes-secret-nixon +era-blueprint-for-fox-news.

44 Lanny Ebenstein, *Milton Friedman: A Biography* (New York: Palgrave MacMillan, 2007).

45 Interview, Commanding Heights, PBS, October 1, 2000, http://www.pbs .org/wgbh/commandingheights/shared/minitext/int_miltonfriedman.html.

46 Milton Friedman, *Capitalism and Freedom* (University of Chicago Press, 1962).

47 Naomi Klein, *The Shock Doctrine: The Rise of Disaster Capitalism* (New York: MacMillan, 2010).

48 Orlando Letelier, "The Chicago Boys in Chile: Economic Freedom's Awfull Toll," *The Nation*, August 28, 1976, http://www.ditext.com/letelier/chicago.html.

49 Milton Friedman and Rose Friedman, "One Week in Stockholm," *Hoover Digest* 1998, No. 4 (October 30, 1998), http://www.hoover.org/publications /hoover-digest/article/6969.

50 *The Works of Thomas Jefferson*, Volume 12, Federal Edition (New York and London: G. P. Putnam's Sons, 1904–5).

51 Thomas Jefferson, Letter to Samuel Kercheval, July 12, 1816, in *Memoirs, Correspondence and Private Papers of Thomas Jefferson, Late President of the United States*, Volume 4 (London: Colburn and Bentley, 1829).

Notes

52 Thomas Jefferson, Letter to James Madison, October 28, 1785, http://press
-pubs.uchicago.edu/founders/documents/v1ch15s32.html.

53 "Analysis of U.S. Census Bureau Data" in *The State of Working America
1994–95*, Economic Policy Institute (M. E. Sharpe, 1994), 37.

54 Michael Linden, "The Myth of the Lower Marginal Tax Rates," Center for
American Progress, June 20, 2011, http://www.americanprogress.org/issues
/tax-reform/news/2011/06/20/9841/the-myth-of-the-lower-marginal-tax
-rates/.

55 Franklin Delano Roosevelt, 1936 Democratic National Convention speech,
June 27, 1936, Philadelphia, Pennsylvania.

56 Franklin Delano Roosevelt, 1944 State of the Union Address, January 11, 1944.

57 Teddy Roosevelt, the New Nationalism speech, August 31, 1910.

58 Elizabeth J. Magie, "The Landlord's Game," reprinted from *The Single
Tax Review*, Autumn 1902, http://www.cooperativeindividualism.org/magie
-elizabeth_landlords-game-1902.html.

59 U.S. Council of Economic Advisors, 2000, *Economic Report to the President,
2000* (Washington, DC: U.S. Government Printing Office, 2000), 279.

60 Grover Cleveland, 1888 State of the Union Address, December 3, 1888,
Washington, DC.

61 Elizabeth J. Magie, "The Landlord's Game," reprinted from *The Single
Tax Review*, Autumn 1902, http://www.cooperativeindividualism.org/magie
-elizabeth_landlords-game-1902.html.

62 Charles J. Adams III, "Monopoly: From Berks to Boardwalk," *HISTORI-
CAL REVIEW OF BERKS COUNTY WINTER 1978*, Volume XLIV,
Number 1 (Winter 1978–79), http://landlordsgame.info/articles/berks2
boardwalk.html.

63 Chrystia Freeland, *Plutocrats: The Rise of the New Global Super Rich and the Fall of
Everyone Else* (New York: Penguin Press, 2012).

64 Henry George, *Progress and Poverty* (Gloucestershire, UK: Dodo Press, 2009).

65 "Essay: The FUTURISTS: Looking Toward A.D. 2000," *TIME*, February 25,
1966, http://www.time.com/time/magazine/article/0,9171,835128,00.html.

66 Richard Wolff, "The Keynesian Revival: A Marxian Critique," October 23,
2010, http://rdwolff.com/content/keynesian-revival-marxian-critique.

67 Ronald Reagan, First Inaugural Address, January 20, 1981, Washington, DC.

68 Jude Wanniski, "Taxes and a Two-Santa Theory," *National Observer*, March
6, 1976, http://capitalgainsandgames.com/blog/bruce-bartlett/1701/jude
-wanniski-taxes-and-two-santa-theory.

69 Interview with David Stockman, *The Big Picture with Thom Hartmann*, September 21, 2011, http://www.youtube.com/watch?v=FdZpOMpFf18.

70 Bill Clinton, the New Covenant speech, October 23, 1991, Georgetown
University.

Notes

71 Bill Clinton, 1996 State of the Union Address, January 27, 1996, Washington, DC.

72 Marie Diamond, "On the 15th Anniversary of 'Welfare Reform,' Aid Is Not Getting To Those Who Need It Most," ThinkProgress, August 22, 2011, http://thinkprogress.org/economy/2011/08/22/301231/tanf-15-anniversary/.

73 Bob Woodward, *The Agenda: Inside the Clinton White House* (New York: Simon & Schuster, 2005).

74 Dwight Eisenhower, Letter to his brother, November 8, 1954, http://www.snopes.com/politics/quotes/ike.asp.

75 John Kenneth Galbraith, *The Great Crash 1929* (New York: Mariner Books, 2009).

76 Tom Philpott, "Foodies, Get Thee to Occupy Wall Street," *Mother Jones*, October 14, 2011, http://www.motherjones.com/environment/2011/10/food-industry-monopoly-occupy-wall-street.

77 Ibid.

78 Interview with Susan Crawford, *The Big Picture with Thom Hartmann*, March 4, 2013, http://www.youtube.com/watch?v=PlO2IGTCHiU.

79 Interview with Chris Hedges, *The Big Picture with Thom Hartmann*, December 20, 2010, http://www.youtube.com/watch?v=By88H5vNMqk.

80 John Ralston Saul, *The Collapse of Globalism* (New York: Viking, 2005).

81 "America, Wake Up!" Americawakeup.net, http://americawakeup.net/.

82 Ibid.

83 David Wessel, "Big US Firms Ship Hiring Abroad," *Wall Street Journal*, http://online.wsj.com/article/SB10001424052748704821704576270783611823972.html#project%3DMULTINATL0419_part2%26articleTabs%3Dinteractive.

84 Dustin Ensigner, "Economy in Crisis," February 2011, http://economyincrisis.org/content/trade-deficit-south-korea-autos-continues-rise.

85 US Census, http://www.census.gov/foreign-trade/balance/c5330.html.

86 Eamonn Fingleton, *In the Jaws of the Dragon* (New York: St. Martin's Griffin, 2009), 66.

87 Ibid., 67.

88 Ibid., 294.

89 Ibid., 27.

90 Chrystia Freeland, "The Rise of the New Global Elite," *The Atlantic*, http://www.theatlantic.com/magazine/archive/2011/01/the-rise-of-the-new-global-elite/308343/.

91 James Goldmsith, *The Trap* (New York: Carroll & Graf Publishers, 1994).

92 Jeff Bercovici, "Why (Some) Psychopaths Make Great CEOs," *Forbes*, June 14, 2011, http://www.forbes.com/sites/jeffbercovici/2011/06/14/why-some-psychopaths-make-great-ceos/.

Notes

93 Pub.L. 97-320, H.R. 6267, enacted October 15, 1982, http://hdl.loc.gov /loc.uscongress/legislation.97hr6267.

94 Matt Taibbi, *Griftopia* (New York: Spiegel & Grau, 2011).

95 Ibid.

96 Ibid.

97 Frederick Kaufman, "The Food Bubble: How Wall Street Starved Millions and Got Away with It," *Harper's*, July 2010, http://harpers.org/archive/2010/07 /the-food-bubble/.

98 Ibid.

99 Ibid.

100 Noah Mendel, "When Did the Great Depression Receive Its Name," History News Network, http://hnn.us/articles/61931.html.

101 Frederick Lewis Allen, *Only Yesterday: An Informal History of the 1920's* (New York: HarperCollins, 2000).

102 Ibid.

103 Ibid.

104 http://www.westegg.com/inflation/infl.cgi.

105 Interview with Steve Keen, *The Big Picture with Thom Hartmann*, March 18, 2013, http://www.youtube.com/watch?v=-n-X4RQqJcs.

106 Saskia Scholtes and Michael Mackenzie, "Hedge Funds Hone In on Housing," *Financial Times*, September 27, 2006, http://www.ft.com/intl/cms /s/0/b78c0fdc-4e40-11db-bcbc-0000779e2340.html#axzz1NfIFsOZS.

107 James Mackintosh, "Alfred Hitchcock's 'The Bankers,'" *Financial Times*, June 23, 2011.

108 Ibid.

109 Thomas Jefferson, Letter to James Madison, September 6, 1789, http:// press-pubs.uchicago.edu/founders/documents/v1ch2s23.html.

110 Thomas Jefferson quote revolution.

111 John F. Kennedy quote, violent revolution.

112 Robert Draper, *Do Not Ask What Good We Do: Inside the U.S. House of Representatives* (New York: Free Press, 2012).

113 Daily Kos member keepmehonest, "Eric Cantor, Paul Ryan & Kevin McCarthy: Plot to Sabotage US Economy with Frank Luntz," DailyKos, June 8, 2012, http://www.dailykos.com/story/2012/06/08/1098434/-Eric-Cantor -Paul-Ryan-Kevin-McCarthy-Plot-To-Sabotage-US-Economy-with-Frank -Luntz.

114 CNBC, February 19, 2009.

115 http://tobaccocontrol.bmj.com/content/early/2013/02/07/tobaccocontrol -2012-050815.abstract.

116 Robert Draper, http://legacy.library.ucsf.edu/tid/vbi08b00/pdf.

Notes

117 Bob Davis, "Rule Breaker," *Wall Street Journal,* July 16, 2004, http://mercatus .org/media_clipping/rule-breaker-washington-tiny-think-tank-wields-big -stick-regulation.

118 http://www.tampabay.com/news/business/billionaires-role-in-hiring -decisions-at-florida-state-university-raises/1168680.

119 Ibid.

120 Ben Dimiero, "LEAKED EMAIL: Fox Boss Caught Slanting News Reporting," Media Matters for America, December 9, 2010, http://mediamatters.org /blog/2010/12/09/leaked-email-fox-boss-caught-slanting-news-repo/174090.

121 Ibid.

122 Media Matters Staff, "Luntz Births Another GOP Talking Point: It's a 'Government Option' Not a 'Public Option,'" MediaMatters for America, August 19, 2008, http://mediamatters.org/video/2009/08/19/luntz-births -another-gop-talking-point-its-a-go/153496.

123 Ben Dimiero, "FOXLEAKS: Fox Boss Ordered Staff to Cast Doubt on Climate Science," Media Matters for America, December 15, 2010, http:// mediamatters.org/blog/2010/12/15/foxleaks-fox-boss-ordered-staff-to-cast -doubt-o/174317.

124 "Fox News' Chris Wallace: Is Obama Even President?" *Los Angeles Times*, January 20, 2009, http://latimesblogs.latimes.com/showtracker/2009/01 /fox-news-chris.html.

125 "Why Obama Voted Against Roberts," *Wall Street Journal*, June 2, 2009, http://online.wsj.com/article/SB124390047073474499.html.

126 Lee Epstein, William Landis, and Richard Posner, "How Business Fares in the Supreme Court," http://www.minnesotalawreview.org/wp-content /uploads/2013/04/EpsteinLanderPosner_MLR.pdf.

127 http://www.spiegel.de/international/europe/greek-debt-crisis-how -goldman-sachs-helped-greece-to-mask-its-true-debt-a-676634.html.

128 http://www.youtube.com/watch?v=Ps5JL268ZQE.

129 http://www.reuters.com/article/2011/10/28/us-goldmansachs-lawsuit-id USTRE79R4JE20111028.

130 http://www.cbsnews.com/8301-503544_162-20003526-503544.html.

131 Ross Douthat, "Conspiracies, Coups and Currencies," *New York Times*, November 19, 2011.

132 http://dailyreckoning.com/goldman-bets-against-the-assets-it-sold-to-aig/.

133 http://www.huffingtonpost.com/2011/09/26/trader-to-bbc-goldman -sachs-goldman-sachs-rules-the-world_n_981658.html.

134 Interview with Rev. David Bullock, *The Big Picture with Thom Hartmann*, January 5, 2012.

135 Ibid.

136 http://www.mackinac.org/14756.

Notes

137 ALEC website, http://www.alec.org/about-alec/.

138 Interview with Mark Pocan, Radio Show, August 5, 2011.

139 Common Cause, http://www.commoncause.org/atf/cf/%7Bfb3c17e2-cdd1
-4df6-92be-bd4429893665%7D/MONEYPOWERANDALEC.pdf.

140 ThinkProgress, http://thinkprogress.org/green/2011/08/05/288979/revealed
-bp-is-top-funder-of-alec-annual-meeting-in-oil-soaked-louisiana/.

141 Mark Pocan, "Inside ALEC," http://progressive.org/inside_alec.html.

142 Mark Pocan interview.

143 Ibid.

144 Common Cause, http://www.commonblog.com/2012/01/31/alec-exposed
-for-24-hours/.

145 ALEC website, http://www.alec.org/about-alec/history/.

146 Mark Pocan radio interview.

147 Common Cause, http://www.commoncause.org/atf/cf/%7Bfb3c17e2-cdd1
-4df6-92be-bd4429893665%7D/MONEYPOWERANDALEC.pdf.

148 Common Cause, http://www.commonblog.com/2011/08/03/have-you-met
-alec-in-minnesota/.

149 The Uptake, http://www.theuptake.org/2012/02/11/mn-governor-vetos-alec
-template-bills/.

150 Heritage Foundation, December 18, 2008, http://blog.heritage.org/2008
/12/18/conservative-leader-paul-weyrich-dies-first-to-lead-heritage/.

151 Paul Weyrich, Youtube: RWW blog, August 1980, http://www.youtube
.com/watch?v=pN7IB-d7Hfw&feature=player_embedded.

152 PBS, http://www.pbs.org/wgbh/pages/frontline/shows/fixers/reports/primer
.html.

153 *Roll Call*, http://www.rollcall.com/issues/56_75/-202990-1.html.

154 http://www.huffingtonpost.com/2012/07/12/cash-hoarding-companies
-spend-lend-economy_n_1666424.html.

155 http://online.wsj.com/article/SB10001424127887323894704578115180435
402750.html.

156 http://online.wsj.com/article/SB10001424052702304724404577297610717
362138.html.

157 http://www.youtube.com/watch?v=dxhyUAWPmGw.

158 *New York Times*, http://www.nytimes.com/2012/02/19/magazine/the-way
-greeks-live-now.html?_r=1.

159 http://qz.com/28535/proof-that-austerity-measures-are-making-european
-economies-worse-not-better/.

160 http://www.spiegel.de/international/europe/profiting-from-pain-europe
-s-crisis-is-germany-s-blessing-a-808248.html.

161 Camilla Louise Lyngsby, "George Soros Blasts Germany for Its Role in Europe
Crisis," CNBC, March 1, 2013, http://www.cnbc.com/id/100512946.

Notes

162 Ibid.

163 Interview with Richard Wolff, *The Big Picture with Thom Hartmann*, September 27, 2012, http://www.youtube.com/watch?v=N5kS9btTY-Q.

164 http://www.bbc.co.uk/news/business-20322746.

165 James Kirkup, *The Telegraph*, Nov. 25, 2011, http://www.telegraph.co.uk /news/politics/8917077/Prepare-for-riots-in-euro-collapse-Foreign-Office -warns.html.

166 "Arthur Young's Travels in France During 1787, 1788, 1789," http://www .econlib.org/library/YPDBooks/Young/yngTF.html.

167 Gordon Chang, "China's Property Sector, Just Before The Crash," *Forbes*, March 3, 2013, http://www.forbes.com/sites/gordonchang/2013/03/03 /chinas-property-sector-just-before-the-crash/.

168 http://www.tikkun.org/nextgen/a-conversation-with-jeremy-rifkin-on-the -third-industrial-revolution.

169 James Madison, from "Political Observations," April 20, 1795, in *Letters and Other Writings of James Madison*, Volume IV (Forgotten Books, 2012), 491.

170 Barbara Starr, "Pentagon Reports Record Number of Suicides," CNN, January 16, 2013, http://www.cnn.com/2013/01/15/us/military-suicides.

171 http://www.youtube.com/watch?v=0HTkEBIoxBA&feature=player _embedded.

172 http://www.economicpolicyjournal.com/2013/03/debt-in-america-details .html.

173 Berkshire Hathaway Inc, 2002 Annual Report, p. 15, http://www.berk shirehathaway.com/2002ar/2002ar.pdf.

174 Thomas Kostigan, "The $700 Trillion Elephant," *MarketWatch*, March 6, 2009, http://www.marketwatch.com/story/the-700-trillion-elephant-room theres?dist=TNMostRead.

175 http://gawker.com/the-next-housing-bubble-is-about-to-pop-all-over-you -510108728.

176 Thomas Jefferson, Letter to Spencer Roane, 1819, Library of Congress, http://www.loc.gov/exhibits/jefferson/137.html.

177 Thomas Jefferson, Letter to Charles Jarvis, September 28, 1820, http:// www.yamaguchy.com/library/jefferson/jarvis.html.

178 http://news.harvard.edu/gazette/story/2009/09/new-study-finds-45000 -deaths-annually-linked-to-lack-of-health-coverage/.

179 http://www.apfc.org/home/Content/aboutFund/aboutPermFund.cfm.

180 http://www.commondreams.org/view/2012/02/17-4.

181 http://www.powerlineblog.com/archives/2012/02/who-makes-the-most -from-oil-and-gas-leases-on-public-land.php.

182 http://insideclimatenews.org/news/20100518/research-shows-federal-oil -leasing-and-royalty-income-raw-deal-taxpayers.

Notes

183 http://www.commondreams.org/view/2012/02/17-4.

184 http://money.cnn.com/2008/01/29/news/economy/stimulus_analysis/index.htm.

185 http://www.youtube.com/watch?v=xhYJS80MgYA.

186 http://www.americanprogressaction.org/issues/labor/news/2009/03/11/5814/the-employee-free-choice-act-101/.

187 http://www.theatlantic.com/business/archive/2012/05/here-is-the-full-inequality-speech-and-slideshow-that-was-too-hot-for-ted/257323/.

188 http://money.cnn.com/2012/09/11/news/economy/wealth-net-worth/index.html.

189 http://www.senternovem.nl/mmfiles/The%20100.000%20Roofs%20Programme_tcm24-117023.pdf.

190 http://www.folkecenter.dk/en/articles/EUROSUN2000-speech-PM.htm.

191 http://en.wikipedia.org/wiki/Solar_power_in_Germany.

192 Resources & Stats, Nuclear Energy Institute, http://www.nei.org/resources andstats/nuclear_statistics/usnuclearpowerplants/.

193 http://en.wikipedia.org/wiki/Solar_power_in_Germany.

194 http://en.wikipedia.org/wiki/German_Renewable_Energy_Sources_Act.

195 Mark Landler, "Germany Debates Subsidies for Solar Industry," *New York Times*, May 16, 2008, http://www.nytimes.com/2008/05/16/business/worldbusiness/16solar.html.

196 http://www.latimes.com/business/la-fi-energy-china25-2010mar25,0,356464.story.

197 http://www.nytimes.com/2009/10/14/business/energy-environment/14oil.html.

198 Wallace S. Broecker, "CO_2 Arithmetic," *Science* 315 (2007): 1371, and comments as *Science* 316 (2007): 829; and Oliver Morton, "Is This What It Takes to Save the World?" *Nature* 447 (2007): 132.

199 http://www.eia.gov/oiaf/aeo/electricity_generation.html.

200 http://solar.gwu.edu/index_files/Resources_files/epstein_full cost of coal.pdf.

201 http://www.chattanoogan.com/2013/1/23/242786/Volkswagen-Chattanooga-Powers-Up.aspx.

202 http://www.cleanenergyactionproject.com/CleanEnergyActionProject/Wind_Power_Case_Studies_files/Alta Wind Energy Center.pdf.

203 http://topics.nytimes.com/top/news/business/energy-environment/wind-power/index.html.

204 Kevin Zeese, "Cooperative: The Co-op Alternative to Corporate Capitalism," It's Our Economy, August 28, 2011, http://itsoureconomy.us/2011/08/cooperatives-the-co-op-alternative-to-corporate-capitalism/.

INDEX

Adams, John, 10, 12, 121, 268
Affordable Care Act, 135–37, 141
AIG, 114, 165, 200
Ailes, Roger, 40–42, 135
Alaska, 222–24
Allen, Frederick Lewis, 15, 109, 110
Alperovitz, Gar, 256, 258
America Beyond Capitalism (Alperovitz), 256
American Dilemma, An (Myrdal), 53
American Enterprise Institute, 134
American Legislative Exchange Council
   (ALEC), 43, 134, 168–73
American Recovery and Reinvestment
   Act, 140
American Revolution, xix, 10, 11, 14, 121, 159–60;
   Tea Act of 1773 and, 5, 11–12, 126–27
American Revolution of 1800, The (Sisson), 12
Americans for Prosperity, 130, 134
Anderson, Jack, 36
Angle, Sharron, 126
Apple Corporation, 179
Argentina, 256–58
Aristotle, 220
Astor, John Jacob, 73
austerity measures, 25, 161, 162, 181–88
Australia, 161, 235, 250, 251, 252, 267
automobile industry, 100, 244, 248–49,
   260–62

Bain Capital, 105, 237
banking, 13, 17, 71, 92, 106, 111, 112, 121, 164,
   201, 269; anti-Obama position of, 154–55;
   bank failures, 3, 14, 76, 105; debt financing,
   112–13; deregulation and abuses, 104–6;

in Europe, 24–25, 182, 187; global coup
   d'état and, 164–67; hoarding cash by, 180;
   "madness of," 112, 114, 161; monopolies in,
   96; Robin Hood tax and, 226–27; Warren
   on, 181
Bank of America, 201
Barnes, Peter, 225
Beak of the Finch, The (Weiner), 94
Beck, Glenn, 134
Beinhart, Larry, 65
Bennet, Michael, 209
Benton Harbor, Michigan, 166
Bercovici, Jeff, 104
Berlusconi, Silvio, 162
Berman, Morris, 27
Black, Hugo, 153
Blodget, Henry, 188
Boehner, John, 173
BP (British Petroleum), 168
Bradley Foundation, 44
Brazil, 186, 248
Brennan Center for Justice, 173
Breyer, Stephen, 155
Buchanan, James, 213
Buckley, William F., 29, 33
Buffett, Warren, 181, 200
Bullock, David, 166
Burgin, Rachel, 171
Bush, George H. W., 40, 83, 107, 123, 196
Bush, George W., 7, 77, 83, 91, 99, 110, 129;
   deregulation and, 107, 109, 132; tax cuts for
   the rich, 84, 237; U.S. Supreme Court and,
   147, 217, 218; war and, 196–97
Butler, Smedley, 20

Index

Camden, New Jersey, xxvi, 102, 201
Canada, 88, 136, 221–22, 235, 245
Cantor, Eric, 124
Capitalism and Freedom (Friedman), 50
Captive Audience (Crawford), 97
Carnegie, Andrew, 73
Carson, Rachel, 32, 123
Carter, Jimmy, 56, 104, 107, 131, 196, 240;
    green energy programs, 240–41, 245, 246n
CATO Institute, 43, 131–32, 134
cellular phone market, 97
Center for American Progress, 66
Chang, Gordon, 192, 193
Cheney, Dick, 7, 132, 197
Chevron, 168
Chicago, Illinois, xxvi–xxvii, 33, 128
"Chicago Boys," 50, 51, 52, 56, 160, 162
Chile, 45–46, 51–53, 54, 160
China, 100, 101, 186, 193; commercial airliner,
    101; flex-fuel cars, 247–48; housing bubble,
    191–94; oil and, 108, 195–96; renewable
    energy, 244–45; U.S. technology sold to, 101
Christmas Carol, A (Dickens), 33–34
Citizens for a Sound Economy (CSE), 129,
    130, 134
Civil War, xix, 5, 10, 14–15, 72, 76, 122,
    190, 269
Cleveland, Grover, 15, 26, 59, 74, 122
climate change, 139–40, 141, 251
Clinton, Bill, 86, 113, 155, 196; deregulation
    and, 106, 107; First Inaugural Address, 86;
    free-trade deals, 88–91; New Covenant,
    86–91; welfare reform of, 87, 123
Clinton, Hillary, 146
Cobb, David, 210
Coburn, Tom, 124
Collapse of Globalism, The (Saul), 98
Commanding Heights (Yergin), 53–54
"Conspiracies, Coups and Currencies"
    (Douthat), 163–64
Cook, John, 40–42
Coolidge, Calvin, 16, 38–39, 109, 143
"Coolidge Prosperity," 16, 109, 110, 111
cooperative economy, 255–66
Cornyn, John, 154–55
corporations, 11, 15, 82, 153; ALEC and,
    168–73; Big Tobacco, 40, 129; cash
    stashed overseas, 180; CEOs and, 95–96,
    104; China policies and, 101–2; *Citizens
    United* and personhood of, 26, 44, 145–58,
    160, 174, 175, 206–12; "corporate death
    penalty," 70–71; deregulation and M&A
    frenzy, 104–5; election spending by, 157–58;

174–75; globalism and, 98–103; lobbying
    by, 42–44; monopolies, 70, 96–98; 112th
    Congress and, 174; "private equity," 105;
    railroads, 149–53; revolution of, 122–23; as
    shadow government, 166–75; Taft's trust-
    busting and, 70; Tea Party and, 129, 141–42;
    Tillman Act of 1907, 15, 72, 122
Crash of 2016, xviii, xx–xxvii; author's letter
    to his great-children, 267–72; banking runs,
    201–2; beginning (2009), 117–18, 123–25;
    cancer stage of capitalism and, 175–76; card
    check and unions, 230–32; China and, 193–94;
    Citizens United and, 206–12; cooperatives
    triggered by, 266; court decisions
    promoting, 143–58; debt forgiveness and,
    234–35; early stages, as seen in Greece,
    182; elections of 2010 and, 158; Europe
    and, 181–91; Great Crash of 1929 and, 4–5;
    green energy and, 238–53; health care and,
    220–22; housing market and, 201–2; oil and,
    194–96; outlawing billionaires, 235–37;
    printing money, 232–33; Reaganomics
    and, 56; reclaiming the commons, 224–25;
    reinvesting, 228–30; Robin Hood tax,
    226–27; U.S. and, 199–202; U.S. Supreme
    Court and, 212–15
Crawford, Susan P., 97
Curtis, Adam, 86
Cyprus, 187–88

Darwin, Charles, 94
Davis, Harold E., 190, 191
Davis, John Chandler Bancroft, 153
Days of Destruction, Days of Revolt (Hedges), xxvi
debt: consumer, 200, 234–35; middle class, 199,
    200, 234–35; mortgage, 128, 234; national,
    82–83, 86; student loan, 200, 234
Debunking Economics (Keen), 112
Delmas, Delphin, 151–53
DeMint, Jim, 124
democracy, 26–27, 159–60, 164; ALEC and
    undermining, 169–73; cooperative economy
    and, 255–60; Economic Royalists' assault on,
    160–76; Greek financial crisis and, 162; loss of
    pillars of, 91; neo-liberalism as threat to, 45;
    plutocracy replacing, xviii, 26; political fund-
    raising in U.S. and, 174–75; shadow corporate
    government and, 166–75; voter ID laws and,
    172–73
Democratic Socialism, 47, 267–68
deregulation, xxvii, 43, 104–6, 110, 271
Detroit, Michigan, 54–55, 102, 167, 185
Deutch, Ted, 209

Index

Dickens, Charles, 33–34
Dickinson, Tim, 40
Dirksen, Everett, 33
Dodd-Frank Wall Street Reform bill, 141
Doherty, Brian, 131–32, 134
Do Not Ask What Good We Do (Draper), 124
Douthat, Ross, 163–64
Draghi, Mario, 164–65
Draper, Robert, 124
Drexel Burnham Lambert, 105
Dunlap, Al, 104
DuPont Corporation, 20
Durbin, Dick, 209

East India Company, 11, 14, 126–27
Ecology and Evolution of Darwin's Finches
   (Grant), 94
Economic Royalists, xxi, xxii, xxvii, 9–15,
   16, 19–20, 22, 26, 29, 33, 76, 86; as "the
   1 percent," 10, 34, 82; assault on democracy
   by, 160–76; attack on education, 38–39; deals
   with universities, 132–33; destruction of the
   middle class and, 59; European technocrats,
   24–25, 162, 164, 166, 167, 170; FDR and,
   xxvii, 3, 8, 9–10, 15, 17–22; financial crisis
   of 2007–2008 and, 24–25; globalism and,
   98–103; Goldsmith's questions to, 103;
   the Great Forgetting and, xxvii, 9, 11, 15;
   Greece's economy and, 160–64; hoarding
   cash by, 179–80; judiciary and, 145–48;
   Koch family and, 130–35; madness of, 93–94,
   103–6, 109; media and, 39, 40–42, 135–40;
   1960s as threat, 31–34; outlawing billionaires,
   235–37; political majorities in Congress, 25;
   Powell memo and, 34–39, 42–44, 49, 56, 86,
   105, 125, 129, 168; Reaganomics and, 76,
   78–88; as shareholders, 223–24; tax cuts for,
   16, 37, 43, 65–66, 78–79, 80, 84, 235, 237;
   Tea Party and, 127–30, 127n; think tanks of,
   43, 105, 131–32, 168; war and, 22–24, 197,
   198, 238–39; Warren Harding and, 15–16;
   wealthiest one hundred, net worth, 235;
   wealth of, vs. the average American, 237
education, xxii, 234; Economic Royalists
   and, 38–39, 132–33; GI Bill, 59, 60. 68;
   government investing in, 229
Eisenhower, Dwight D., 6, 32, 60, 91; "military-
   industrial complex," 32, 238, 271
Ellsworth, Oliver, 215
Emanuel, Rahm, 117
energy, 238–53; solar and wind, 240–45, 253;
   stripping oil of its strategic value, 246–50. *See
   also* oil industry

Enron, 105–6
Europe, 25; austerity measures, 23, 25, 161–62,
   187–88; banks hoarding cash in, 180; cell
   phone costs, 97; Central Bank, 162, 164–65,
   181, 183, 187; Commission, 181; Democratic
   Socialism in, 47, 267–68; Eurozone collapse
   predicted, 187–88; German response to
   the financial crisis of 2007–2008, 183–85;
   Goldman Sachs in, 161; Greek financial
   crisis, 160–64; health care systems, 136,
   220–21; right wing extremism in, 25, 191;
   road to World War II, 22, 23, 25; technocrats
   in, 24–25, 162, 164, 166, 167, 170
ExxonMobil, 168

Fascism, 10, 16, 18, 24, 25, 28
Fear and Loathing in Las Vegas (Thompson), 34
Federal Deposit Insurance Corporation,
   17, 71
Federalists, 10, 12, 13, 121, 215–16, 268–69
Federalist Society, 44
Field, Stephen J., 149, 150
Fighting Bob Fest, 254–55
financial crisis of 2007–2008, xxvii–xxviii, 6, 7,
   106, 109, 183–85, 189, 195, 233
financialization, 106–9
Fingleton, Eamonn, 102
Florida State University, 132–33
food industry, 108–9
Fourth Turning, The (Strauss and Howe), xix, 6
Fox News, 40–42, 124, 135–40, 144
France, xviii, 49, 118, 164, 182, 186, 189–90,
   226, 227
Freeland, Chrystia, 75, 102
free-market economists, 37, 43, 48, 49–50, 51,
   53, 63, 107, 110, 132, 168, 170, 270
Friedman, Milton, 48–51, 52–53, 54, 56
Friesen, Steven, 82
Froomkin, Dan, 180
Fuller, Richard, xxv–xxvi

Galbraith, John Kenneth, 92–94, 103, 109
GATT, 89, 98
Geithner, Tim, 165
generational cycles (of revolution and crisis),
   xviii–xix, xxvii, 5–9, 24–25, 29, 94–96;
   Jefferson's cycle of revolutions, 118–21
George, Henry, 73, 75
George Mason University, 132
Germany, 183, 183n; banking, 182;
   democratizing capital, auto industry,
   260–62; as driver of austerity agenda, 182,
   183–84; economic policy, 182–84, 186;

Index

green energy initiatives, 242–44; right wing extremism in, 25; trade and, 182, 186; Treaty of Versailles and, 23–24

GI Bill, 59, 60, 68

Giftopia (Taibbi), 107

Gilded Age, 34, 65, 72, 73, 74, 75, 96, 122, 141–42, 174

Gingrich, Newt, 123, 125

Ginsburg, Ruth Bader, 155

Glass-Steagall Act, 71, 106

globalism, xxv–xxvi; Clinton free-trade deals and, 88–91; ideology of, 98–99; looting of America and, 99–103

Goldman Sachs, 114, 160–61, 170, 201, 227; Greece and, 160–61; role in global coup d'état, 164–65; Timberwolf deal, 161

Goldman Sachs Commodity Index, 108

Goldsmith, Sir James, 103

Gramm, Phil and Wendy, 105–6

Gramm-Leach-Bliley Act, 106

Grant, Peter and Rosemary, 94–95

Great Crash of 1857, 5, 14, 25, 72, 76, 269

Great Crash of 1929, 4, 8, 10–11, 29, 269; causes, 43, 66; five weakness of the economy and, 92–93; housing-market meltdown (1926), 109–12

Great Crash of 1929, The (Galbraith), 92–93

Great Depression, xix, 3–5, 9, 11, 16, 47, 73, 109, 112; Hoovervilles, 205–7; road to war and, 22–24. *See also* Roosevelt, Franklin D

Great Forgetting, xxvii, 5–9, 8; Economic Royalists and, xxvii, 9, 11, 15, 30, 96; of the Great Depression, 29, 113; Reagan tax cuts and, 79; World War II and, 189

Greece, 25, 160–64, 181–82, 185

green revolution, 238–53; Australia, 250; carbon taxes and, 250, 252; in China, 244–45; in Germany, 242–44; government investing in, 229; renewable energy vs. fossil fuel, 250–53; solar or wind energy, 240–45, 252; stripping oil of its strategic value, 246–50

Greenspan, Alan, 86, 92, 113

Gregory, Dick, 159

Hamilton, Alexander, 69, 215; eleven-point plan of, 10, 69, 88

Hanauer, Nick, 235, 236

Hannity, Sean, 138

Harding, Warren, 15, 38–39, 43, 105

Harkin, Tom, 209

Hayden, Tom, 31–32

Hayek, Friedrich, 47–48, 49, 50, 53, 54, 131

health care, xxiv–xxv, 135–38, 141, 162–63, 220–22

Hedges, Chris, xxvi, 176

Heritage Foundation, 43, 134, 168, 173

Hoover, Herbert, 4, 16, 38–39, 206

housing: adjustable rate mortgages, xxiii, 105, 128; bubbles, 6, 110–11, 113, 161, 191–94, 201; government guaranteed mortgage, 61; meltdown of 1926, 109–12, 113; mortgage assistance programs, 138, 234, 235; mortgage debt, 234

Howe, Neil, xix, 6

Hudson, Michael, 159

Hunter, Vernon, xx

Ibsen, Henrik, xv

Icahn, Carl, 104

ICANN, 97

Immelt, Jeffrey, 100

"In a Message to Democrats, Wall St. Sends Cash to G. O. P." (Kirkpatrick), 154

India, 100, 102, 195–96, 247

infrastructure, 229–30

Institute of International Finance, 180

International Forum on Globalization, 134

International Monetary Fund (IMF), 162, 181

Ireland, 181, 187–88

Israel, 55

Italy, 18, 24, 25, 102, 160, 162, 163, 164, 182, 186, 188, 235, 246, 246n

Jackson, Andrew, 13–14, 121

Jackson, Jesse, 205–7

Jarvis, William Charles, 214

Jay, John, 215

Jefferson, Thomas, xviii–xix, 12, 21, 63–65, 74, 191, 214, 271; cycle of revolutions, 118–21, 123; on the judiciary, 216–19

Jetsons, The (cartoon), 78

John Birch Society, 130, 131

Johnson, Lyndon B., 30–31, 68, 84; Great Society, 35, 68

JPMorgan Chase, 201

Judis, John, 191

Katz, Earl, 89, 90

Kaufman, Frederick, 108–9

Keen, Steve, 112, 113, 199, 233

Keller, Helen, 254

Kelton, Stephanie, 233

Kemble, Rebecca, 262–63

Kennedy, Anthony, 154

Kennedy, John F., 123

Index

Kercheval, Samuel, 63
Keynes, John Maynard, 23–24, 46
Keynesian economics, 46–47, 51, 56
Kirk, Russell, 29, 33
Kirkpatrick, David D., 154
Klein, Naomi, 50
Koch, David and Charles, 26, 43, 129, 130–35, 142, 237; affiliations, 133–35, 168, 169; Koch Industries, 101, 130, 133, 168; Tea Party, 134–35; university deals, 132–33
Kostigen, Thomas, 200
Kreitner, Ricky, 191
Kroll, Andy, 167–68
Krugman, Paul, 27
Kyl, Jon, 124

Lansing, Michigan, 60–61
Latrobe, Benjamin, 144
Lay, Kenneth, 105–6
LeFevre, Robert, 131
Lehman Brothers, 189
Letelier, Orlando, 51
Lewis, Hyrum S., 33
libertarianism, 62, 105, 131
Liebreich, Michael, 250–51
Limbaugh, Rush, 134
Lincoln, Abraham, 14, 122, 212–13
lobbying/lobbyists, 42–44, 86, 99, 133, 134, 175; ALEC and, 168–73
Locke, John, 63
Luntz, Frank, 124, 138

MacGuire, Gerald, 20
Mackinac Center for Public Policy, 167–68, 173
Madison, James, 64, 74, 119, 196, 196n, 215
Magie, Lizzie, 73, 74
Making of a Radical, The (Nearing), 75
Manners, John, 63
manufacturing, 70, 106; Clinton free-trade deals and, 88–91; decline of U.S., 88–91, 99, 102; in Germany, 182, 183, 260–62; Hamilton's eleven-point plan, 69, 88; Perot's warning, 88–89; U.S. industrial assets sold, 99–100
Marshall, John, 156, 215–16, 218
Mayer, Jane, 131, 133
McCain-Feingold Act, 146, 147, 156
McCarthy, Kevin, 124, 125
McChesney, Robert W., 45
McCormick, Anne O'Hare, 18
McGuire, Bill, 137
McKinley, William, 122
McNamara, John, 263, 264, 265

media, 39, 40–42, 124, 135–40, 144
Medicare, 31, 68, 84; "Part E," 221
Mellon, Andrew, 16, 43, 66, 79, 111
Mendel, Noah, 109, 109–12
Mercatus Center, 132
Merkley, Jeff, 209
Michigan, 166–68
middle class, xvii, xviii, 29, 59–76, 85; author's father and, 59–62; debt and, 199, 200, 234–35; Economic Royalists and, 29, 33, 179; government necessary for, 62–64; labor unions and, 61, 70; manufacturing decline and loss of, 89–91; marketplace rules and, 70–72; New Deal and, 64, 76; post-World War II, 64; progressive taxation and, 64–66; protectionist trade policies and, 88; protections for, 28–29, 69–70; Reagan's destruction of, 59, 81; rise of, 1960s, 50; Robber Barons' destruction of, 76; social safety net and, 66–68, 86–91; wealth tax to help, 237
Milken, Michael, 104
Miller, Samuel F., 149, 152–53
monopolies, 26, 70, 73–74, 96–98, 137
Monopoly board game, 72–73, 74–75, 76
Mont Pelerin Society, 48–50, 51, 56
Moore, Michael, 179
Morgan, J. P., 73
MoveToAmend. org, 210, 211
Moyers, Bill, xxvi, 26–27
Mulloy, Patrick, 101–2
Mund, Horst, 261, 262
Murdoch, Rupert, 40
Mussolini, Benito, 18, 102
Myrdal, Gunnar, 53, 54

Nader, Ralph, 32, 123
NAFTA, 89, 98
National Committee for Responsive Philanthropy, 133–34
Nearing, Scott, 75
neoliberalism, 45, 48, 56, 132
New Deal Economics, 47, 56
1960s, 30–34; "The Leisure Society," and, 77–78, 79; Reagan Revolution and, 122–23; SDS and Port Huron Statement, 31–32
Nixon, Richard, 34–35, 40, 42, 55, 246n

Obama, Barack, 8, 134, 146, 155; administration vs. Bush's, 27; Affordable Care Act, 135–37, 141; compared to FDR, 140–41; First Inaugural Address, 7–9, 124; Immelt and, 100; Inauguration 2009, 117;

Index

insurgency against, 123–25; mortgage assistance program, 128; presidential oath bungle, 143–45; State of the Union Address (2013), 238; stimulus and, 140–41; thwarted progressive agenda, 140–42, 157

Occupy Movement, 206

oil industry, 55, 107–8, 194–96, 222–26; in Alaska, 222–24; stripping oil of strategic value, 246–50, 246n

Olson, Ted, 146–47

Only Yesterday (Allen), 15

On the Commons, 225

organized labor (unions), 29, 38–39, 61, 70; ALEC and attacks on, 171; card check, 231–32; decimation of, 230–31; German car manufacturers, 260–62; Michigan's contract breaking, 166; Reagan's crackdown, 81; Walker's attack on, 255

Origin of Species, The (Darwin), 94

Palin, Sarah, 135–36, 223

Papademos, Lucas, 162, 164, 165

Papandreou, George, 160, 162, 164

Paulson, Henry, 164, 165

Paulson, John, 181

Perot, Ross, 88–89

Philpott, Tom, 97

Pickens, T. Boone, 248

Pinochet, Augusto, 45–46, 51, 52, 160

plutocracy, 9, 10, 12–13, 26, 29, 39, 75, 160. *See also* Economic Royalists

Plutocrats (Freeland), 75

Pocan, Marc, 168–69, 170–71

Portugal, 162, 181, 182, 184

poverty, xxvi, 38, 59, 75, 102, 103; Clinton's welfare reform and, 87; FDR on, 267; food insecure and, 108–9; LBJ's Great Society reducing, 68, 84, 87; social welfare programs and, 230; wealth tax to fight, 237

Powell, Lewis F., Jr. and Powell memo, 34–39, 42–44, 49, 86, 105, 123, 125, 129, 131, 168

privatization, 22, 43, 51

Progress and Poverty (George), 75

Progressive Era, 15, 20–21, 76

Psychopath Test, The (Ronson), 104

Quinn, Daniel, 5

Rand, Ayn, 62

Rastani, Alessio, 165

Reagan, Ronald, 33, 40, 76, 77–91, 196, 230, 270; deregulation and, 104, 105, 107; environmental programs and, 241, 246n;

Farewell Address, 83; federal land leases and, 224; First Inaugural Address, 82–83; Friedman and, 56; middle class destruction and, 59; national debt and, 82–83; Revolution (Reaganomics), xviii, xxvii, 88, 122–23, 199, 271; tax cuts for the rich, 78–79, 80, 81, 84, 235, 237; trade policies, 89; Two-Santa Theory, 85; Wanniski and, 84

Rebooting the American Dream (Hartmann), 245

Reich, Robert, xviii

Remington Corporation, 20

Republican Party: "Coolidge Prosperity," 16, 109, 110, 111; as frontmen for Economic Royalists, 269; GOP TV, 40–42; majority in the House, 83, 158; national debt and, 82–83; New Deal Republicans, 91; pact to derail Obama, 123–25; Tea Party, 127–30, 127n; Wanniski ideas and, 84–85

revolution, 117–25; internal, American, 121–23; Jefferson's cycle of, 118–21, 123

Rifkin, Jeremy, 195

"Rise of the New Global Elite, The" (Freeland), 102

Robber Barons, 10, 20, 65, 70, 73–74, 76, 122, 142

Roberts, John, 143–48, 155–56

Robin Hood tax, 226–27

Rockefeller, John D., 4, 70, 73

Rome, ancient, 33, 69, 82, 198, 246, 246n

Romer, Christina, 140–41

Romney, Mitt, 104, 105

Ronson, Jon, 104

Roosevelt, Franklin D. (FDR), 18–19, 24, 29, 48; banking regulations, 71; Business Plot against, 19–20, 142, 160; Economic Royalists, war against, xxvii, 17–22, 23, 28; First Inaugural Address, 3, 8, 9–10, 19; Great Depression response, 9, 17–22, 183; Keynesian economics and, 46–47; middle class and, 59–60; mortgage assistance program, 128, 234; New Deal, 35, 44, 49, 59, 64, 66–68, 76, 84, 140, 270; Powell memo and, 36; as a Progressive, 20–21; progressive taxation and, 64–66, 68; protections for working people, 69–70; revolution of, 122; Second Bill of Rights, 67–68; Second Inaugural Address, 267; Social Security and, 28–29, 66–68, 84; speech (1936), 3, 21, 22, 23, 67, 157; unemployment insurance, 29, 66–67, 84

Roosevelt, Teddy, 20–21, 66, 71–72, 122, 146

Rousseau, Norman, xxii–xxiv

Rubin, Robert, 86

Rutledge, John, 215

Ryan, Paul, 124, 125

Index

"sacrific zones," xxvi–xxvii
Sammon, Bill, 135, 137–40
Sanders, Bernie, 209–10
Sanderson, S. W., 150
Santelli, Rick, 127–28, 127n, 151
Sarkozy, Nicolas, 226
Saul, John Ralston, 98
Schiedel, Walter, 82
Schumer, Chuck, 209
Schwarzenegger, Arnold, 222
"Serious People Are Starting to Realize That
   We May Be Looking at World War III"
   (Kreitner), 191
Sessions, Pete, 125
Shell Oil, 168
Sherman Antitrust Act, 70, 96, 104
Shock Doctrine, The (Klein), 50
Silent Spring (Carson), 32
Sisson, Daniel, 12
Smith, Adam, 11, 46
Snyder, Rick, 166–67, 168
Socializing the Right (Lewis), 33
Social Security, 28–29, 66–68, 84
Soros, George, 181
Sotomayer, Sonia, 155
South America: as corporatocracy, 45–46;
   Friedman's Chilean experiment, 52–53;
   globalism and, 102. *See also specific countries*
South Korea, 97, 100, 267
Soviet Union, 130, 198
Spain, 160, 162, 181, 182, 183, 184, 185,
   186, 188, 235; Mondragón Cooperative,
   258–60
Spengler, Oswald, 103
Square Deal, 66, 67
Stack, Joe, xx–xxi
Stahl, Leslie, 191
Stevens, John Paul, 155–56
Stockman, David, 85
stocks, commodities, and derivatives, 161,
   200, 223–24; billionaires dumping, 180–81;
   Commodity Futures Modernization Act,
   106; crash of 1974, 55–56; deregulation
   and, 106, 107–8; derivatives, 199, 200–201;
   dot-com bubble, 113; Glass-Steagall Act, 71;
   hedge funds, 113–14; 1920s, 109–10, 111–12;
   Robin Hood tax, 226–27
Strauss, William, xix, 6
Sydnor, Eugene, Jr., 35, 36, 131
Syrigos, Kostas, 163

Taft, Robert, 70
Taibbi, Matt, 107–8

taxes: carbon taxes, 250, 252; cuts for the
   wealthy, 16, 37, 43, 65–66, 78–79, 80, 84,
   235; Economic Recovery Tax Act of 1981,
   78–79; economic stability and, 65, 66; fair,
   middle class and, 63; FDR's tax hikes for
   the rich, 65; Johnson's tax hikes for the
   rich, 31; Obama's proposed tax hikes, 124;
   progressive, 64–66, 68, 78; Robin Hood tax,
   226–27; wealth tax, 236–37
"Taxes and a Two-Santa Theory"
   (Wanniski), 84
Tea Party, 126, 127–30, 127n, 134–35, 141–42,
   158
Thatcher, Margaret, 54
Third Industrial Revolution, The (Rifkin), 195
Thompson, Hunter S., 34
Thoreau, Henry David, 33
Tillman Act of 1907, 15, 72, 122, 146
TIME magazine, 77–78, 79
Tocqueville, Alexis de, 64, 189, 190, 191
Toobin, Jeffrey, 145–46
Toynbee, Arnold, 5
trade deficit, 88, 102
Trap, The (BBC series), 86
Trap, The (Goldsmith), 103
Truman, Harry, 60
Twilight of American Culture (Berman), 27

Udall, Tom, 209
unemployment, 3, 7, 76, 104; Great Depression
   and, 16; insurance, 29, 66–67, 84; job
   programs, 17–18, 232; outsourcing of
   American jobs and, 100
Union Cab, 263–66
United Healthcare, 137
United Kingdom, 54, 69, 164, 188–89
Unsafe at Any Speed (Nader), 32
U.S. Chamber of Commerce, 35, 37, 39, 131, 134
U.S. Congress: Constitutional powers of, 215,
   216; "Do-Nothing" Congress, 83, 173;
   lobbying and, 42–44; 112th session, 173–74;
   Republican majority and, 83–85, 158; as
   responsive to Royalists, 173–74
U.S. Constitution: amendments, 148–53, 154,
   157, 208–9; amendment to overturn *Citizens
   United*, 209–12; Jefferson's view, 120–21;
   Supreme Court and, 214
U.S. economy: average hourly work week, 80–81;
   crash of 1893 and, 76; democratizing, 254–66;
   economic inequality and, 82; employment
   growth, 66; financialization of, 106–9; GDP,
   200; geared to benefit Wall Street profits, 165;
   Germany vs., 89–90; globalism and, 98–103;

Index

government spending, 228–30; high tax rates on the rich and stability, 65–66; housing bubbles and, 6, 110, 113, 161; industrial assets sold, 99–100; inflation and, 233; manufacturing, 70, 88–91, 99, 100, 102, 106; Michigan's financial managers and, 166–68; middle class and, 72; military spending, 198; mortgage debt, 200; per capita income, 1900, 74; poorest Americans, income drop, 81–82; printing money, 232–33; productivity, 29, 78, 79–80, 81; Productivity vs. Wage Growth, 1947–2010 (chart), 79; rules for the marketplace and, 70–72; S&P's downgrade, 174; self-employment, 74; top one percent, 10, 34, 82; trade deficit, 88, 100; wages, 29, 77–80, 81, 88, 199; Wall Street bailout, 164; war and, 196–98, 229, 238–39; wealth of average American vs. one-percenters, 237. See also debt; unemployment

U.S. Supreme Court, 32, 143–58; Brown v. Board of Education, 30, 53, 206, 219; Buckley v. Valeo, 44, 210; Bush v. Gore, 147, 217, 218; Chief Justice Roberts, 143–48, 155–56; Citizens United, 26, 145–48, 154–58, 160, 174, 206–12; 218; Constitutional powers of, 214–15; corporations given person rights, 147–53; Crash of 2016 and, 212–15; *Dred Scott v. Sandford*, 207, 213–14; Economic Royalists and, 43–44, 145–48; *First National Bank of Boston v. Bellotti*, 44; Justice Powell, 35; *Marbury v. Madison*, 156, 216, 217; *Plessy v. Ferguson*, 218, 219; *Roe v. Wade*, 31, 206, 218, 219; *Santa Clara County v. Southern Pacific Railroad*, 148, 150–53, 212; taking the power of kings, 217–19; *United States v. Martin Linen*

Supply Co., 44; *Virginia State Board of Pharmacy v. Virginia Citizens Consumer Council*, 44

Verone, James Richard, xxiv–xxv
Vietnam War, xx, 30, 31, 34, 38, 208
Villard, Henry S., 111
Visa, 168

Wachovia Bank, xxii
Walker, Scott, 255
Wallace, Chris, 144
Wallace, Henry, 10, 28
Wal-Mart Stores, 82, 97, 168
Wanniski, Jude, 84–85
Warren, Elizabeth, 181
Washington, George, 69
Wealth of Nations (Smith), 11
Weiner, Jonathan, 94
Weissman, Robert, 209
Wells Fargo Bank, xxii–xxiii
Weyrich, Paul, 173
Whitehouse, Sheldon, 143, 209
"Why (Some) Psychopaths Made Great CEOs" (Bercovici), 104
Wikipedia, 30
Wilson, Woodrow, 70
Wolff, Richard, 185, 193, 199
Woodward, Bob, 91
World Trade Organization (WTO), 89, 98, 191
World War I, 15, 23, 24, 122
World War II, 3, 4, 5, 10, 24, 25, 47, 60, 64, 68, 113, 122, 140, 143, 146, 155, 181, 182, 189, 222

Yergin, Daniel, 53–54
Young, Arthur, 190

ABOUT TWELVE

TWELVE

TWELVE was established in August 2005 with the objective of publishing no more than twelve books each year. We strive to publish the singular book, by authors who have a unique perspective and compelling authority. Works that explain our culture; that illuminate, inspire, provoke, and entertain. We seek to establish communities of conversation surrounding our books. Talented authors deserve attention not only from publishers, but from readers as well. To sell the book is only the beginning of our mission. To build avid audiences of readers who are enriched by these works—that is our ultimate purpose.

For more information about forthcoming TWELVE books, please go to www.twelvebooks.com.